Typical and Atypical Child and Adolescent Develop

Cognition, Intelligence and

This concise guide offers an accessible introduction to cognitive development in childhood and adolescence. It integrates insights from typical and atypical development to reveal fundamental aspects of human growth and development, and common developmental disorders.

The topic books in this series draw on international research in the field and are informed by biological, social and cultural perspectives, offering explanations of developmental phenomena with a focus on how children and adolescents at different ages actually think, feel and act. In this volume, Stephen von Tetzchner explains key topics including: theories of cognitive development; attention, memory and executive function; conceptual development and reasoning, theory of mind; intelligence; and learning and instruction.

Together with a companion website that offers topic-based quizzes, lecturer PowerPoint slides and sample essay questions, *Typical and Atypical Child and Adolescent Development 4: Cognition, Intelligence and Learning* is an essential text for all students of developmental psychology as well as those working in the fields of child development, developmental disabilities and special education.

Stephen von Tetzchner is Professor of Developmental Psychology at the Department of Psychology, University of Oslo, Norway.

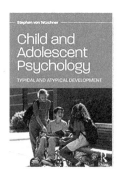

The content of this topic book is taken
from Stephen von Tetzchner's core textbook *Child and Adolescent Psychology: Typical
and Atypical Development*. The comprehensive volume offers a complete overview of
child and adolescent development – for
more information visit www.routledge.
com/9781138823396

Topics from Child and Adolescent Psychology Series
Stephen von Tetzchner

The **Topics from Child and Adolescent Psychology Series** offers concise guides on key aspects of child and adolescent development. They are formed from selected chapters from Stephen von Tetzchner's comprehensive textbook *Child and Adolescent Psychology: Typical and Atypical Development* and are intended to be accessible introductions for students of relevant modules on developmental psychology courses, as well as for professionals working in the fields of child development, developmental disabilities and special education. The topic books explain the key aspects of human development by integrating insights from typical and atypical development to cement understanding of the processes involved and the work with children who have developmental disorders. They examine sensory, physical and cognitive disabilities and the main emotional and behavioral disorders of childhood and adolescence, as well as the developmental consequences of these disabilities and disorders.

Topics books in the series

Typical and Atypical Child and Adolescent Development 1
Theoretical Perspectives and Methodology

Typical and Atypical Child and Adolescent Development 2
Genes, Fetal Development and Early Neurological Development

Typical and Atypical Child and Adolescent Development 3
Perceptual and Motor Development

Typical and Atypical Child and Adolescent Development 4
Cognition, Intelligence and Learning

Typical and Atypical Child and Adolescent Development 5
Communication and Language Development

Typical and Atypical Child and Adolescent Development 6
Emotions, Temperament, Personality, Moral, Prosocial and Antisocial Development

Typical and Atypical Child and Adolescent Development 7
Social Relations, Self-awareness and Identity

For more information on individual topic books visit www.routledge.com/Topics-from-Child-and-Adolescent-Psychology/book-series/TFCAAP

Typical and Atypical Child and Adolescent Development 4

Cognition, Intelligence and Learning

Stephen von Tetzchner

LONDON AND NEW YORK

Cover image: John M Lund Photography Inc

First published 2023
by Routledge
4 Park Square, Milton Park, Abingdon, Oxon OX14 4RN

and by Routledge
605 Third Avenue, New York, NY 10158

Routledge is an imprint of the Taylor & Francis Group, an informa business

© 2023 Stephen von Tetzchner

British Library Cataloguing-in-Publication Data
A catalogue record for this book is available from the British Library

Library of Congress Cataloging-in-Publication Data
A catalog record for this book has been requested

ISBN: 978-1-032-27394-5 (hbk)
ISBN: 978-1-032-26775-3 (pbk)
ISBN: 978-1-003-29250-0 (ebk)

DOI: 10.4324/9781003292500

Typeset in Bembo
by Apex CoVantage, LLC

Access the companion website: www.routledge.com/cw/vonTetzchner

Contents

Introduction

Development can be defined as an age-related process involving changes in the structure and functions of humans and other species. Cognition is part of these structures and functions; it is a mental apparatus that differentiates between species and may also differentiate between individual members of a species. The six parts in this topic book concern core issues related to human cognitive development and build on the models of development and the developmental way of thinking presented in Book 1, *Theoretical Perspectives and Methodology*. They include both typical cognitive development, which is the most common course, with unimpaired functions and ordinary individual differences between children, and atypical development, which represents various degrees of unusual or irregular cognitive development, including the development of children and adolescents who have cognitive disabilities. The issues presented in this topic book are particularly relevant for teachers, special educators and other staff in preschool and school.

Human development to maturity stretches over about 20 years. Most individual differences in mental and physical features and abilities do not emerge directly from a particular biological or environmental factor but rather as a result of *interaction effects*, where biological and environmental factors are moderated by one or several other factors. The basic cognitive apparatus is shared by all humans, but there are considerable individual differences in cognitive abilities and skills. Some children have cognitive disabilities and never reach the intellectual level of their peers. The individual differences in cognitive development emerge from interactions between genes and experience. Development is never a one-way process: it is a *transactional process*, characterized by reciprocal influences between the child and the environment over time. Readers may find it useful to consult the part on developmental models in Book 1, *Theoretical Perspectives and Methodology*, or the corresponding chapters in the complete book before reading the present topic book.

Cognition comes from the Latin *cogitare*, which means to think or to ponder. Cognition is a representation or symbolization of the world, an inner recreation of things in the outer world. It includes functions such as attention, memory, processing of new and stored experiences, calculation, decision-making and planning of actions. All animals have memory and other cognitive functions that enable them to plan and adapt to and function in their ecological niche. For example, birds must build nests before they lay eggs, remember places with food and find their way back to the nest with food. Squirrels must remember where they stored food for later use. Their cognitive abilities are reflected in everything humans do, such as going for walks, playing, eating, solving academic tasks, designing spaceships, sending messages on mobile phones or reading books. Human cognition is varied and complex and differs between individuals in various ways; the differences are related to biology, experience and culture. Children are not small adults – cognitive development involves qualitative changes in concept formation, thinking and reasoning.

Part I Theories of Cognitive Development introduces the concept of cognition and diverse views on the structure and functions of the human mind, such as assumptions about inborn modularity or domain-general and domain-specific functions. The cognitive abilities of infants are limited and adapted to ensuring survival of the baby, who is totally dependent on competent caregivers. Adult cognition is complex and constitutes a basis for independence in thinking, reasoning and acting. The most important theoretical task is to explain how infants, children and adolescents develop new ways of mental processing, thinking and reasoning. Part I presents four main theoretical schools of cognitive development that differ in their assumptions about cognitive structures and processes and mechanisms underlying development, the role they attribute to genes and experience, and their research methodologies. The variety of theoretical explanations and their small and large disagreements about even the basic cognitive functions reflect the complexity of the human mind. The reader may consult Book 1, *Theoretical Perspectives and Methodology*, for more general features of the theoretical schools included here.

Part II Attention, Memory and Executive Function presents basic cognitive functions that are involved in almost all human activities. *Attention* is about selectivity and regulation of perception and thinking and is crucial for exploration and learning. Children gradually become able to focus on specific aspects of the situation and disregard others, motivated by their own interests and feelings and by social guidance from others. Infants are attentive to other people, and the emergence of the ability to follow attention direction and to direct the attention of others to specific targets and engage in *joint attention* is a significant milestone in the development of communication and language (see Book 5, *Communication and Language Development*).

Memory development is about the changes in gathering, organizing and retrieving one's own experiences and information provided by others. The memory system performs mental elaboration and storage and enables the integrated use of current and earlier positive and negative experiences. All species have a memory system that ensures that they remember what may be important in their ecological niche, such as the location of food, shelter and dangers. The memory system of infants is quite simple, but its capacity and functionality grow fast. What children remember depends on their understanding and cultural background. The memory system contains not only particular events but also a representation of how things and procedures usually are, for example a typical school day or a birthday party. Moreover, human memory is special owing to the language abilities that allow humans to establish autobiographic memory and conscious reflection on past and future events.

Executive functions have to do with planning, organizing and executing actions. Attention and memory are part of these functions. Executive functions are necessary for children's enculturation and coping in societies with physical and social structures of varying complexity. In children's early years, parents, teachers and other adults give much support to children's executive functions by helping them plan and perform everyday activities such as eating, dressing and playing. With age, children become more autonomous and responsible for planning and executing their daily activities, including getting to school, doing homework, organizing leisure activities with peers and so on. The capacity and functionality of the executive functions increase through childhood and adolescence, but so do the demands on these functions. Some children and adolescents struggle with the demands on planning and persistence, for example those with attention deficit disorders or autism spectrum disorder.

Part III Conceptual Development and Reasoning is about the changes in children's categorization of the world around them and their reasoning. This includes the basic dimensions of space and time and the understanding of causality, of cause and effect. This part presents different theoretical views on how children categorize animals, objects, places and people. Increased experience and knowledge lead to qualitative changes in categorization, enabling children and adolescents to form gradually more abstract and complex concepts. For example, it takes time before children learn the internal structure of their families, how fathers and mothers, sons and daughters, siblings, and uncles and aunts are related to each other.

Children's *reasoning* interacts with and builds on their knowledge and concept formation. Early reasoning may involve assumptions and inferences based on what the child observes here and now. With age, reasoning comes to include mental problem solving involving real and imagined situations. The basic features of reasoning development are also relevant for moral reasoning (see Book 6, *Emotions, Temperament, Personality, Moral, Prosocial and Antisocial Development*, Part III).

Social interaction requires social cognition and an understanding of social relationships and processes. Mental evaluation of the situation – as pleasant, funny, insecure, dangerous and so on – is an inherent element of emotions (see Book 6, *Emotions, Temperament, Personality, Moral, Prosocial and Antisocial Development*, Part I). Cognition is therefore also a foundation of social and emotional functioning. Mind understanding is an insight that sets the human species apart from others species and is essential to human social interaction and collaboration. *Part IV Mind Understanding* presents the emergence of perspective-taking abilities and social inferencing in childhood. There are different theories of the development of mind understanding, but there seems to be agreement that humans have a species-specific ability to understand other people's minds, with an implicit assumption that it is people's subjective evaluations of the environment that determine their emotional reactions, decisions and choices of action. The subjective mind of another person is not directly observable, and children need to develop the insight that knowledge and beliefs – whether false or correct – will determine how people act in a particular situation. Central to mind understanding is the recognition that people with different knowledge or background can perceive the same situation differently, sometimes also wrongly. Children with different disabilities may be delayed in their development of mind understanding, and experimental studies of children with autism spectrum disorder have contributed particularly to the insights into emergent mind understanding in general.

Children and adults think and reason differently, but there are also considerable individual differences in cognitive abilities within an age cohort, differences which may be important for learning and adaptation. Some children solve problems quickly; other children are slower. The role of genes in development is a major issue in developmental psychology (see Book 2, *Genes, Fetal Development and Early Neurological Development*, Part I), and there is an enormous research literature on the effects of genes and environment on intellectual development, including associations with social and economic background. There is a main divide between age-typical and age-atypical abilities, lower or higher than the average. There are children with cognitive impairments who will never be able to solve mental tasks that most of their peers solve quite easily. *Part V Intelligence* is about individual differences in cognition and cognitive profiles. It presents the concept of IQ and the design and functions of intelligence testes. Intelligence tests for children were originally designed to help schools identify pupils who are delayed in some aspect of cognitive development and therefore may need special education services. To be able to provide functional educational activities, teachers need to understand how children think, reason and feel, and why they act the way they do. This applies to children of all ages and with different abilities, both children with typical development and children with learning disorders. Teachers' task is to support children's learning and knowledge acquisition, and insight into the developmental possibilities and constraints presented by cognitive impairments is important for adapting educational strategies to each pupil's needs.

Informal and formal learning are essential elements of human development. *Part VI Learning and Instruction* presents different forms of individual and group learning at different age levels and two developmental perspectives on education. Many children struggle with academic skills such as reading, writing and mathematics, which may have a lasting impact on their education and later work life. Measures for preventing and remediating learning disorders are therefore important for children's and adolescents' mental health and well-being.

Some of the terminology used in developmental psychology may be unfamiliar to some readers. Many of these terms are highlighted and can be found in the Glossary.

Part I

Theories of Cognitive Development

I

Cognition

Cognition plays a role in everything human beings do – playing, eating, working out school assignments, designing space crafts, developing strategies for a football game, taking a walk and enjoying the view, sending messages on a cell phone or reading a book. Cognitive development is an essential part of developmental psychology. Children are not merely "incomplete" adults, and theories of cognitive development aim to explain how children's cognitive processes initially arise and develop into adult comprehension, thinking and problem solving (Newcombe, 2013).

The theories are as complex as cognition itself. They describe dissimilar processes and emphasize different factors in explaining the **development** of a mature mind. The current chapter discusses four main approaches to cognitive development: **logical constructivism**, **information processing**, **nativism** and **social constructivism**. (Their main features are presented in Book 1, *Theoretical Perspectives and Methodology*, Part II, and will not be repeated here.) Comparisons between them provide an insight into the different ways of understanding changes in children's cognitive functioning and a sound basis for discussing the various aspects of cognitive development presented in the following chapters. Piaget's theory is the most influential as well as the most criticized among the theories, and most other theories incorporate elements from Piaget's theory, challenge it or both (Barrouillet, 2015). Therefore, it is presented first and treated in some detail, and the others are discussed in relation to it.

DOI: 10.4324/9781003292500-2

2

Domains, Modules and Activities

Cognitive development concerns the organization, structure, and biological and cultural basis of cognition. One of the key questions is whether all areas undergo a general change in level or whether development varies between different knowledge areas, or **domains**. **Domain-general** development means that knowledge areas share the same foundation and evolve more or less in parallel. When development is **domain-specific**, it progresses differently in separate areas, such as language, spatial perception or mathematics. Therefore, the question is whether cognition is driven by a single large "machine" or by multiple "machines" of varying size for each individual domain.

Modules

Some theorists believe that domain-specific development has its basis in **modules**, neurological units with a specific function that include a set of categories and processes capable of interpreting external stimulation in one particular way only, just as the heart, the liver and other organs have their specific **functions**. One module perceives language only, another spatial relationships, a third social relationships and so on. A module can cover a broader or narrower area of knowledge, and modules can incorporate independent sub-modules. These modules are considered important for development because they are specialized to deal with particular aspects of the world and thereby put restrictions on **learning** and lead it in the right direction. Without such restrictions, human experience would be too ambiguous and inadequately structured, the world would appear chaotic, and children would be unable to distinguish aspects of the environment that are and are not relevant for a particular task (Butterfill, 2007). There is, however, considerable disagreement about the number of modules. Spelke and Kinzler (2007)

DOI: 10.4324/9781003292500-3

believe there are four or five, while Carruthers (2006, 2008) and Sperber (2001) argue in favor of "massive modularity," meaning that the mind (and the brain) contains a large number of modules.

Because modules are independent, they can be damaged without affecting the function of other modules. Both **developmental disorders** and acquired injuries are used as an argument for the possible existence of modules. For example, many theorists assume there is a module for language, as brain injury can result in impaired **language function** (aphasia) without affecting other areas in any significant way. The same applies to the ability to recognize faces.

Most modularists adopt a nativist view and believe that modules were formed in the course of evolution, as they led to skills that ensured a higher survival rate. They mainly develop through maturation, while experience merely functions as a "trigger mechanism." Chomsky (2000) and Pinker (1994) for example believe that human beings have an innate language module, and that children, under normal circumstances, only need to be exposed to linguistic stimulation in order to develop language (see Book 5, *Communication and Language Development*, Chapter 6). Other theorists argue that any potential modular properties of the brain are not present at birth but emerge through a *process of modularization* where experience and genes interact. The modules are thus the result of development rather than being mechanisms that determine the developmental course of knowledge, such as the nativists claim (Karmiloff-Smith, 2015). In line with this view, **atypical development** can occasionally lead to inadequate modularization. While persons with **typical development** activate different areas of their brain when they see faces and other objects, people with **Williams syndrome** seem to activate the same area when looking at cars and faces (D'Souza & Karmiloff-Smith, 2011).

Activities

An alternative to the notion that the mind consists of domains or modules is the view that different abilities have their origin in experiences related to various activities, and that the developmental process may be **activity-specific** in some areas. Activities here are not isolated acts but constitute a stable and complex system of practices that have evolved in response to society's needs and opportunities. Play, education and different types of work are examples of activities (Cole, 2006; Karpov, 2005). A tailor may be good at calculating how much fabric is needed for a dress, or a butcher at calculating the weight of a piece of meat, without either of them being able to solve a problem of similar difficulty outside their professional activities, for example when presented in a classroom (see Chapter 6). The math skills of the tailor, the butcher and the pupil in the classroom belong to the same knowledge domain, but develop in different ways nonetheless. Domain-specific knowledge exists independently of a given **activity**, and it would therefore be incorrect to say that their math skills are domain-specific. Instead, learning arithmetic appears to be activity-based and, to some extent, remains activity-specific knowledge.

Embodiment

Although cognitive psychology has largely focused on the brain, cognitive development is not a process that merely occurs in the brain, independent of the body. Many theorists emphasize how human (and other species') **perception** of the world, thinking and problem solving are determined by the very design of the body, its interaction with the physical forces of nature and participation in social interaction. According to this view, the human body itself imposes limitations on the development of the human mind. Organisms with different bodies would also have had a different type of cognition and other ways of categorizing, thinking and solving problems. The nervous system is the body's connection with the environment. Human beings do not have "a brain or a mind in a box" but are organisms with a nervous system that exists *within* rather than separate from the environment. Children do not learn to perform an action isolated from a situation but as an **adaptation** to and within the situation. Hence, the body and the physical and social environment are part of the human cognitive apparatus and development (Clark, 2008; Glenberg, 2010).

3

Logical Constructivism

This chapter discusses Piaget's **standard theory**, including the cognitive structure, the developmental processes and the **stages**, its critical reception and "**the new theory**."

Cognitive Structure

According to Piaget (1950, 1952), cognitive development involves the formation of a **cognitive structure** based on logic and mathematics that enables increasingly complex and abstract thinking. The cornerstones of this structure consist of **schemas** that are formed when actions become generalized and transformed through mental processing. *Action schemas* can be compared with action strategies. When children face obstacles in achieving a goal, their past actions – previously incorporated into schemas – will determine how they try to overcome these obstacles, for example by using a stick to get hold of something that is out of reach. Schemas are **abstractions** that include aspects of actions that are not specifically related to a given situation and can be transferred to other situations. "Throwing" is an example of an action schema formed early in life. A child can throw a rattle, a ball, a cap or something else. Since the act of throwing is adapted to different objects, it can vary a good deal – high or low, long or short and so forth. However, the schema includes only what is common to or *constant* in throwing. Activating a schema rather than merely repeating the execution of an earlier action allows the child's execution to be more flexible and adapted to the situation.

According to Piaget's theory, action and thinking have the same function: to achieve goals and overcome obstacles. Thoughts are internalized actions, and action knowledge provides the foundation for all thinking. It is by exploring and engaging with objects in space and

DOI: 10.4324/9781003292500-4

time that children discover how they can predict, understand and master the world around them.

Symbolic schemas represent something other than themselves. Words are an example of symbolic schemas. When children pretend that a wooden block is a toy car, the block becomes a non-linguistic **symbol** for "car." The development of symbolic schemas enables children to solve problems and think about objects and events without directly linking them to actions.

Action schemas and symbolic schemas involve abstraction, meaning that certain characteristics are extracted and reassembled into new categories. *Operational schemas* keep track of the changes that occur when experiences are transformed from concrete experience to mental categories. Operational schemas are necessary for children to understand the connection between events and to construct a coherent and consistent world.

The assumption that children develop the same cognitive structure independent of their specific experiences is one of the cornerstones of Piaget's standard theory. Just like the other schemas, operational schemas are not products of learning in the conventional sense, but mental constructs formed by abstracting and processing physical and mental actions. The knowledge children acquire is neither determined by an innate mental structure nor a replica of the world formed through sensory experiences. Instead, it arises from the interaction between the child and the external environment. According to Piaget, it is the human biological equipment that makes abstraction possible, but children must have experience in order for abstraction and the formation of structure to take place (Piaget, 1950, 1983).

The Development Process

Children's quest to understand the world is a basic life function, a *process of adaptation* whereby mental schemas and processes undergo a gradual change as children respond to challenges and gather new experiences. According to Piaget, development is determined by three factors: maturation, training and social transfer. **Maturation** is of particular importance during early development and is also a prerequisite for the particular order between the stages (see below). Development based on maturation alone would, according to Piaget, be static and fail to provide a sufficient basis for the adaptive abilities that distinguish children's development. Thus, development is not simply the result of learning or social transfer, but requires the presence of a cognitive structure able to perceive and interpret – humanize – experience.

An attempt to determine what may be the result of maturation and what is learned is considered to be of little importance by Piaget. It is the *interaction* between maturational processes and children's active interaction with the environment, their adaptation to constantly new surroundings and conditions, that determines development in Piaget's theory: experience leads to challenges, mastering challenges leads to new experiences that provide new challenges, and so on.

Assimilation and Accommodation

When children perceive events, objects and people, they select or interpret things and events in the external world based on the schemas they have acquired. Piaget calls this **assimilation**. Because younger children's cognitive schemas and structures differ from those of adults and older children, they perceive the physical and social world in a different way. In order for children to gain new knowledge and develop new actions, their schemas must be adapted to experiences with new people, objects and events. Piaget calls this process **accommodation**. It is accommodation that leads to changes in cognitive schemas, but assimilation entails adaptation as well. The assimilation of new objects and events forces children's thinking to adapt, to be accommodated. Assimilation and accommodation thus are complementary aspects of the same process, rather than distinctly separate processes. The internal structure (accommodation) and children's perception of the world (assimilation) change in tandem with each other.

Equilibration and Conflict

According to Piaget, cognitive development is driven by an innate ability to perceive cognitive contradictions and seek to create *equilibrium* between established schemas and new experiences. When children experience a *conflict* between beliefs they have formed, they encounter a state of cognitive *disequilibrium* that leads them to resolve the problem. Disequilibrium represents a state of incomplete adaptation but enables the child to perceive the contradiction. Based on their own schemas, children are unable to perceive the same contradictions as adults. An adult knows, for example, that an object cannot float one moment and sink the next. Toddlers might claim that a toy they have just observed sinking will float the next time they throw it into the water. It is only once children understand that these two events are incompatible that a cognitive conflict takes place and becomes a problem they can relate to. Children must have acquired the necessary prerequisites to recognize a problem before they can solve it.

Piaget's theory thus views development as being driven by an intrinsic motivation to establish equilibrium or structural order. Children's perceptions are constantly challenged by new experiences, and they actively seek out such challenges. When a child has solved the problem created by a given state of disequilibrium, the new understanding brought about by **equilibration** forms the basis for new insights, which in turn lead to new conflicts and disequilibrium. A final state of equilibrium is essentially impossible to achieve, as new and unresolved problems will emerge on new levels.

Organization

The earliest schemas evolve individually and independently of one another. They represent knowledge about the world that is as yet fragmented and disjointed. It is the *organization* process that makes the cognitive structure function as a whole. It coordinates established schemas and creates superordinate schemas in accordance with logico-mathematical principles. This is the logic in logical constructivism. Reorganization leads to a greater degree of equilibrium by solving former contradictions or conflicts and, at the same time, leads to disequilibrium as the child discovers new contradictions. One consequence of this model is that new experiences affect the structure and organization of past experiences, which in turn are adapted to the new knowledge. Following each new organization, the child is unique and different from the person he was before and will be in the future. Some reorganizations imply a transition to a new cognitive stage.

Stages

Piaget describes four domain-general stages of cognitive development. Each stage represents an extensive reorganization and a qualitatively new way of thinking and reasoning that enables children to understand and solve new tasks. Since the completion of a stage leads to the ability to recognize new cognitive conflicts, one stage always functions as preparation for the next.

The Sensorimotor Stage (0–2 Years)

In this stage, children develop *sensorimotor schemas* based on perception and external actions. It includes approximately the first 2 years of life and is divided into six substages. In the first substage (0–1 months), the child has a small repertoire of reflexive actions that are elicited by primary needs. Adaptation to the environment begins as early as during the first few days of life. Newborns quickly improve at finding their mother's nipple and beginning to suck.

In the second substage (1–4 months), children produce spontaneous actions they can perceive to lead to a goal. Piaget (1952) describes how his son Laurent learned to suck his thumb after accidentally putting it into his mouth for the first time. However, children do not yet distinguish between means and ends. The goal is achieved because a particular sequence of movements leads to it. It is only during the third substage (4–8 months) that children are able to use the same action to achieve other goals. At the same time, this substage forms the basis for being able to distinguish between means and ends and choose from a variety of actions to reach a goal, something children do during the fourth substage (8–12 months). In the fifth substage (12–18 months), children are able to use tools to achieve a goal, such as grasping the edge of a tablecloth and pulling it toward them to reach an object (Figure 3.1).

The acquisition of **object permanence** is an important cognitive milestone in the fourth substage. At 7–8 months, children will stop looking for a toy when it has been hidden under a blanket so they cannot see it. Children who are 2 months older will search for the object and look underneath the blanket. This reflects an understanding of the permanent existence of objects and shows that children are beginning to "handle" objects mentally. Their understanding remains limited, however, and the search is unsystematic. During the fifth substage, children begin to show understanding of how objects behave under

(a)   (b)

Figure 3.1 Using a tool to achieve a goal.

Once children have reached the fifth **sensorimotor stage**, they are able to pull on a tablecloth to reach an object placed on it (Willatts 1989, p. 162). (Thanks to Peter Willatts.)

different conditions. In the sixth substage (18–24 months), children will also look in other places if they cannot find the toy where they thought it would be (see Part III, this volume).

The sixth substage represents the completion of basic sensorimotor skills and lays the groundwork for the development of operational thinking. Of particular importance is the development of mental **representations** and symbolic schemas. Children no longer need to perform concrete actions, but are able to solve problems mentally by imagining actions and objects. They can show sudden insight and make use of new solutions as the result of thinking without physical trial and error. This marks the beginning of dissociation from the immediately perceptible situation. Once children have developed object permanence, they are able to look for objects they have just observed being hidden, such as a toy under a pillow. Symbolic representation enables them to look for objects that were not part of a given situation some moments earlier.

According to Piaget's theory, the ability to *imitate* plays an important role in cognitive development. Although children show imitation-like behavior as early as the first sensorimotor stage, Piaget does not consider this to be *genuine* **imitation**. During the second and third substage, children repeat their own actions when these are imitated by adults. True imitation emerges in the fourth stage, first in the form of **immediate imitation**, followed by **deferred imitation**, meaning that an action is carried out some time after the original action, such as when a child sweeps the floor like dad did the day before. Children show deferred imitation of simple actions toward the end of the sensorimotor stage (see Part IV, this volume). Imitation is not a passive form of replication – deferred imitation requires the child to store an action mentally and recreate it completely or in part. It is an active and creative process that leads to independently constructed mental representations.

A tremendous development takes place during this first stage, "no less than a conquest by perception and movement of the entire practical universe that surrounds the small child," to quote Piaget (1968, p. 9). External actions have become internalized mental actions, and children have acquired and organized basic knowledge of the physical and social world around them.

The Preoperational Stage (2–7 Years)

The **preoperational stage** forms the transition from sensorimotor to operational thinking. Piaget calls this stage "preoperational" because the cognitive structure includes schemas that are not aimed at coordinating external actions and thus are not sensorimotor, but are not abstract enough either to be operational. During this stage, thinking begins to detach itself from action but continues to be unstable and characterized by the immediate perception of a situation: children think what they see.

Object permanence is the understanding that objects continue to exist even when they cannot be seen at the moment. This stage sees the development of a new type of **constancy** that enables children to retain specific qualities of objects, such as color and shape. They are able to categorize objects by a single property but unable to take into account several at the same time (Inhelder & Piaget, 1964). A 5-year-old (B) shows typical preoperational thinking in conversation with the experimenter (E):

E: *What do we have here?*
B: *Blue circles and blue and red squares.*
E: *Are all the circles blue?*
B: *No, because there are blue circles and squares.*
E: *Are all the squares red?*
B: *Yes, because there are only squares.*
E: *Are all the circles blue?*
B: *No, there are circles and squares.*

The development of *symbolic function* is one of the key elements of this stage. It allows children to influence the coordination of perception and action-based knowledge with their own thought processes and thereby overcome the limits of sensorimotor knowledge and free their thought from their actions. This is reflected in children's deferred imitation, use of words and **symbolic play**. Words are symbols, but the use of symbols is not necessarily related to language. A piece of clay is also a symbol when it represents the mother or the baby during play. According to Piaget, language does not structure thinking; it is the cognitive development that lays the foundation for a child's understanding of complex linguistic content. Nonetheless, Piaget considers language important for children's acquisition of knowledge.

In the course of this extended process, while the cognitive structure is still incomplete, children solve a number of tasks by using "intuitive" prelogical thinking and mental trial and error. Children often know the answer, but are unable to explain it. The following answers are typical:

PIAGET: *What is wind?*
CHILD: *Something that blows in the sky.*

PIAGET: *How do you know that?*
CHILD: *I just know.*

An incomplete cognitive structure thus characterizes children's thinking during this stage. This is also apparent in their failure to fully separate between fantasy and reality – both their thoughts and their dreams can appear real to them.

The Concrete Operational Stage (7–11 Years)

It is the formation of *operational schemas* that distinguishes the cognitive structure formed during the operational stages from the structure of the first two stages. These schemas enable children to organize and link together other schemas and provide them with a "mental space" to move around in and solve new problems in entirely new ways.

In contrast to earlier stages, descriptions of children's problem solving during the **concrete operational stage** place greater emphasis on what they are capable of rather than not. Many advanced cognitive skills emerge for the first time during this stage. For example, children become able to arrange objects according to a given dimension and eventually also to compare information. They can draw a map that shows the way to school, something younger children are unable to do, even if they know the way and can walk to school on their own. Five-year-olds can usually differentiate between the right and left sides of their body, but, during the concrete operational stage, they are able to do so for others as well for the first time. Yet children's thinking continues to be limited and relies on being supported by experience. The stage is concrete operational because they are only able to carry out operations in relation to "concrete" objects.

During this operational stage, children begin to master various forms of **conservation**. This is a type of *mental constancy*, an understanding that the material or mass of an object does not change even if external aspects of the object do. This underscores that children's perception of the world is not a passive registration of external characteristics. Conservation of number is usually acquired first, followed by mass, weight and volume. Figure 3.2 shows two typical **experiments** studying conservation in children.

In experiments on conservation, younger children are unable to pay attention to more than one aspect at a time. They fail to understand that quantity, weight and volume remain constant even if the object's outward appearance changes. They focus on the characteristics that

Figure 3.2 Two conservation experiments.

(1) Number: Together, the experimenter and the child place two rows of buttons so they lie in pairs of two. The experimenter asks whether both rows contain an equal number of buttons and receives a positive response from the child. The experimenter then increases the distance between the buttons in one row so the row becomes a little longer. He asks which of the rows contains most buttons. Children below the age of 6–7 years usually respond that there are a greater number of buttons in the longer row.

(2) Mass and weight: The child is given a lump of clay that is divided into two precisely equal parts by the experimenter and rolled into two clay balls. He asks the child whether there is an equal amount of clay in each ball and gets an affirmative answer. Next he rolls one of the balls into a sausage and asks which of them contains the most clay. Children below the age of 7 years point to the sausage. Older children respond that there is an equal amount. A corresponding procedure is used for weight, with the experimenter asking what weighs the most. Children are usually 7–8 years old before they are able to correctly answer the question on mass, and 9–10 years before they correctly answer the question on weight.

attract their attention the most and experience no cognitive conflict due to lack of constancy. At the age of about 7 years they are first able to overcome the object's immediate visual impact.

At about 7–8 years, children begin to understand that an object can belong to two classes simultaneously, such as being both black and round, and can therefore be assigned to both piles if the task is to categorize objects by shape and by color. A related conceptual development is the understanding of **class inclusion**, the fact that one class of objects can be a subcategory of another class. Tulips and roses are two distinct categories, but also subcategories of the category "flowers" (Chapter 14, this volume).

The Formal Operational Stage (11+ Years)

Around the age of 11, children begin to think more like adults and, at the age of 15, they have acquired a stable system of formal mental **operations**, according to Piaget. The **formal operational stage** is characterized by a new ability to combine several features or elements. "Formal" here means that operations can be applied to abstract and hypothetical problems. Concrete operations involve thinking about the world; formal operations involve thinking about thinking.

Adolescents who have reached this stage therefore do not need concrete support. Thought is liberated from specific content, and adolescents are able to deduce logical consequences of an issue or a situation without first deciding whether it is true or false. They are, for example, able to reason about what would happen *if* they were in a different country. Whereas children in the concrete operational stage will dismiss such a counterfactual question by answering that they are not in the other country, thought is only limited by possibilities rather than by what actually is during the formal operational stage. Adolescents begin to understand proportion, probability and analogy and are able to take into account several dimensions at the same time, such as the width and the height of a glass to estimate its contents. In addition to actual problems, the final cognitive structure is capable of processing hypothetical obstacles and objectives.

In this stage, adolescents also become able to form theories and make use of **hypothetical-deductive reasoning**, formulating hypotheses and testing them out in a systematic manner. It is precisely this capacity for "scientific" thinking that characterizes the formal operational stage, the culmination of Piaget's description of cognitive development. Thinking becomes more advanced and complex even after the age of 15, but, according to Piaget, later development is characterized only by an increase in knowledge, not by **qualitative changes** in cognitive structure. When adults draw incorrect conclusions it is due to a lack of knowledge rather than an inadequate logical structure (see also Part III, Chapter 15, this volume).

Domain-General Development

According to Piaget, development is domain-general (see Chapter 2, this volume). Once the cognitive structure has been established and conservation can be demonstrated in one area, children will also be able to master similar tasks in other areas. However, the ability to solve different tasks does not always occur at the same age, a fact Piaget explains by suggesting that children's thinking in the concrete operational stage is not yet fully detached from concrete situations, but more or less related to specific types of experiences. Because the occurrence of such experiences varies, some areas may be delayed compared with others. Only once children enter the formal operational stage does their thinking become entirely liberated from specific objects and experiences and reach the same general cognitive level.

Status of the Standard Theory

Piaget's theory was the major theory in the twentieth century, and, in the twenty-first century, neo-Piagetians and others continue to develop theories and conduct research building directly on it (Barrouillet, 2015; Morra et al., 2008). However, Piaget's standard theory and his empirical findings have been challenged by all the other theoretical views on cognitive development. Criticism of him is as essential to the debate as his theory. Yet Piaget continues to occupy a central position, both because his theory remains the only comprehensive and detailed theory of cognitive development and because it includes many positions that can be scientifically verified (see Book 1, *Theoretical Perspectives and Methodology*, Chapter 10). The basic assumption that children develop a cognitive structure based on logic is generally disputed, but many of Piaget's concepts and his terminology are still frequently used to describe children's cognitive development. The experimental tasks used by Piaget have in themselves been important for an understanding of cognitive development. Piaget described them in great detail, and they represent an original and well-founded approach to children's thinking and reasoning.

Age

Much research has been aimed at establishing whether the various age specifications Piaget arrived at are correct. A common objection to Piaget is that he underestimates younger children. Studies show that, by using other methods or changing the instructions, children are able to solve similar tasks at a lower age level than specified by Piaget. For example, using the visual **preference method**, Baillargeon (1987) found evidence of object permanence in children much younger than Piaget found (Chapter 10, this volume). McGarrigle and associates (1978) studied class inclusion in an experiment involving a teddy bear walking up a staircase made up of red and white steps to reach a table. Children were able to determine whether there were a greater number of red steps or total steps at a much earlier age than in Piaget's study, in which they were asked whether there were more red flowers or more flowers (Chapter 14, this volume). McGarrigle believes the difference can be explained by the fact that the teddy bear task was based on a play activity the children were familiar with. A similar difference was found between Piaget's and Donaldson's studies of children's ability to adopt different visual perspectives (Chapter 18, this volume).

However, not all tasks are mastered simply because the instructions change, and the age levels Piaget found for mastering certain tasks still generally hold true (Bjorklund, 1995). What the studies conducted by Hundeide (Box 3.1), Donaldson and others show is that changes in the conditions of tasks may change the age at which children are able to master them. Together, Piaget's and the other studies contribute to an understanding of what it takes for children at various age levels to solve different types of tasks. The fact that studies show children to be capable of solving many tasks at an earlier age when combined with familiar activities emphasizes the importance of designing tasks that are meaningful to children based on their own experience. This also indicates that children's ability to solve many cognitive tasks is more *activity-based* than suggested by Piaget's standard theory.

Box 3.1   How a Problem Is Presented May Influence Reasoning (Hundeide, 1977)

The experimenter showed a picture of five cups and two glasses to **preschool-age** children and asked them whether there were more cups or more things to drink from. Seventeen of the 36 children who were shown the picture before they were asked the question answered correctly. Thirty-six other children were asked the question before they saw the picture, and 31 of them answered correctly. Hundeide's explanation of the results is that the children who were shown the picture first were naturally aware that it included two types of objects, and many had therefore formed an *expectation* that the two objects were going to be compared, since this is something adults often ask children to do. They expected a question about the differences between cups and glasses and "forgot" that both are used to drink from. The children who had not seen the photograph first had no such expectation to influence their reasoning.

While Piaget underestimates younger children, he seems to overestimate the capacity for systematic and logical thinking among adolescents and adults. Far from all teenagers are able to master formal operational tasks (Shayer & Wylam, 1978). Also, adults frequently provide answers that reflect a concrete operational way of thinking, especially in connection with tasks related to areas they have little experience with (Chapter 15, this volume). Most people never develop a fully consistent level of logical thinking, but their reasoning to some extent remains dependent on the given situation.

Piaget himself was relatively uninterested in specifying age. He considered age indications to be approximate, and mastering a skill earlier or later than usual is not critical to his theory as such. Only a change in the sequence of skills associated with the different stages would represent a decisive blow to his ideas. When differences in the age at which children acquire a particular skill show major discrepancies, the question nevertheless arises whether cognitive development truly is domain-general and can be explained based on the acquisition of a higher-level cognitive structure relatively independent of children's concrete experiences.

Stages and Domains

Developmental stages must comply with certain formal criteria. Children have to acquire a certain competence that differs qualitatively from the competence they have previously shown. The transition from one stage to another should occur relatively quickly and be accompanied by changes in several aspects of children's thinking. Every child must move through the stages in the same order (Flavell, 1971). Research shows that these criteria are not always met, and most developmental theorists reject the types of stages described by Piaget. However, stages are still considered useful for describing children's cognitive development (Carey et al., 2015; Lourenço, 2016). The models of neo-Piagetians Case (1985, 1998) and Feldman (2004) represent an adaptation of Piaget's theory by integrating the concept of stages with more recent research about children's thinking and conceptual formation. According to Feldman's model, the first half of each stage is used to build new skills and structures, the second to develop the ability to apply them. The distinction between construction and application provides more room for individual and cultural differences.

The stages in Piaget's theory are domain-general, but research suggests that many areas involve domain-specific and activity-specific development. Tasks that according to Piaget reflect the same cognitive structure are mastered at different age levels (Bidell & Fischer, 1992). There is also cultural variation as to when children master different tasks. Price-Williams and colleagues (1969) compared children from two Mexican villages. The **population** in one of the villages made a

morphisms. They can compare a subcategory with the category it is part of, such as "raspberries" and "berries," and correctly answer that there are mostly berries. Children process the simple correspondences they have discovered in the world around them. Consequently, the new theory is able to explain why children at this level manage this type of task better with known than with unknown materials. It is, for example, more difficult for children to include "ducks" in the category "animals" than to include "yellow flowers" in "flowers." They don't usually refer to ducks as animals. Such results were critical to the standard theory, which was based on domain-general development, while the new theory opened up for domain-specific and activity-specific knowledge (Acredolo, 1997; Barrouillet & Poirier, 1997).

A *qualitative* change takes place in children's thinking from the intermorphic to the transmorphic level. Children at the intermorphic level are merely able to coordinate morphisms. At the *transmorphic* level, they are capable of generalizing this knowledge and changing – transforming – morphisms into more abstract correspondences. Transmorphisms are also *operations*, processing of mental content. Children can link morphisms together into a comprehensive system so that their knowledge exceeds the specific content of these morphisms, which is based on their individual experiences. This marks the transition to a general system similar to **formal operational thinking**, but via a process that is more varied and whose results are less predetermined than in the standard theory.

Roughly speaking, preoperational thinking is comparable to the intramorphic level, concrete operational thinking to the intermorphic level, and formal operational thinking to the transmorphic level. An important difference however lies in the fact that the three levels of Piaget's new theory do not represent general stages of development. Compared with the standard theory, cognitive functioning is to a greater extent determined by the child's individual experiences. A child's thinking can involve different levels in different areas, depending on the child's specific experiences. The performance of different tasks may furthermore depend on the material being used and is therefore, to some extent, activity-specific (Acredolo, 1997).

4

Information Processing

The common denominator of information-processing theories is the notion that all cognitive phenomena can be described and explained based on a model whereby *information flows through one or more processing systems*, and increasing *complexity* is a major organizing principle of cognitive development (Halford & Andrews, 2011). According to Cohen and associates (2002), six principles explain how children come to understand the world:

1   Infants are endowed with an innate information-processing system.
2   Learning is hierarchical – infants form higher units from lower units.
3   Higher units serve as components for still-higher units.
4   Children will always take advantage of the highest-formed units.
5   If higher units are not available, lower-level units are utilized.
6   This learning system applies throughout development and across domains.

Thus, information processing can involve individual processes. An example of this is memory, which can be broken down into **encoding**, *decoding*, *storage*, **recall** and *feature identification* (see Chapter 10, this volume), while executive processes and other metacognitive processes monitor and regulate the processing. Metacognitive processes can be compared with Piaget's operations, although the underlying approach is quite different. In Piaget's theory, cognitive development centers on the formation of a unified structure. Information processing takes the opposite view and searches for a set of individual processes involved in all forms of cognitive functioning. Some mental tasks can be solved by individual processes, while others require coordination and multiple parallel processes (Welsh et al., 2006). Complexity may be defined as

DOI: 10.4324/9781003292500-5

the number of relations that can be processed in parallel and schemes needed to coordinate (Halford & Andrews, 2011).

The Developmental Process

Information-processing theorists have different views on *what* it is that changes during cognitive development. One view is that basic processes increase in speed or capacity with age, while at the same time children acquire more knowledge and better strategies and use of rules (Demetriou et al., 2002; Kail & Miller, 2006; Luna et al., 2004). Pascual-Leone (1970) for example argues that changes in children's thinking are the result of maturational increases in memory capacity that allow children to store more information in their **working memory** and encode it into **long-term memory**. Information processing can also become more complex and efficient as the result of *parallel processing*, a gradual increase in the ability to perform multiple processes simultaneously. Others, such as Case (1985), believe that after **infancy** the fundamental processes remain the same throughout life, and that development is a result of more efficient use of the capacities. Many tasks require more conscious attention and cognitive resources in children than in adults, where the performance of the task has become automatized, a development that entails that much routine processing takes place outside of the individual's conscious attention. When fundamental processes are constant and cannot be affected by the environment, they are per definition innate (Halford & Andrews, 2011).

Also, the view on domains varies within this tradition. When children solve mental tasks faster as they grow older, it may be owing either to the increasing speed of individual cognitive processes or to a general speed increase across different processes. In some models, basic processes operate across domains and therefore are domain-general (Cohen et al., 2002; Gathercole et al., 2004). Other models include differential processing of domains, and domain-specific development (Demetriou et al., 2002). Kail (2004) suggests that development includes both global (domain-general) and domain-specific processes.

Knowledge

From the perspective of information theory, knowledge is information, and changes in the extent and organization of information are important elements in cognitive development. Multiple processing allows the information to become more efficiently organized and take up fewer resources. An individual with extensive experience of a particular type of information becomes an "expert." Experts in a particular area have more knowledge of a certain type and are therefore able to solve problems in this area faster than non-experts – novices. According to Chi, problem solving, which in Piaget's model is assumed to reflect qualitative changes in cognitive structure, can be the result of a child's expanding knowledge and an increase in the speed of processing information when the subject area is known. Adults usually have more knowledge than children, but children are nevertheless able to surpass adults in certain areas. Many children know more about dinosaurs than adults do. Children who are good at chess remember the position of more pieces on the board than adults who know the rules but have little experience with the game (Chi & Koeske, 1983). Knowledge and strategies for organizing information thereby affect how it is perceived, memorized and processed.

Rules and Strategies

The use of strategies for managing cognitive tasks is an important element of information processing (see Box 4.1). New rules and strategies for solving tasks lead to changes in cognitive performance. Throughout **childhood**, children acquire a large repertoire of action strategies and create rules that can be more or less useful for different types of problem solving tasks. Younger children have few strategies, and their application is often inefficient or inappropriate. As they get older, they adopt and reject new rules and strategies. Some of these are short term, others long term, and they are used to varying degrees at different age levels (Figure 4.1). The particular strategies children choose depend on previous experience, the types of problems they intend to solve and how successful they eventually turn out to be (Siegler & Jenkins, 1989; Siegler, 1994).

Strategic choices and the establishment of rules gradually become better adapted with age. School-age children adopt various strategies spontaneously, and many strategies are explicitly communicated by teachers at school. The use of rules is not always permanent however, and some strategies are rarely applied unless children are reminded of them. One explanation may be that complex strategies demand too great a part of children's limited cognitive resources. Therefore, the use of new strategies does not always lead to improved performance in younger children, and sometimes they perform even worse. In one study, children in third and seventh grade were taught a memory

Box 4.1   Rule Development in the Acquisition of Counting (Kail & Bisanz, 1992, p. 252)

The development of early arithmetic skills can progress from applying a rule to a specific problem via a set of rules for similar problems to the formulation of general rules:

Rule 1: If the goal is to add (1 + 2), then count one finger, followed by two fingers, and say the result

Rule 2: If the goal is to add (3 + 4), then count three fingers, followed by four fingers, and say the result

Rule 3: If the goal is to add two numbers, m and n, then count m fingers, followed by n fingers, and say the result

Rule 1 is only valid for solving the problem 1 + 2 = ? Rule 2 is a new unique rule with an equally narrow scope (3 + 4). Rule 3 is a general rule, but is restricted by confining itself to the number of available fingers. When children learn higher numbers, they need new rules because Rule 3 is not broad enough.

strategy based on collecting words into categories and trying to recall all the words in the category, such as animals, clothing or furniture. Having received instruction, all of the children used the strategy they

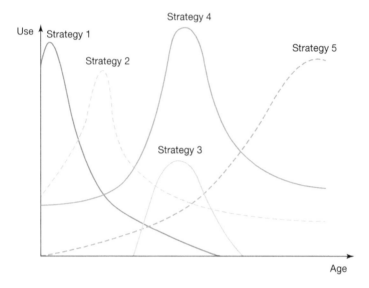

Figure 4.1 Siegler's developmental model for strategy choice.

According to Siegler, children develop a repertoire of strategies to choose from over time. In this example, Strategy 2 fairly quickly takes over from Strategy 1. Strategies 3 and 4 occur simultaneously, while Strategy 4 is used the most. In the end, Strategy 5 almost completely takes over, but Strategies 2 and 4 continue to be used (based on Bjorklund, 1995, p. 117).

had been taught, but only the seventh-graders recalled more words. Bjorklund and Harnishfeger (1987) interpret this to mean that the third-graders spent so many of their cognitive resources on applying the strategy that there were few resources left for the memorization task itself. This shows that there is little point in teaching children conscious strategies before they have developed the capacity to handle both task and strategy at the same time.

The path to using adult rules and strategies is a long one. Children must choose between different strategies and identify the one that fits best. The ability to inhibit strategies that do not fit the situation and abandon previously acquired strategies that no longer are suitable is also part of development. Particularly during **adolescence**, the monitoring of one's own deliberate choice and use of strategies – metacognitive strategies – becomes progressively more pronounced (Kuhn & Franklin, 2008).

Connectionism

Connectionism is an approach within the information-processing tradition. Connectionists attempt to describe the fundamental processes behind various functions and their development by **modeling** and simulating these processes using computer programs. They believe that computer simulations can help bridge the gap between cognitive models of the mind and neurological models of the brain and nervous system. Connectionist models of cognitive functions consist of networks of processing units that are assumed to correspond to similar units in the brain. When simulating an external stimulation, the model's units are activated to varying degrees and transmit activating or inhibitory impulses to other units in the network, thereby generating a *representation* or "model" of the incoming stimulation. Similarly, the model incorporates networks of units that activate or inhibit simulated action. When combined, the networks replicate the perception and actions of a simulated "child" (Elman et al., 1996; Schultz, 2003).

There are similarities between unit patterns of connectionist models and Piaget's schemas. Both describe how sensory stimulation and action are represented in the mind. Many connectionists have a background in the Piagetian tradition and view the simulation of children's learning processes as one of assimilation and accommodation (see Chapter 3, this volume). Unlike Piaget, however, they make no assumptions about predetermined structures or stages. Connectionists have demonstrated that the simulation of skill acquisition can result in a developmental curve similar to that of stages, as many small developmental changes can lead to sudden higher-level changes. An example of this is the simulation of the "**vocabulary spurt**," an increase in the rate of word learning that usually occurs at the end of the second year of life (see Book 5, *Communication and Language Development*, Chapter 6). According to connectionist simulations, the rate of word acquisition will increase once the system has learned a certain number of words (Elman et al., 1996). However, connectionist models never deal with domain-general development, but rather a stage-like development within clearly defined domains.

Connectionists are generally critical of assumptions about innate domain-specific knowledge. They acknowledge the existence of certain genetic factors but, by using computer simulations, they have been able to show that cognitive skills can be acquired through experience in areas where nativists insist on the presence of certain innate abilities because a given skill cannot be learned. For example, the use of simulations has made it possible to demonstrate that children can quickly learn to recognize faces, an ability that consequently need not be innate, as many nativists claim (see Book 3, *Perceptual and Motor Development*, Chapter 3).

Status of the Information-Processing Tradition

Information processing is the dominant school of thought in twenty-first century cognitive psychology. Although many scientists base their study of development on information and processing systems, the tradition remains somewhat incomplete in its perspective on development. Greater focus has been placed on identifying individual processes than on the developmental changes they bring about, and on creating models and simulating processes than on theoretical explanations of development (Munakata, 2006). No single unified model exists; it is rather a general approach to the understanding of cognitive functioning that slowly introduces developmental aspects, and there is considerable disagreement as to what development actually involves. This may be the very reason that information processing is often integrated with other approaches, including logical and social constructivism (Halford & Andrews, 2004; Morra et al., 2008; Russell, 1999).

Although the strength of connectionist simulations lies in their ability to specify all processes and elements of development, it simultaneously limits the type of development that can be simulated. They primarily center on the acquisition of relatively simple perceptual, cognitive and language skills, but include atypical development. Additionally, the simulations do not sufficiently account for the child's own active role in development (Elman, 2005). Many critics have raised the question of whether the computer **metaphor** is suited to describe the cognitive development of children. Computers neither grow nor change in the way children do. The information-processing tradition makes little allowance for the learning situation itself and for social and cultural factors that have proven to be important for cognitive functioning. The focus is on isolated processes and information, and socially constructed meaning is not considered to be central to an understanding of cognitive functioning (Nelson, 2007a).

5

Nativism

According to nativist views on cognitive development, infants are born with a pre-programmed, or "hard-wired," mental "model" of various aspects of the world. Modern nativists ascribe some degree of importance to the environment, but nativism is based on the fundamental assumption that the development of many cognitive functions are *experience-independent* or *experience-expectant* (see Book 2, *Genes, Fetal Development and Early Neurological Development*, Chapter 15). In their view, human genes impose **constraints** on what children can perceive and learn and provide a framework for the development of *domain-specific* processing modules, but not for their detailed contents. The rationale behind this is that these constraints ensure a **developmental pathway** that is domain-relevant rather than domain-irrelevant (Newcombe, 2002). Strong and weak forms of nativism are distinguished by the specific degree to which development is determined by genes.

Strong Nativism

Strong forms of nativism ascribe the basis of cognition to genetic factors. There are no structural cognitive changes as a result of experience as described by Piaget and others. The emergence of neurological processes and the way in which knowledge is represented are predetermined. Experience may be necessary for a given function to be utilized, but has little significance for the design of the function, for example how human beings perceive spatial relationships. Children's acquisition of knowledge depends solely on an input that allows processing by the module.

Assumptions about pre-programmed modules are central to strong nativist theories (see p. 165). According to Fodor (1983, 1985), the sensory system translates information to fit the relevant module. For

DOI: 10.4324/9781003292500-6

example, stimulation of the eye is translated in a way that enables the geometry module to process it. Following such processing, knowledge is forwarded to higher cognitive processes that guide the actions of children (and adults). Gardner (2006) believes there are different forms of intelligence with a basis in a limited number of modules (see Chapter 25, this volume).

Some theorists distinguish between *core domains*, with a genetic basis that leaves little room for variation, and *non-core domains* that are more dependent on experience. Core domains have developed because they represent areas in which the human species and its predecessors have needed to solve specific problems over a large number of generations (Gelman & Williams, 1998). Carey (1992), for example, suggests that the ability to distinguish and recognize members of one's own species has been of such great advantage that, in the course of evolution, humans have formed a separate neurological module to process facial information. This allows newborn infants to quickly learn to differentiate between the face of their own mother and that of another female. Specific problems with facial **recognition** due to brain injury during adulthood are also considered evidence of an innate modular ability (see Chapter 2, this volume). Spelke and Kinzler (2007) propose that children are born with four or five modules constituting a **core knowledge** that forms the basis for further cognitive development. These are modules for understanding objects, actions, numbers and spatial relationships (geometry), and perhaps also social relationships (**social cognition**).

Weak Nativism

In weaker forms of modern nativism, development is more affected by experience. The most important innate cognitive function in Gopnik and Meltzoff's (1997) *theory-theory* is the ability to form "theories." A theory can be defined as a coherent conceptual system used to understand and explain a set of related conditions and to predict future events (see Book 1, *Theoretical Perspectives and Methodology*, Chapter 10). A theory arguing that infants form "theories" is based on the assumption that infants possess cognitive resources enabling them to form hypotheses, make inferences about specific causal relationships in the outside world and determine whether the theory's inferences are correct or not, based on their own experience.

The ability to develop and try out theories is domain-general and used to produce theories in different areas of knowledge, according to Gopnik and Meltzoff. Infants are born with certain innate assumptions or "theories" about the world that they use as the basis for analyzing "data" from different domains, including an implicit **"theory of mind."** These theories are not permanent but subject to later modifications and revisions. To begin with, they provide an insufficient basis, and infants draw conclusions that future experience or "evidence" will show to be incorrect. When the infant gains new evidence, she creates new theories, which in turn are tried out and revised. The theories an individual ends up with as an adult may therefore have very little in common with the infant's initial theories. The earliest theories are nevertheless required in order to initiate the developmental process and enable children to recognize the world and form new theories.

The theory-theory represents a weak form of nativism because it does not assume that children are born with modules or "theories" that represent final cognitive functions. Instead, they constitute an innate starting point. In this way, the theory-theory allows more room for developmental variation and qualitative changes in children's thinking not determined by maturation. It nevertheless stands in sharp contrast to Piaget's theory by claiming that children are born with a cognitive structure that enables them to form and try out hypotheses. Piaget's theory views this type of "scientific" ability as the final result of development, first acquired through the development of operational schemas late in childhood. Yet the theory-theory's conjecture that children's theories – and consequently their conceptual system and reasoning – are changed through experience is not entirely unlike Piaget's theory of equilibration. The theory-theory hypothesizes that qualitative changes occur in children's thinking because the "data" (what children learn about the world) require a new theory and way in which to perceive the world, just as Piaget's theory states that children's experiences lead to the formation of new cognitive structures that cause them to perceive the world differently than before. According to the theory-theory, the types of theories children form depend to some extent on their specific experiences. The theory thus allows for different developmental pathways and **individual differences** in abilities and knowledge.

No clear boundaries exist between weak forms of nativism and what are considered to be non-nativist points of view. All theories assume that genetic factors play a determining role in the development of human cognition and thinking, but weak nativists place greater emphasis on these predetermined factors than non-nativists.

Status of Nativism

Nativism plays a significant role in twenty-first-century developmental psychology, but no one today views cognitive development as being exclusively determined by maturation. Nor does anyone entirely reject the importance of genes. A key objection to nativist assumptions is that they do not contribute to a better understanding of development by sidestepping the developmental process and ascribing all essential factors to the influence of genes. Strictly speaking, there is no development when all is predetermined (Kuo, 1967; Stotz, 2008). This is also Piaget's objection to a theory based exclusively on maturation. Others have pointed out that nativists underestimate the structural importance of children's actions and their environment, and the brain's ability to form patterns within these structures (Blumberg, 2008; Elman et al., 1996).

Many nativist theories are based on infant studies using **habituation** and visual preference (see Book 1, *Theoretical Perspectives and Methodology*, Part III). Infants have certain ways of organizing their experiences of the environment, but the nature of this organization and the associated competence is uncertain (Newcombe, 2002). Critics argue that nativists ascribe greater cognitive skills to infants and toddlers than empirically warranted. After all, cognitive development does not end at birth. Compared with older children and adults, infant knowledge is partial and as yet unfinished. Something must be developed, and maturation does not sufficiently explain the process (Campos et al., 2008; Kagan, 2008a; Karmiloff-Smith, 2007). Studies show, for example, that much of the mind understanding ascribed to toddlers on the basis of visual **exploration** is not yet explicit or consciously accessible at the age of 4 years (see Chapter 20, this volume). Just as important as establishing what perceptual and cognitive knowledge infants have is being able to explain *how* this initial knowledge can develop into mature cognitive functioning and reflection (Halford, 1989). This is precisely what developmental models attempt to do. Innate knowledge in itself is relatively inflexible. The more genetically specific one assumes early recognition to be, the more important it is to explain the flexibility that characterizes later cognitive development. The development of specific modules furthermore requires interaction between an extremely large number of genes. Researchers with a background in biology believe it is unlikely that the human organism would use a large proportion of its 23,000 genes or so (Ezkurdia et al., 2014) to develop dedicated processes for number comprehension or facial recognition. Genes have to take care of many other tasks (Nelson et al., 2006b).

Karmiloff-Smith (2009) points out that many theorists seem quick to assume that something is innate when a developmental process is difficult to describe, rather than searching for alternative *developmental* explanations. The nativists' claim that certain forms of knowledge cannot be taught or acquired seems paradoxical in light of their view that the basis of this knowledge can be formed through evolution. The explanation of why evolution has led to a higher occurrence of some genes than of others is that they contribute to properties that improve the individual's chance of survival. As the wheels of biology grind slowly, such properties must be useful over a large number of generations. Because environmental conditions tend to constantly change, it is likely that the evolutionary process has taken place based on general environmental characteristics, rather than producing highly specialized knowledge that mostly improves the chance of survival within a limited ecological niche.

6

Social Constructivism

From a social constructivist perspective, the deductive reasoning children grow up in affects their thinking through informal interaction as well as formal training (Vygotsky, 1935a, b). One of the key points is that children construct knowledge on their own: "An individual's abilities do not arise from the exercise of individually possessed 'cognitive processes,' but are constructed out of the social interactions an individual is immersed in" (Service et al., 1989, p. 23). *Dialogue, cooperation with others* and the *internalization of* **cultural tools** provide the main basis for cognitive development, rooted in the activities that incorporate these tools and strategies (Karpov, 2005; Vygotsky, 1962, 1978). Development is therefore characterized by a greater degree of *activity-specific* processes. When social constructivists criticize Piaget for failing to account for social conditions, it is not primarily his lack of interest in the importance of social factors for the development of individual differences that is the concern. The criticism is directed at the fact that he underestimates the role of social and cultural aspects in cognitive development in general.

Development

Although social constructivists, too, argue that children are born with a biological makeup that determines much of their early cognitive development, it is more a matter of processes that contribute to a child's social orientation rather than of domains of abstract knowledge (Gauvain & Perez, 2015). Individual cognitive resources are not sufficient for the development of higher forms of cognitive functioning. Children depend on adults to convey the knowledge their culture considers important, as well as mental tools and how to use them. It is

DOI: 10.4324/9781003292500-7

worth noting that this is the same argument used by nativists to argue that knowledge must be innate – that children are unable to acquire enough knowledge through individual experience with the physical environment alone (see Book 1, *Theoretical Perspectives and Methodology*, Chapter 14).

In social constructivist explanations, cognitive development occurs on two levels: first on the social and second on the psychological level. Initially, it is an interpersonal (intermental) process, followed by an individual (intramental) process. Children are guided to acquire the culture's knowledge and interpretation of the environment, and their cognition changes qualitatively with the activities and social interactions they engage in (Vygotsky, 1962). This point of view differs radically from the Piagetian tradition, in which the child herself develops knowledge at increasingly higher and more conscious levels by processing and organizing experiences.

Cultural Tools

While Piaget emphasizes the development of the child's own cognitive structure, the social constructivist theories emphasize the way in which cultural cognitive tools facilitate thinking. Tools such as symbols, calendars and mathematics reflect human knowledge developed over many generations. Children must acquire the use of these tools just as they must learn to use a hammer, a spade and other tools of labor the culture has developed for use by human hands (Karpov, 2005). The most important mental tool is language: children solve practical tasks as much by using language as with their eyes and hands. Language enables children to plan actions and carry out mental actions and causes human memory to work fundamentally differently from that of other species. It is a tool for autonomous thinking and reflection, but also a tool that makes it possible to gain and communicate knowledge, and that facilitates the acquisition of other tools. According to Vygotsky, language is a requirement for developing higher mental functions, while Piaget attributed less importance to language precisely because it is socially acquired, through observing the outside world.

Internalization

Internalization may be the most important process in Vygotsky's developmental model. It entails the transformation of external processes, for example in the form of dialogue or collaboration on problem solving, into internalized psychological processes. The internalization of tools depends on children's participation in social interaction and adult guidance and mediation, as children are unable to "discover" these tools on their own. The internalization of language and other cognitive tools mediates increased awareness and higher cognitive functioning. By engaging in conversations and collaboration, children acquire new ways of solving problems and gradual mastery of the tools used by their culture. They use language initially in interaction with others and subsequently as a tool for abstract reflection. The process of internalization happens gradually, and, during early development, children speak out loud when planning and regulating their own behavior or solving tasks because the tool is not yet fully internalized (see Chapter 19, this volume).

This process is illustrated by the development of memory. While the memory of toddlers is based purely on a biological ability to store what is being perceived, adults use language and various other strategies and aids to remember (for example by categorizing things or writing them down). Through interaction with adults, children gradually learn the memory strategies of their culture and integrate the basic functions of memory with conceptual skills, reasoning and narratives.

The types of tools that shape cognition vary from culture to culture. The way in which a culture organizes knowledge forms the basis for the developmental reorganization of categories and the structure of thought. Therefore, the internalization of cultural tools and knowledge from more competent peers and adults is an important basis for continuity across generations as well as cultural variation.

The Zone of Proximal Development

According to Vygotsky, the gradual process of social internalization makes it necessary to distinguish between what children master independently and what they are able to do in collaboration with adults and more competent peers. Things children are unable to master on their own, but can together with others, are within their **zone of proximal development**. In Vygotsky's own words: what children are capable of with help today, they do on their own tomorrow. Children will always be able to do more with help than on their own, but two children capable of doing equally much independently may not be equally susceptible to help – they have different zones of proximal development. Take for example two 8-year-olds, both capable of independently solving arithmetic problems typically mastered by children of their age. With help, one of the children can solve arithmetic problems that children are usually able to solve when they are 9 years old, that is, 1 year older. The other child can solve problems that children usually are unable to master before the age of 12. Within this domain, the first child has a zone of proximal development of 1 year, and the second child has one of 4 years. It is within the zone of proximal development that learning can take place (see Chapter 36, this volume). When Mary is able to do more than John, and both receive equal help, Mary has a greater *learning potential* in that particular area and at that particular moment than John. Vygotsky believes that what children are able to do with help is a better measure of cognitive development than what they can do on their own. This principle is used in **dynamic assessment** (see Book 1, *Theoretical Perspectives and Methodology*, Chapter 27).

In other words, internalization is the result not of a passive intake of socially mediated knowledge, but of a collaborative effort that gradually changes character. Help and guidance from adults (and more competent peers) are part of children's cognitive development and mastery of new tasks. To begin with, it may be the adult who is in charge of nearly all the cognitive resources necessary to solve a task. By interacting, children receive confirmation of previously established skills, acquire new tools and knowledge and gradually need less help to solve the task. In the end, the necessary tools and their use become internalized and provide children with sufficient cognitive resources to master tasks on their own.

The beginning of the zone of proximal development is defined based on what a child is able to do independently. The point at which children no longer master a task on their own marks the beginning of the zone. Its extent is defined by what the child can do with help. When a maximum amount of help from more competent peers and adults does not enable the child to attempt to solve a task, it means that the task lies outside the child's developmental zone. The child must be able to understand the task and have a strategy in order to try to solve it. The strategy may well be incorrect, but, for a task to lie within the zone of proximal development, the child must show an understanding of what the task is about and somehow attempt to approach the task. It is not enough that an adult solves the problem while the child looks on with interest.

In social constructivist theory, development is not domain-general – either independent performance or the zone of proximal development. Instead, different zones are associated with separate domains and skills, and children can have strengths and weaknesses in different areas (see Figure 6.1). When children acquire new competence,

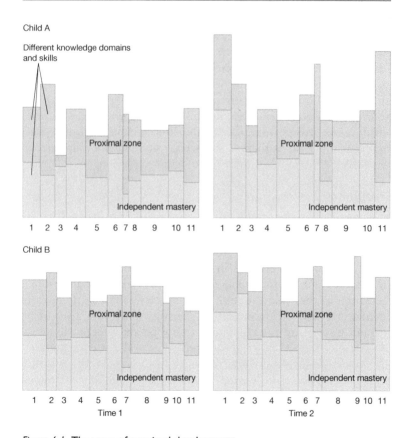

Figure 6.1 The zone of proximal development.

The figure shows independent performance and the zone of proximal development (what children are able to do with help) for two children at different ages within several knowledge domains and skills. At time 1, these areas show a difference in "width" and "length," and the development within the different domains is also somewhat dissimilar until time 2. In domain 1, both independent performance and the developmental zone (problem solving with help) have increased from time 1 to time 2 in both children. Independent performance has increased in domain 2, and the developmental zone has decreased correspondingly in both children. They have become more independent, but are unable to do more with help than at time 1. In domain 4, the developmental zone of Child B has increased (can do more with help), but there is no increase in the child's independent performance. For Child A, neither independent performance nor the developmental zone has increased in this domain, but Child A shows a similar development in domain 11 as Child B in domain 4. Child B shows a corresponding development in domain 5 to that of Child A in domain 4. Consequently, the children have different strong and weak domains and skills and also show a dissimilar development between the two times.

their independent competence increases, and their zone of proximal development changes. Children do not move through the zone; it is the zone itself that changes with the child's growing expertise. For a period of time, a child's development in a given area may consist of an increase in independent performance, while the developmental zone for that domain decreases correspondingly. At other times, only the developmental zone increases. The child is able to do more with help, but does not master more tasks within the domain more independently. At other times, there is an increase in children's independent performance and in what they can do with help (see Figure 6.1).

Scaffolding

According to social constructivist developmental theories, it is mediation by adults that enables children to acquire the cognitive tools and knowledge of their culture, and the collaboration between adults and children represents an important part of the developmental process. Adults must be able to introduce "tasks" and adapt their mediation to the child's zone of proximal development. If children encounter a task with a degree of difficulty above this zone, they will not understand the task and thus not be able to contribute to its solution. If the task is too easy, solving it will not contribute to the children's development or changes in their zone of proximal development. For tasks located within a given zone, the strategies contributed by adults are known as **scaffolding**; they constitute a flexible external structure that can support the development of the child's ability to solve problems. Scaffolding is mediation: adults attempt to clarify what is required to solve a task, limit those aspects of the task that the child is unable to master – for example by holding an object stationary while the child tries to take something from it – and shield the child from distractions that can draw attention from the task at hand. The scaffold – help and support – is gradually disassembled or reduced, and, once the child is able to master a task independently, scaffolding is no longer needed. This means that adults guide the child toward tasks at the child's own level *as well as* offer help that the child actually benefits from. Too little help can prevent children from being able to solve the task. Too much help can reduce children's trust in their own ability, because the help provided by adults also reflects an evaluation of the child's competence (von Tetzchner, 2009). Both task and help must therefore lie within a child's zone of proximal development if adults are to contribute to the child's development.

Development of Leading Activities

From a social constructivist point of view, children's cultural participation and activities are part of their cognitive development. Vygotsky and Elkonin describe six phases of children's participation in activities, from intuitive and emotional contact between children and adults to the acquisition of vocational expertise (Box 6.1). Each phase is comprised of a *leading activity* with specific *motives*, *goals* and *actions* that are central to a particular age level and prepare the child for the next phase with a new leading activity. The particular activities are not predefined and will depend on the culture a child grows up in. In industrialized societies for example, **role-play** prepares preschool-age children for school, while children in many other societies participate in adult activities from an early age (Morelli et al., 2003). These phases also reflect the way in which social constructivist theories describe children's cognitive functioning on two levels. One level includes the activities children engage in together with more competent adults or peers. This represents children's "external" thinking. The second level incorporates the changes that occur in children's "internal" thinking. Because the activities in a society are not stable over time, Rogoff (1998) suggests that an understanding of development requires a third level, the *community level*, which includes the technological and cultural development of a society. The cell phone for example has changed the patterns in children's social interactions (see Book 7, *Social Relations, Self-awareness and Identity*, Chapter 38). Leontiev and other neo-Vygotskians are further developing the phases in **activity theory** (Karpov, 2005).

When knowledge is acquired only within a specific area or activity, it is not automatically transferred to other activities. One study found that 9–15-year-old street vendors in Brazil were able to solve math problems when they sold fruit on the street but were unable to do so outside the confines of their familiar street vending activities, even if the problems by and large required the same level of math skills (Box 6.2). Similarly, British children who have learned to work out pre-formulated math exercises may encounter difficulties when confronted with practical math problems in text form (Desforges, 1998).

Other studies have demonstrated that different cultural activities can lead to cognitive differences, for example in the development of conservation (see Chapter 3, this volume). Moreover, Vygotsky himself emphasizes the importance of formal education and considers it to be part of the cultural foundation that shapes cognitive development (Karpov, 2014).

Box 6.1   Phases of Leading Activities

Vygotsky and Elkonin describe six phases in children's development that are characterized by different leading activities:

1   The activity of intuitive and emotional contact between the child and adults (0–1 years)

   This includes a feeling for the need to interact with other people, the expression of emotions, learning to grasp things and a variety of perceptual actions.

2   Object-manipulation activity (1–3 years)

   Children adopt socially acceptable ways of handling things and through interaction with adults they develop speech and visual-perception thinking.

3   Game-playing activity (3–7 years)

   Children engage in symbolic activities and creative play. They now have some comprehension of how to cooperate together in group endeavors.

4   Learning activity (7–11 years)

   Children develop theoretical approaches to the world of things, a function that involves their considering laws of reality and beginning to comprehend psychological preconditions for abstract theoretical thought (intentional mental operations, schemes for problem solving, reflective thinking).

5   Social-communication activity (11–15 years)

   Adolescents gain skills in initiating types of communication needed for solving life's problems, understanding other people's motives and submitting to group norms.

6   Vocational-learning activity (15–17 years)

   Older adolescents develop new cognitive and vocational interests, grasp elements of research work and attempt life projects.

The development of activities is characterized by fluctuations between periods of **stability** and periods of change. The transition from one **developmental phase** to another disrupts the stability of the child's thinking and interaction with the environment, thereby producing crises as the child struggles to comprehend the next activity that is to occupy the leading role (based on Thomas, 2005).

Box 6.2   Street Mathematics and School Mathematics (Nunes et al., 1993)

The study includes four boys and one girl from the poor quarter of the city of Recife in northeastern Brazil. They were between 9 and 15 years of age and had received 1–8 years of schooling, but classroom teaching had been limited. Their arithmetic skills were studied using both informal and formal **tests**. The informal test was conducted in their natural environment – on the street corner or in the market where they sold coconuts and other goods. The experimenter was the "customer" and purchased goods or inquired about the price of goods she considered buying. The formal test took place at the children's home. The math problems were dictated to the subject (for example 105 + 105) or presented in word form of the type: *Mary bought x bananas; each banana cost y; how much did she pay altogether?* The results showed that the children were able to solve a far greater number of problems in the natural street vending situation than in the more formal tests.

Subject	Informal test	Arithmetic operations	Word problems
M	10.0	2.5	10.0
P	8.9	3.7	6.9
Pi	10.0	5.0	10.0
MD	10.0	1.0	3.3
S	10.0	8.3	7.3

Example I (M, I2 Years)

Informal test

CUSTOMER: I'm going to take four coconuts. How much is that?
M: There will be one hundred five, plus thirty, that's one thirty-five ... one coconut is thirty-five ... that is ... one forty!

Formal test

M solves the item 35 × 4, explaining out loud: *Four times five is twenty, carry the two; two plus three is five, times four is twenty.* Answer written: 200.

Example 2 (MD, 9 Years)

Informal test

CUSTOMER: *OK, I'll take three coconuts* (at a price of 40 cruzeiros each).
MD (calculates out loud): *Forty, eighty, one twenty.*

Formal test

MD solves the item 40 × 3 and obtains 70. She then explains the procedure: *Lower the zero; four and three is seven.*

Example 3 (MD, 9 Years)

Informal test

CUSTOMER: *I'll take twelve lemons* (one lemon is 5 cruzeiros).
MD: *Ten, twenty, thirty, forty, fifty, sixty* (while separating out two lemons at a time).

Formal test

MD has just solved the item 40 × 3. In solving 12 × 15, she explains what she does while trying to solve the problem, and proceeds by lowering first the 2, then the 5 and then the 1, obtaining 152.

Example 4 (S, I I Years)

Informal test

CUSTOMER: *What would I have to pay for six kilos* (of watermelon at 50 cruzeiros per kilo)?
S (without any appreciable pause): *Three hundred.*
CUSTOMER: *Let me see. How did you get that so fast?*
S: *Counting one by one. Two kilos, one hundred. Two hundred. Three hundred.*

Formal test

The task: A fisherman caught 50 fish. The second one caught five times the amount of fish the first fisherman had caught. How many fish did the lucky fisherman catch?

S writes down 50 × 6 and 360 as the result, then answers *36.* Examiner (E) repeats the problem, and S does the computation again, writing down 860 as the result and answering: *86.*

E: *How did you calculate that?*
S: *I did it like this. Six times six is thirty-six. Then I put it there.*
E: *Where did you put it?* (S had not written down the number to be carried.)
S (points to the digit 5 in 50): *That makes eighty-six* (apparently adding 3 and 5 and placing this sum in the result).
E: *How many did the first fisherman catch?*
S: *Fifty.*

Individual and Social Exploration

By focusing on social and cultural activities, social constructivists have made a unique contribution to the understanding of cognition and cognitive development. Piaget is frequently criticized for his view of children as self-reliant explorers of the physical world and for failing to take sufficient account of the social context that provides a framework for cognitive development. Yet a similar criticism of bias can be directed at many theorists within the social constructivist tradition. They place little emphasis on the independent and direct exploration of objects that characterizes early development in particular. Children engage with other people, but it takes time before they realize that they can use others to solve the problems they encounter. Even when they are able to ask for such help, they do not always want it. "Do it myself" is virtually a standard phrase among 2–3-year-olds. More often it is older children who seek help with problems they are unable to cope with. Part of the reason that children's independent exploration of the physical environment has received little attention within this tradition may be found in the fact that Vygotsky himself rarely studied children under the age of 4 years. Moreover, social constructivist studies have focused specifically on language and cultural activities that involve interaction, such as **group play** and meals. A theory of cognitive development must include both the exploration children engage in on their own *and* the knowledge that is communicated through cooperation with adults (Gauvain & Perez, 2015).

Status of Social Constructivism

Social constructivism plays a central role in modern developmental psychology and is often applied as a counterweight to both logical constructivism and nativism. Although many researchers base their study on the concepts of this tradition, it has lead them down somewhat different paths in Russia, Europe and the US. Many theorists of the Russian school are critical of Western European and North American interpretations of Vygotsky's writings, which they found to be too static (Karpov, 2005). Compared with the other theories, social constructivist ideas seem to have somewhat less influence on research based on brain functioning, which today represents a significant part of developmental science.

The social constructivist tradition has had a major influence on educational theories and practices. At the same time, it has been criticized for its bias toward adult-communicated knowledge. Damon (1984) emphasizes that cooperation with peers also provides a unique contribution to children's cognitive development through the exchange of ideas with equal partners. In addition, many studies based on social constructivist theory focus on the interaction between a single adult and child, a fact that most likely reflects the small family size of industrialized countries. Many activities involve numerous participants, particularly in developing countries, but, in highly industrialized societies as well, children's activities occur in the context of larger groups, such as educational settings (Sommer, 2012).

7

Disparity and Integration

Today, the four main traditions of developmental cognitive psychology continue to evolve in different ways. The complexity of cognitive development is reflected in the fact that so far no single description or explanation exists that all can agree on. At the same time, the different theories are expanded and integrated with ideas that lie outside the individual tradition. Several current approaches combine Piaget's constructivist ideas with concepts based on information processing (Barrouillet, 2015; Morra et al., 2008). Concepts from neuroscience are commonly included as well. Both *neuroconstructivism* (Mareschal et al., 2007a, b) and *neoconstructivism* (Johnson & Hannon, 2015) integrate elements from Piaget's theory, connectionism and neuroscience. Nelson's developmental theory (1996, 2007a) uses *events* as a basic unit and is inspired by both Piaget and Vygotsky. Children begin by participating in and learning to master events that are part of their social and cultural world and subsequently form an understanding of these events. The most important cognitive task is to create *meaning* out of events, and it is this search for meaning that drives children's cognitive development.

A discussion of the basic ideas behind these traditions is important in order to reveal disparities between their various explanations (Sokol & Martin, 2006). Nelson (2007a) points out that each tradition in itself is insufficient to explain cognitive development. She is critical of nativism, owing to its lack of focus on development, as well as the information-processing tradition, which she believes describes isolated mental processes without accounting for the sense of meaning and coherence that characterizes the human mind.

DOI: 10.4324/9781003292500-8

Summary of Part I

1 The central question of theories of cognitive development is how children perceive and adapt to the world around them, retain experiences and develop new knowledge and new ways of categorizing, thinking and reasoning.

2 The theories place varying emphasis on modules, domains and activities. Cognitive processes can be *domain-general*, *domain-specific* or *activity-specific*. Some theorists argue for the existence of innate *neurological modules* that correspond to specific areas of knowledge. Others believe that development is based on a *process of modularization*.

3 *Piaget's theory* has had a decisive impact on most approaches to cognitive development. His is the only major theory to describe the development from infant to adult as a coherent developmental pathway of qualitative changes in thinking and reasoning, and to explain how this development takes place. Piaget's key concepts are that thought has its roots in action, and that children *construct* their understanding of the world through their experiences with the physical and social environment. Children develop a *cognitive structure* that consists of *schemas*, enabling children to abstract and store experiences. The basic processes are *assimilation*, *accommodation* and *organization* – mental schemas and processes undergo change as children solve problems and acquire new experiences. Development is driven by an innate ability to perceive contradictions and a search for *equilibrium* between established schemas and new experiences. Piaget divides cognitive development into four universal stages: *sensorimotor*, *preoperational*, *concrete operational* and *formal operational*. The cognitive structure manifests itself in the types of tasks children are able to understand and solve in the different stages.

DOI: 10.4324/9781003292500-9

4   Piaget's theory has also received more criticism than any other in the field of cognitive development. Many are sceptical about the role of domain-specific processes and the division into stages, but stage thinking is still present in many theories. Studies show that children are capable of solving similar tasks at a much earlier age than Piaget found by facilitating a different set of circumstances, and often there are significant differences in age levels at which tasks with the same presumed operational structure are mastered. Additionally, there are major differences in how various cultures solve cognitive tasks. Piaget's ideas are being further developed by neo-Piagetians, including his **stage theory**.

5   The main principle behind Piaget's *new theory* is that schemas are formed when children discover *correspondences* in the external world. Correspondences that go beyond a comparison of identical features are called *morphisms*. They are tools for establishing *constants*, conditions that do not vary across the phenomena in question. Thinking traverses three levels: *intramorphic*, *intermorphic* and *transmorphic*. They do not represent general stages of development; instead, a child's thinking can involve different levels in different domain-specific areas.

6   *Information-processing theories* build on the assumption that all cognitive phenomena can be described as information that flows through one or more processing systems, and they search for a set of *basic processes* of human cognition. There are different views on what development consists of. As children develop, they may increase their capacities, perform several processes simultaneously, gain more knowledge and organize it in new ways, develop metacognition and acquire new strategies for solving problems. Critics claim that the computer is not suitable as a model for children's cognitive development, and that information processing has a biased focus on children's performance of isolated tasks without placing them in the social and cultural context in which they belong.

7   *Connectionism* uses computer models and simulations to investigate the basic processes underlying different abilities, based on models where external stimulation leads to various activating or inhibitory processes. These processes determine what an individual perceives and how he or she acts. Critics point out that connectionism to date has focused mainly on the acquisition of relatively simple perceptual, cognitive and linguistic skills and has not taken sufficient account of the child's own active role in development.

8   *Nativism* is based on the assumption that children are born with a mental "model" of various aspects of the world, and that the brain "knows" something about how to interpret certain forms of stimulation. Genes impose *constraints* on what children can perceive and learn. Studies of cognitive abilities in infants and toddlers constitute an important but also disputed empirical basis. In *strong forms of nativism*, it is largely genes that determine the design of cognition, often in the form of *neurological modules*. Spelke and Kinzler suggest that children begin with a core knowledge of four or five modules that form the basis for further development. *Weaker forms of nativism* attribute a somewhat lesser role to genes. According to Gopnik and Meltzoff's *theory-theory*, children are born with a domain-general cognitive structure that enables them to form hypotheses and try them out. Children begin with *innate theories* that are revised as the children gain more experience. Nativism has a strong position in twenty-first-century cognitive developmental psychology. Critics point out that there is little room for development because the structure is predetermined. They also argue that nativists ascribe greater cognitive skills to infants than empirically warranted, and that there are major differences between the infant competence inferred from indirect methods and the explicit understanding and ability to apply knowledge in older children.

9   From a *social constructivist* perspective, cognitive development is the result of collaboration between children and adults. Social interaction and cultural knowledge and activities become a part of a child's cognitive structure, and there are cognitive differences between children who grow up under different social and cultural conditions. The acquisition of *cultural cognitive tools*, such as language and other symbolic systems, facilitates thinking and makes it possible for children to plan actions, act mentally and reflect, and develop higher mental functions. The internalization of cultural tools requires social interaction, as children are unable to create these tools on their own. The social process of internalization makes it necessary to distinguish between what children master independently and what they are able to do in collaboration with others, their *zone of proximal development*. The strategies contributed by adults are figuratively known as *scaffolding*, a flexible external structure that can support and promote the child's functioning and development. Vygotsky and Elkonin describe six phases or levels of children's participation in activities, further developed by Leontiev

and other neo-Vygotskians. Social constructivism has been criticized for placing too little emphasis on the independent exploration that characterizes an infant's early development in particular,
and for its bias towards adult-communicated knowledge and the
interaction between a single adult and child. Many child activities
involve numerous participants, such as in educational settings.

10 There is today no single description or explanation of cognitive
development that everyone can agree on. All the four main traditions of cognitive development continue to be developed today.
They represent significant theoretical and empirical differences,
but are also further expanded and integrated with ideas that lie
outside the individual tradition.

Core Issues

- The presence of domain-general, domain-specific and activity-
  specific processes.
- The role of nature and nurture in cognitive development.
- The role of culture in cognitive development.

Suggestions for Further Reading

Acredolo, C. (1997). Understanding Piaget's new theory requires assimilation and
accommodation. *Human Development, 40,* 235–237.

Cohen, L. B., Chaput, H. H., & Cashon, C. H. (2002). A constructivist model of
infant cognition. *Cognitive Development, 17,* 1323–1343.

Karmiloff-Smith, A. (2015). An alternative to domain-general or domain-specific
frameworks for theorizing about human evolution and ontogenesis. *AIMS Neuroscience, 2,* 91–104.

Karpov, Y. V. (2005). *The neo-Vygotskian approach to child development.* Cambridge:
Cambridge University Press.

Morra, S., Gobbo, C., Marini, Z., & Sheese, R. (2008). *Cognitive development: Neo-
Piagetian perspectives.* New York, NY: Lawrence Erlbaum.

Nunes, T., Schlieman, A. D., & Carraher, D. W. (1993). *Street mathematics and school
mathematics.* Cambridge: Cambridge University Press.

Piaget, J. (1954). *The construction of reality in the child.* New York, NY: Routledge &
Kegan Paul.

Spelke, E. S., & Kinzler, K. D. (2007). Core knowledge. *Developmental Science, 10,*
89–96.

Vygotsky, L. S. (1962). *Language and thought.* Cambridge, MA: MIT Press.

Part II

Attention, Memory and Executive Function

8
Basic Cognitive Functions

Attention, memory and **executive functions** are the basis for all daily activities and are necessary for the child to adapt to and cope with the environment. Attention has to do with being alert, obtaining an overview of one's surroundings and focusing on what is important and relevant to the situation. Experiences are processed and stored; they can be recognized or recalled or otherwise influence children's thoughts and actions. Executive functions serve to regulate attention, plan and monitor the performance of voluntary actions, and inhibit inappropriate action impulses. As executive functions include attention and working memory, there are no clearly defined boundaries between them.

DOI: 10.4324/9781003292500-11

9

Attention

Attention is about directing awareness toward what is relevant – like a spotlight – and limiting or expanding the attention depending on the activity and the objective. When playing football, broad attention is functional, while focused attention is more appropriate when solving math problems. Attention is important in the regulation of thoughts and feelings, but the ability to disengage and shift attention to something else can be just as important as focusing attention (Reynolds et al., 2013; Ristic & Enns, 2015). While research on early attention often centers on how long children look at something (Colombo, 2001), hearing and other senses are also governed by attention (Karns et al., 2015).

Attention in the First Year of Life

The development of attention proceeds through three phases that reflect the different functions of attention (Colombo, 2001). The first phase includes the first 2 months of life and is characterized by increasing alertness and the ability to sustain attention over gradually longer periods of time. Infants gradually look at things for longer, but they have difficulty shifting attention away from something once they have become aware of it (Reynolds et al., 2013).

During the second phase, from 3 to 6 months, there is an increase in infants' ability to orient themselves and explore their surroundings. Owing to faster and more efficient processing of sensory information, they are able to shift attention more frequently. The third stage begins around 7 months; the time infants need to familiarize themselves with new things becomes more stable and increases in duration for more complex stimulation. Throughout the first year of life, infants learn to

DOI: 10.4324/9781003292500-12

use attention to regulate their own emotional arousal and distress, for example by looking away when they get too emotionally aroused by what they are looking at or shifting visual attention away from stimulation that makes them distressed to neutral or positive stimulation (Swingler et al., 2015).

The child's attention focus is also important for the infant's interaction with adults. Parents observe their child's focus of attention, interpret the child's behavior and general state and direct the child's attention to something neutral or positive when the child seems upset or agitated by something. Development thus progresses from attention controlled by external stimulation to a greater degree of voluntary attention regulation. Children also improve at filtering stimulation and focusing on what is relevant (Ristic & Enns, 2015) and, toward the end of the first year, they begin to become attentive to the attention of others as well (see Book 5, *Communication and Language Development*).

There are considerable differences between children with typical development, and research has found a relationship between early individual differences in attention and the development of language, cognition and play during later childhood (Reynolds et al., 2013).

Solving a puzzle requires attention and working memory

Attention Development during Childhood and Adolescence

Younger children have difficulties adapting their attention. With increasing age, their ability to maintain and shift focus improves – they become better at both limiting and expanding the boundaries of their attention to a given activity or situation, and to perceiving what is relevant and maintaining attention there. Children's ability to filter and prioritize stimulation gradually improves during early school age. They are increasingly able to refrain from reacting to stimulation that is not relevant to what they are engaged in and thus less distractible. There are, however, individual differences in how well children are able to sustain attention on a task and how easily they become distracted by more peripheral stimulation (Ristic & Enns, 2015).

The ability to regulate attention is important in school, where children need to sit still and maintain focused attention on the subject in the classroom. Research shows that young schoolchildren perform many tasks involving attention as well as adults, such as finding specific letters or patterns on a page. However, their attention depends on motivation and content, and on the ability to understand context and meaning. For example, children notice a change in pictures better when the change makes sense or is central than when the change is more peripheral (Fletcher-Watson et al., 2009). Even for adolescents, it is difficult to sustain attention when they do not understand the meaning of what is being taught. There may be quite different reasons why a teacher struggles to maintain the attention of a class, but it might be because the children do not understand what the teacher is trying to tell them.

Certain types of stimulation promote attention more than others. Children (and adults) generally react differently to social and non-social stimulation, for example faces and geometric shapes. They are more attentive to faces that express fear or anger than to faces with a neutral or positive emotional expression and find it difficult to ignore faces that look angry or frightened, perhaps because they convey information that can create both fear and **empathy** (see Book 6, *Emotions, Temperament, Personality, Moral, Prosocial and Antisocial Development*, Chapter 6). Children are more likely to discover spiders and snakes hidden among mushrooms and flowers in a picture than mushrooms and flowers hidden among spiders and snakes (Waters et al., 2008). However, although infants show high attention to snakes, there is no evidence that they are afraid of snakes or find them aversive (Thrasher & LoBue, 2016).

Children also develop general attention tendencies that determine how they filter stimulation and weigh different cues. This in turn affects how they perceive or misperceive their surroundings. Social cues are often ambiguous, and children develop different tendencies in regard to perceiving emotional cues. Physically aggressive children for example tend to be particularly aware of social hostility and to perceive others as threatening (see Book 6, *Emotions, Temperament, Personality, Moral, Prosocial and Antisocial Development*, Chapter 27) (Arsenault & Foster, 2012; Gouze, 1987). Children who have developed such a tendency may find it difficult to filter out or not react to potential signs of hostility, even when other aspects of the situation indicate that they are irrelevant (Ristic & Enns, 2015). Similarly, shy children tend to be aware of potential cues for social rejection. They have fewer expectations that others might be glad when they look at them and are more likely to perceive interactions as negative (Kokin et al., 2016).

Attention in Atypical Development

Children with **ADHD** have problems sustaining attention and are easily distracted by more peripheral stimulation but do not necessarily perform poorly on tasks that require them to be alert and orient themselves. Problems are evident in daily life, especially in the educational domain, and many children and adolescents with ADHD perform below their skill level at school (Rogers et al., 2015). Even when symptoms of inattention and **hyperactivity** decline, children may have significant academic difficulties throughout school, possibly because early inattention has impeded acquisition of the basic knowledge and skills that form the basis for later learning (Pingault et al., 2011, 2014; Sasser et al., 2016).

Helping children gain better control over their attention may be effective in early intervention (Posne & Rothbart, 2000). The trajectories of ADHD are related to family characteristics, and inconsistent parenting may negatively influence development (Sasser et al., 2016). Early parent education can affect parents' response to their child's behavior and thereby contribute to preventing the development of behavioral problems (Campbell et al., 2014; Danforth et al., 2016). The effectiveness of cognitive behavior therapy for children with ADHD is well documented, but only in connection with the presence of behavioral problems (Antshel & Olszewski, 2014; Tamm et al., 2014). There have been many attempts at attention training, but results are modest (Cortese et al., 2015; van der Donk et al., 2015).

Studies suggest that some children with ADHD are sensitive to certain food substances and can benefit from a change in diet (Pelsser et al., 2011). ADHD is often treated with medication, but the use of medication is controversial. For some children, drugs can be of help, but they should only be administered once other treatment initiatives have been tried for several months without satisfactory results and should also always be accompanied by other therapeutic approaches (Rothenberger & Banaschewski, 2004; Sibley et al., 2014). Additionally, drugs have a greater impact on behavior than on learning (Doggett, 2004). Therefore, both with and without medication, it is important to tailor education at school and adopt strategies that reduce the cognitive load to allow children with ADHD to master the daily academic and social challenges they face (Hinshaw & Scheffler, 2014; Tannock, 2007). Many children with ADHD struggle with learning to read and may benefit from intensive reading intervention, independent of their use of medication (Tannock et al., 2018).

Attention deficits are classified as a separate group of disorders (see Book 1, *Theoretical Perspectives and Methodology*, Part IV), but problems with attention are also associated with other neurodevelopmental disorders (Karns et al., 2015). They are not always a matter of attention regulation being better or worse but can be of what children and adolescents pay attention to (Burack et al., 2016). Children with **autism spectrum disorders** are characterized by atypical filtering and focus and they are often attentive to other aspects of the situation than their peers (Fan, 2013; Keehn et al., 2013). An intervention study with heterogeneous groups of children with intellectual and developmental disabilities did not find positive effects of attention training (Kirk et al., 2017). Attention and distractibility are furthermore affected by problems related to vision (Tadić et al., 2009) and hearing (Dye & Hauser, 2014). Behaviorally inhibited children and adolescents with anxiety tend to pay attention to threat and not to reward, and attentional bias modification is used in anxiety intervention (MacLeod & Clarke, 2015; Shechner et al., 2012).

10

Memory

The mind always makes use of earlier experiences and learning. Memory makes it possible to anticipate the future and create continuity between past, present and future. Speech, writing and other cultural tools also allow for the organization and storage of knowledge beyond the limits of each individual's memory.

The human memory consists of several elements with different functions. The function of short-term memory is to store information for a short period of time, seconds or minutes, often in connection with the performance of another task, such as when children think of the shape of a puzzle piece cut-out while looking for the piece that fits. Working memory also stores information for a short time, but additionally involves some type of processing or organizing information, such as when children learn to pronounce and use a new word. Working memory is about the here-and-now and has a limited capacity for storing and processing information. It registers information from both the environment and long-term memory and helps tie together new and previously stored information. At any given time, working memory only contains what is needed at the moment and forms an integral part of all learning and thinking (Cowan, 2014).

Long-term memory stores information over time, in some cases throughout life. It is considered to have unlimited capacity and represents the individual's personal and cultural knowledge base. In order to make use of what is stored, children must be able to recall the information whenever it is needed. *Recognition* may be measured by asking children to indicate whether they have seen a particular photograph or action before. Infants, for example, will typically look longer at an unfamiliar image than at one they have seen before (see Book 1, *Theoretical Perspectives and Methodology*, Chapter 25). *Recall* is a process of recreation or reconstruction: the individual tells or shows what was

DOI: 10.4324/9781003292500-13

observed or experienced. The focus of attention, knowledge and past experiences determine what is being recalled. However, forgetting and unlearning are also important functions of the memory system. They are necessary so that children do not act the same way all the time but are capable of adapting to constantly changing environments (Bauer, 2014; Cuevas et al., 2015).

From a developmental point of view, the question is how the various parts of the memory system change with age. The most important developmental changes seem to happen between birth and early school age, but changes in memory function continue all the way until adulthood.

Memory in Infancy

Memory is functional very early, but initially both working memory and long-term memory are severely limited in capacity, and the ability for recall is still lacking.

Working Memory

A common method of measuring working memory is to set up a situation with a time gap between an incident and the child's reaction or response to it, such as looking for something that has been hidden after a short delay. The number of seconds a child can be delayed or distracted and still maintain the search for the hidden object is considered to be a direct measure of working memory capacity. Studies using this method indicate a memory span of about 2 seconds for 7-month-old children, 7–8 seconds for 1-year-olds, and 30 seconds for 2½-year-olds (Reznick, 2009). Six-month-olds are able to hold one thing in mind, while 1-year-olds can maintain about three different things in working memory at the same time (Rose et al., 2004; Oakes & Luck, 2014).

Long-Term Memory

As early as the womb, experiences slowly become embedded in fetal long-term memory. The fact that children only a few days old prefer their mother's voice to unfamiliar voices (see Book 2, *Genes, Fetal Development and Early Neurological Development*, Chapter 9) shows that certain aspects of the mother's voice are represented in the child's mind.

A common experiment with infants aged 2–6 months is to attach a ribbon to one of their ankles so that they trigger a mobile when

kicking with their legs and see how long they remember the mobile
and the movement (Box 10.1). The results show that the duration of
children's memory increases significantly in the first 18 months of life,
but they also show early memory is context-dependent. Objects used
for later recognition had to be identical to those used during training.
It is possible to teach 3- and 6-month-old children to move two different mobiles in two different situations, but the learning from one
context is not transferred to the other. Infants seem to remember them
as independent events (Rovee-Collier & Cuevas, 2009a; Watanabe &
Taga, 2006). However, at this age, context-dependence may also have
certain advantages. It prevents children from resorting to actions they
have learned in situations where they are inappropriate. Infants have
poor control over action impulses, and actions should therefore not be
too easily activated (Rovee-Collier & Cuevas, 2009b). At 6 months of
age, infants begin to draw connections between these types of independent memories, and, by the age of 9 months, their learning begins
to become less context-specific. At this point, infants also become
more mobile and exploratory and need to be able to apply the knowledge they have and adapt their learning to new situations (Campos
et al., 2000).

Box 10.1   Mobile Experiments with Infants (from Rovee-Collier & Cuevas, 2009a)

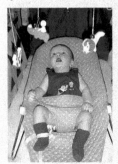

Left: the ribbon is attached to the infant's ankle, but not to the mobile, so the infant can get used to it. The infant looks at the mobile, but the leg is at rest.

Center: the infant has learned how to move the mobile with the leg.

Right: the ribbon is attached to something else. The infant pulls the ribbon with the leg while looking at the mobile, but the mobile does not move.

(Thanks to the child's parents and Carolyn Rovee-Collier for the use of these photos.)

Infants aged 2–6 months had a ribbon attached to one of their ankles, so that the mobile moved when they kicked their legs. Once the infants had learned this motor activity, the ribbon with the mobile was once again attached to the ankle after a certain length of time. If the infants kicked more with their legs than they did in a similar situation without the ribbon and mobile, the action was considered to be remembered.

Two-month-olds remembered the mobile and leg movement for 1 day but not for 3 days. Three-month-olds remembered perfectly for 3–4 days but had forgotten the mobile and the movement after 6–8 days. However, objects in the mobile had to be identical to those used during training. When more than one of the objects on the mobile was replaced, infants no longer showed any retention after 1 day. Three-month-olds recognized the mobile after 1 day, even in a new environment but, after 3 days, they only recognized it as long as an identical ribbon was attached to their ankle or wrist. When the color of the ribbon was changed, the infants' recognition was significantly reduced, and, when it was placed in a different room, they showed no recognition.

After as little as 1 day, even older infants did not recognize the mobile used during training if it was presented in a new context. It is possible to teach 3- and 6-month-old children to move two different mobiles in two different situations, but the learning from one context is not transferred to the other. Infants seem to remember them as independent events.

Infant memory is dependent on repetition. Repeated actions or events are preserved, while anything that is not repeated disappears or becomes difficult to reactivate, consistent with the brain's synaptic processes (see Book 2, *Genes, Fetal Development and Early Neurological Development*, Chapter 15). **Refreshment**, whereby children are exposed to all or part of the same incident, therefore has a major impact on how long infants remember. The best effect is achieved while the infant performs the original task, but even a reminder in the form of short exposure to the mobile without triggering their movement leads to a significant increase in the duration of infants' memories. When the mobile was shown to 3-month-old infants for 2–3 minutes at a later point, they remembered it for about a week – longer than when they initially learned how to set it in motion. The effect is further increased by using several reminders (Rovee-Collier et al., 1999). In one study, 3-month-old infants were given several reminders and showed no sign of forgetting after 6 weeks (Hayne, 1990). In another study, 6-month-olds learned to start an electric train by pushing a lever. At this age, and without refreshment of memory, infants usually remembered the action for 2 weeks. Children who received a 2-minute reminder at the ages of 7, 8, 9, 12 and 18 months showed no signs of forgetting by the age of 2 years (Hartshorn, 2003).

These experiments show that infants can integrate information from two different points in time. However, refreshment must be presented within a certain *window of time*. If no refreshment is given, the original situation will be forgotten, and the next repetition is as a new situation. The retention interval furthermore increases when refreshment occurs at the end, rather than at the beginning, of this time window (Rovee-Collier et al., 1993).

The Development of Memory during Childhood and Adolescence

Throughout childhood, children continue to explore and expand their knowledge base as the memory system becomes more efficient.

Working Memory

The capacity of working memory is commonly measured by the individual's ability to recall numbers. **Memory span** lies at around two at the age of 2 years, four at the age of 5, five at the age of 7 and six at the age of 12. Many adults have a memory span for numbers of around seven (Dempster, 1981). Another way of testing working memory is to ask children to imitate an action sequence. Children as young as 11 months of age are capable of performing a sequence of two tasks that are demonstrated to them and that they have never carried out before, such as putting a button inside a box and shaking it like a rattle. At 20 months of age, children are able to imitate tasks consisting of three parts and, 4 months later, five parts. Children aged 2½ years are nevertheless able to imitate the construction of a house in eight parts: pour sand on the house, put a nail into a precut hole, hammer in the nail, use a saw on the house, load up a truck with blocks, put a pipe on the roof and paint the house (Bauer & Fivush, 1992). This reflects the fact that these types of tasks depend less on language skills and carry more meaning for children.

The development of children's performance on tasks requiring the use of working memory is also linked to the formation of **concepts**. Children aged 7–9 years who know a lot about soccer, for example, remember more objects from an image related to soccer (such as the soccer ball, shoes and goal) than an image with objects unrelated to soccer (such as a bike, a banana and a hammer), while there is no corresponding difference among children who have little knowledge of soccer (Schneider & Bjorklund, 1992). When the things to be remembered are less familiar, more of the capacity of working memory is used for encoding and organization and less for storage (Alexander & Schwanenflugel, 1994).

As they grow older, children improve at making use of *memory strategies*, such as saying aloud or silently the things to be remembered (Bjorklund et al., 2009). In an experiment with 5–10-year-old children, only two 5-year-olds out of 20 verbally articulated what they had seen for themselves, compared with half of the 7-year-olds and 17 of the 10-year-olds (Flavell et al., 1966). Organizing objects that belong together into groups is also a common memory strategy. Younger children who are encouraged to do so, however, or who try to group objects on their own in connection with memory tasks, go about it in such an unsystematic way that it is of little help in practice. Only from about the age of 10 do children begin to apply this type of categorization effectively (Bjorklund et al., 2009). This shows that children's use of strategies is less automatized than that of adults. Even when younger children have learned a number of strategies, they do not always apply the best strategy when performing a task. Working memory capacity and utility therefore continue to develop into adolescence (Isbell et al., 2015; Luciana et al., 2005).

Long-Term Memory

Children are aware of and remember much of what goes on around them, thus keeping what they are learning about the world. At the end of the first year of life, it is not unusual for them to observe someone's action and perform it themselves at a later time. Thirteen-month-olds are to some degree able to remember a sequence of actions shown to them. After 1 week they remember less, although it is still possible to detect some recollection. Twenty-month-olds show few signs of forgetting short actions after 2–6 weeks – their recollection is as good as it was right after the action (Bauer, 1997). Thus, toddlers are able to remember individual actions for a considerable length of time, while the temporal sequence of actions is more difficult to recall, especially if it is non-functional. When preschoolers recount baking cookies together with someone, they follow the course of events. When they talk about a shopping trip, the order is random (Fivush, 1997). This is not only because the sequence of baking cookies must occur in a certain order. Children who had not seen the event sequence were unable to find out how to perform the actions on their own.

It is not always necessary to show an action sequence several times for it to be remembered, but children who have seen it repeatedly will remember more of it for a longer time. Children aged 13–15 months who were shown an action once were able to remember it for a week, but had largely forgotten it after a month. Children who were shown the action three times in the course of 1 week remembered the action just as well after a month as after a week (Bauer et al., 1995). Similarly, children aged 2–2½ who had seen an action twice remembered as much after 3 months as they did after 2 weeks, and far more than children who had seen it only once (Fivush & Hamond, 1989). These findings show that repetition and refreshment continue to be important for memory retention during toddler age as well, especially if the actions are complex and consist of several parts. Repetition also implies that an action is important and worth remembering. Toddlers often ask for stories that engage them to be told over and over again (Nelson, 2014).

Toddlers are not as dependent on similarity with the original situation as infants, but similarity continues to be of importance. Eighteen-month-olds were shown a puppet action with a toy cow and were able to reproduce the action sequence with the cow the next day. But, when the children were asked to perform the action sequence with a toy duck, they seemed to have forgotten everything. Children who were 3 months older had no difficulty performing the action sequence with a different puppet (Hayne et al., 1997). When children aged 3 and 5 years were asked to verbally recall or demonstrate a play action they had participated in, the older children told more about it than the younger ones, but both groups conveyed an equal amount of information by demonstrating the action. This was only the case, however, as long as the situations were identical. When new toys and small changes were introduced to the action during repetitions, the group of 5-year-olds recalled far more than the younger children. When asked to perform a similar but not identical task, 5-year-olds were able to do so without a problem, whereas the 3-year-olds seemed not to know what to do (Fivush et al., 1992).

In order to recall an action, infants must perform or observe it once again on their own, while older children can also be reminded verbally or by using videos and images. Photographs along with verbal narration were an effective reminder for 2-year-olds, but not for children 6 months younger. A verbal reminder about a previous activity had an effect on the memory of 3-year-olds, but not on that of 2-year-olds (Hudson, 1993; Hudson & Sheffield, 1995).

Just like adults, children remember best things that are important and meaningful to them (Nelson, 2007a, 2014). One study found that 4-year-olds remembered more grocery items when this involved foods they were supposed to make lunch with than when they were simply asked to remember items read to them from a list (Mistry et al., 2001). Events that are perceived to be important can be remembered for a long time, such as a popcorn fire (Box 10.2). The earliest interviews suggested that the 4-year-olds had understood far more of the fire situation than the 3-year-olds. Since the incident was more meaningful to them, they had better recall, even at the age of 11. In addition, it is likely that the 4-year-olds talked more about the incident at home and thus established it more firmly in their memory (Neisser, 2004).

During school age, the development of memory is primarily associated with the formation of concepts and cognitive development in general. Throughout childhood, children become faster and more efficient at processing, storing and recalling information and able to remember more complex events and details. In adolescence, memory reaches its peak and has become integrated, coherent and consistent (Howe, 2015; Schneider, 2015).

Memory and Language

Language is important for the organization of memory – it is language that makes it possible for people to "travel" in time and reflect on the past and future. Language also makes it possible to take part in the

Box 10.2   Remembering a Fire in the Kindergarten (Pillemer et al., 1994)

In 1984, a kindergarten at Wellesley College Child Study Center was abruptly evacuated because the popcorn someone was making had caught fire. The children were told to sit by the sandboxes in the outside playgrounds while the firefighters entered the building and turned off the alarm. The teachers and children then returned to their classrooms.

Two weeks later, 12 children with an average age of 3;8 years and 16 children aged 4;7 years were interviewed individually and asked: "What happened when you heard the fire alarm?" This open-ended question was followed by six direct questions about the child's personal circumstances at the time, such as where he or she had been and what they were doing. The narratives of the 3-year-olds and the 4-year-olds differed considerably. Of the 4-year-olds, 15 of the 16 said they were inside the building when the alarm went off, while, of the 3-year-olds, seven of the 12 said they were already assembled outside at that point. Twelve of the older children and four of the younger ones told that they had felt it was important to leave the building. Seven of the 4-year-olds mentioned the cause of the fire alarm, compared with only one of the 3-year-olds.

The children were interviewed 7 years later, when children from the younger group were 10;11 and the older group were 11;11 years old. The children were asked open-ended questions about their memories of (1) anything special or unusual that happened in preschool, (2) a very loud noise at school and (3) hearing the fire alarm. The 25 children who reported having a memory were asked six direct questions about (a) the child's location when the alarm sounded, (b) the child's ongoing activity, (c) the cause of the alarm, (d) the child's feelings at the time, (e) other people's feelings and (f) what happened after hearing the alarm. Eight of the 14 children in the older group remembered the incident, and four were able to provide a coherent description of what had happened. Nine of the 11 younger children had forgotten the incident, and only two children were able to give a fragmentary account of the event sequence.

experiences of others, share one's own experiences and refresh one's memory without reliving the event (Nelson, 2007b, 2014).

Studies show that children can remember some of what they experienced before they learned to speak and in the earliest stages of language development, but also that there is a connection between children's ability to express themselves verbally when they experience something and their ability to tell about it at a later point. Bauer and Werkera (1995, 1997) observed 13–20-month-old children at regular intervals for a year after the children had seen a specific action for the first time, such as someone hanging up a metal gong and striking it. Most of the children spoke spontaneously in all of the situations, and approximately half of what they talked about had to do with the action they had observed. There was a significant statistical relationship between children's verbal ability at the time they observed the action and how much they told about it later on. Their understanding of language, however, had little impact on how much they were able to describe later, and their expressive verbal skills were not decisive for how much of the action they performed, only for what they told about the action. The children who gave the most complete verbal descriptions were not always the ones who performed most of the original action.

Similarly, another study found that 27–39-month-old children were unable to "translate" a spectacular **pre-linguistic** experience into verbal narrative (Box 10.3). The decisive element was the children's ability to express themselves verbally at the time the event was stored, rather than when it was recalled from memory. Nevertheless, children's understanding of language may have an impact on how well they can take advantage of language support from their parents in remembering past events (Lukowski et al., 2015).

Memories of personally experienced events need not be verbal but can include visualizing an event in the form of mental imagery. Nevertheless, language is an important tool for organizing events and

Box 10.3   Toddlers Remembering the Magic Shrinking Machine (Simcock & Hayne, 2002)

Children aged 27–39 months were shown a "magic shrinking machine" that could turn big toys into small ones. Each child was visited at home and invited to play with the machine. First, the child was shown how to turn on the machine by pulling down a lever that activated an array of lights on the front panel. Then, the experimenters took a toy from a large case and placed it inside the Magic Shrinking Machine, where it disappeared from view. The experimenter then turned a handle on the side of the machine to produce a series of unique sounds. When the sounds stopped, the child was shown how to retrieve a smaller, yet identical, toy from a door on the front of the machine.

This was a fascinating experience for the children, and all of them remembered the machine 6 and 12 months later, although fewer details of the event after 12 than after 6 months. The amount remembered increased with the age of the child at the time of the event. The children were asked first to describe (verbally) what they had observed, then asked if they remembered more when they were shown a photograph of the original event, and finally they were asked to reenact it (non-verbally). They remembered the greatest proportion of information when they reenacted the event and the smallest proportion when they had to use language to tell about it. Their performance with the photograph was intermediate between these two. The verbal accounts were related to the children's **expressive language** skills at the time they first observed the "shrinking process." Even though they had acquired the necessary words in the meantime, they were not able to "translate" pre-linguistic experiences into verbal narrative. This shows that the decisive element was children's verbal ability at the time the event was stored, rather than when it was recalled from memory.

a requirement for **personal narratives**. There is, in other words, a close relationship between the organization of event memories and language. The previous studies also demonstrate that the extent to which children are capable of expressing themselves verbally does not always reflect their ability to remember. Several studies have found that 5-year-old children were able to communicate twice as much information when asked to perform what they had seen rather than describe the event in words (Goodman et al., 1990). Younger children's limited language skills can therefore easily result in underestimating their ability to remember.

Scripts

Children's lives do not consist of individual and unique events alone, but include many routines that involve recurring actions with larger and smaller variations (Hudson & Mayhew, 2009). These routines seem to be organized in the form of script-based memory. A **script** is a mental representation of what usually happens within a given context – the sequence of events, what is being said and so on (Nelson, 2007a; Schank & Abelson, 1977). Some scripts reflect special family routines, but many scripts relate to common cultural practices.

The question is: when and how do children begin to acquire this type of knowledge? The earliest scripts consist of simple interaction routines children engage in, such as mealtime, shopping, visiting grandma, various forms of play, dressing and undressing, relaxing, going on a car trip and so on (Nelson & Gruendel, 1981). Over time, children create an extensive inventory of scripts for various events.

A common method of gaining insight into script knowledge is to ask children to describe their everyday events, such as dinner at home, their day at school or a birthday party. When children describe these types of situations, they usually use the second-person singular (you) and present tense, rather than the first-person (I) and past tense, as they do when describing a particular event they have experienced. Younger children have shorter and less elaborate scripts than older children (see Box 10.4).

The question is how script is formed. One possibility is that children initially acquire a large number of experiences and subsequently abstract a script based upon them. However, the fact that children seem to begin to acquire scripts at an early age suggests that the script is a basic way for human beings to organize experiences, with age-related changes in content. Children appear to begin with a schematic script

Box 10.4 Script for Birthday Parties from Children Aged 3–8 Years (Nelson & Gruendel, 1981, p. 135)

3;1   You cook a cake and eat it

4;9   Well, you get a cake and some ice cream and then some birthday (?) and then you get some clowns and then you get some paper hats, the animal hats and then and then you sing "Happy Birthday to you", and then then then they give you some presents and then you play with them and then that's the end and they go home and they do what they wants

6;7   First, uhm … you're getting ready for the kids to come, like puttin' balloons up and putting out party plates and making cake. And then all the people come you've asked. Give you presents and then you have lunch or whatever you have. Then … uhm … then you open your presents. Or you can open your presents anytime. Uhm … you could … after you open the presents, then it's probably time to go home, if you're like at Foote Park or something, then it's time to go home and you have to drive all the people home. Then you go home too

8;10 Well, first you open your mail box and get some mail. And then you see that there's an invitation for you. Read the invitation. then you ask your parents if you can go. Then you … uhm … go to the birthday party and after you get there you usually wait for everyone else to come. Then usually they always want to open one of the presents. Sometimes then they have three games, then they have the birthday cake then sometimes they open the other presents or they could open them up all at once. After that they like to play some more games and then maybe your parents come to pick you up. And then you go home that grows in detail as they gain more experience, rather than a script that arises as an abstraction of several similar experiences. Although older children have more elaborate scripts than younger children – presumably the result of greater experience as well as more advanced linguistic and cognitive development – their scripts have the same basic temporal characteristics. Their scripts are described in essentially the same manner, but older children's experience contributes to more complexity and detail.

Autobiographical Memory

There are major differences between a personally experienced event and one communicated by someone else. Events children have merely been told about, or which they have seen on video, result in far less robust memories. Even stories that are told repeatedly are not remembered as well as those experienced by children themselves (Fivush, 2011).

Autobiographical memory consists of temporal sequences of significant personal events, something that happened to one's **self** – me – at a particular time and place (Prebble et al., 2013). While autobiographical memory forms the basis for the development of a temporally extended self (see Book 6, *Emotions, Temperament, Personality, Moral, Prosocial and Antisocial Development*), this self is also integrated with the organization of memories of personally experienced events (Howe, 2015). This form of memory seems to emerge around the age of 3–4 years (Nelson, 2007a; Peterson, 2002). Fivush and Hamond (1990) found that 2½-year-olds had relatively little interest in talking about their experiences, while the same children were more than willing to do so at the age of 4.

To begin with, children's stories consist of fragments, such as *food for breakfast, luggage for the trip* or *a special toy* (Nelson, 2014). Early representations of personal events are not always chronological but are organized around a theme, such as this monologue by 21-month-old Emmy (Nelson, 1996):

> *The broke, car broke, the . . . Emmy can't go in the car. Go in green car. No. Emmy go in the car. Broken. Broken. Their car broken, so Mommy Daddy go in their their car, Emmy Daddy go in the car, Emmy Daddy Mommy go in the car, broke. Da . . . da, the car . . . their, their, car broken.*

Emmy is using private speech to reflect and make sense of her experiences; the monologue is private in a double sense: it is directed at herself and is recorded without anybody being present (Nelson, 2015). Nine months later, at the age of 2½ years, Emmy was able to describe her experiences in a far more organized and coherent way:

> We bought a baby, . . . cause, . . . the, well because, when she, well, we thought it was for Christmas, but when we went to the s-s-store we didn't have our jacket on, but I saw some dolly, and I yelled at my mother and said I want one of those dolly. So after we were finished with the store, we went over to the dolly and she bought me one. So I have one.

Thus, children's descriptions gradually become more coherent, although they contain little detail during early childhood. One boy summed up his camping trip as follows: *First we eat dinner, then go to bed, and then wake up and eat breakfast.* With increasing age, knowledge of oneself and one's surroundings becomes more firmly integrated and permanent (Howe, 2015).

What children spontaneously talk about when asked to describe earlier experiences becomes curtailed over time, but, if they are shown objects or pictures of the event, they are able to remember many details. *What* they describe can also change. One study found that pre-school children related equally much about holiday trips and birthday parties after a few weeks and after 1 year. Most of what the children described was correct, but relatively little of what they talked about during each of these two periods dealt with the same events (Peterson, 2002). Another study of children who had visited the emergency room between the ages of 12 and 33 months followed up with interviews after 6, 12 and 18 months. The youngest children (12–18 months) did not remember anything about the visit 18 months later, while the middle group (20–25 months) remembered certain details. The older children (26–33 months) remembered a good deal after 1 year and even more after 2 years. They told many things that were incorrect, but the proportion of correct information remained the same. This means that they added both correct and incorrect elements (Peterson & Rideout, 1998). Older children are able to remember events for many years, but they, too, change the content of their stories. Children's accounts of events that lie far back in time often contain more general information (Peterson, 2002), illustrating that children (and adults) combine event-specific knowledge with script elements when describing something they experienced long ago.

Children must learn to talk about the past in general before they can construct a personal narrative. By talking with parents and other adults about events that have occurred, children construct the basis for their autobiographical memory by internalizing these conversations (Nelson, 2007a; Nelson & Fivush, 2004). In the case of preschoolers, personally experienced events and coherent stories in conversation with parents result in the best recall and description by children afterwards. Four-year-olds had better recall of those parts of an event their mothers had talked about than of the rest of the event. In addition, they remembered the information they had discussed with their mother better than that described by the mother or by themselves alone (Tessler & Nelson, 1994). This demonstrates how children create their own world through conversations with adults. Children can remember events they have experienced on their own, but the memories of these events are generally neither as complete nor as accurate.

In line with this, parents' conversational style affects children's autobiographical memory and thus how they perceive themselves, other people and events in the world. When parents use a *high elaborative style*, they help their child remember by expanding and verbally elaborating the child's narratives, emphasizing key elements, providing situational details, evaluating events and asking many questions. A *low elaborative style* means that parents are more passive and ask fewer, more general and partly redundant questions. The parents' style seems to remain relatively stable, even if parents tend to become more elaborative as children get older, but can be changed. Children of mothers who had received elaborative-style training remembered more from a camping trip than children of mothers who had not received such training (Boland et al., 2003). Children of parents with a high elaborative style talk about their experiences in a more coherent and evaluative way (Fivush et al., 2006). In addition, conversations reflect the child's **temperament**, gender and other traits. Both mothers and fathers talk more about shared experiences and use a more elaborative style with their daughters than with their sons, at least in Western cultures. Furthermore, children do not share their experiences with their parents alone – grandparents, siblings and friends also help to shape children's autobiographical memories (Fivush et al., 2006; Fivush & Nelson, 2004).

In childhood and adolescence, the process that began in early infancy is brought to completion, and the autobiography gains more context and detail. Older children and adolescents get better at structuring their descriptions, talk more about the causes and contexts of actions rather than merely describing them, and position their experiences on a personal timeline. In addition to who was involved, what happened, how it was done and where and when it occurred, personal narratives also involve a subjective perspective and evaluation. Seven-year-olds typically include three such narrative elements, while 11-year-olds use twice as many, and girls generally include a few more elements than boys. In adolescence, personally experienced events are increasingly associated with both earlier experiences and possible future events (Bauer, 2013). At this age, the development of **identity** also assumes a central role (see Book 7, *Social Relations, Self-awareness and Identity*, Chapter 24).

Autobiographical memories are about a self in a world of other people, a development that is also shaped by culture (Alea & Wang, 2015; Nelson, 2014). Cultural differences manifest themselves in personal narratives as early as preschool age. In China, mothers typically use conversation to emphasize the moral aspects of an event, whereas mothers in the United States ask more questions and focus more on the child's personal views. US mothers are, in other words, characterized by a higher elaborative style than Chinese mothers. When US and Chinese children were asked to describe an important event such as a birthday or an occasion when their mother scolded them, US school-children told long and detailed stories that focused on themselves and their feelings, while the stories of the Chinese children were more frail and emotionally neutral, with greater focus on social interaction and routines, and their own social role in the event (Wang, 2001, 2004).

Memories of Negative and Traumatic Events

Children's lives consist of minor and major joys and sorrows, of positive, negative and neutral events. Some children experience dramatic and traumatic events such as getting hurt in an accident, being hit by a tsunami or other natural disaster or being subjected to physical and sexual abuse (Quas & Fivush, 2009). When comparing children's memories of emotionally neutral and positive events with their memories of stressful and traumatic events, it appears that moderately stressful events are remembered better than positive and more neutral events (Bauer, 2006). Therefore, it has been speculated that negative events are remembered better because knowledge of such events may be more important for the individual's **protection** and survival than knowledge of positive and neutral events (Howe, 2015; Cordón et al., 2004; Wallin et al., 2009). This may also be related to the fact that increased arousal or motivation leads to better recall – up to a certain point. Beyond this point, memory is weakened. Children who cried a great deal during a stressful medical examination, for example, remembered less than children who did not cry as much, but what they remembered was accurate (Peterson & Warren, 2009). Negative events may create an attentional bias and preparedness for negative events (McLaughlin & Lambert, 2017; see Book 6, *Emotions, Temperament, Personality, Moral, Prosocial and Antisocial Development*, Chapter 9). However, even children growing up in dangerous environments such as the Gaza Strip report more early memories of play and visits to nice places than of traumatic events (Peltonen et al., 2017).

Many dramatic events are remembered for a long time. Sometimes children are able to recall more after a long time than they did immediately following the incident. Children who had experienced Hurricane Andrew in New Orleans in 1992, for example, were able to give twice as much information about the event when they were interviewed at 10–11 years of age compared with their interviews right after the hurricane, at the age of 3–4 years. There was much talk about the event at the time, and it is likely that the children's stories were equally based on the descriptions of others as on their own experiences, in addition to the fact that they had gained more knowledge about the world in general (Fivush, 2009; Fivush et al., 2004). The importance of working through experiences together with adults is also demonstrated by the fact that children of mothers who frequently talk about everyday and non-stressful events remember more details than children whose mothers do not talk as much. However, it is not certain whether the children actually remember more or whether they simply are willing to talk more and therefore also provide more information (Peterson & Warren, 2009).

Childhood Amnesia

The research presented here leaves no doubt that children under the age of 3 years are able to remember and recount specific experiences both verbally and by acting them out. Adults, on the other hand, rarely remember experiences from before the age of 3, although some can remember events from their second year of life (Rubin, 2000). They remember considerably more from the ages of 3–6 years, but memories from this period are difficult to recall for adults and generally fragmented (Hayne & Jack, 2011; Pillemer & White, 1989). In a classic study, Sheingold and Tenney (1982) asked students about events surrounding the birth of a younger sibling that could be verified by the mother and other family members. Students who were under the age of 3 years at the time the sibling was born were unable to answer some of the questions, while those who were 7 years and above at the time of their sibling's birth were able to answer most of the questions.

Early memories seem to begin to fade by the age of 4–6 years; from 8 to 10 years of age, children and adolescents remember approximately as much of their first 3 years of life as adults do (Howe, 2015). In one study on early memories in children aged 4–13 years, many of the youngest children (4–7 years) remembered events from before the age of 2, but most of them did not remember the event 2 years later, even though they had talked about it at the time. New events had taken their place, and the average age for the earliest memory increased from 32.0 to 39.7 months. The oldest children were between 10 and 13 years old at the time of the original interview and, 2 years later, mostly recalled the same events as in the first interview (Peterson, 2012; Peterson et al., 2011). Bauer and Larkina (2014) found that children aged 5–7 years remembered 70 percent of events from the age of 3, while 8–9-year-olds remembered somewhat less than 40 percent of the same events. There was also a marked transition between the age of 8 and 9 years.

Freud (1905) was the first to use the term "**childhood amnesia**" about the fact that individuals rarely remember anything from their first 3 years of life. He believed childhood amnesia was caused by the repression of sexual and aggressive feelings toward the parents. This is an unlikely explanation, as memories of many different types of events are affected, rather than only events involving feelings toward the parents. A more up-to-date explanation is that the neurological structures responsible for storing memories undergo significant development during the first 2 years of life, and that early memories are not adequately stored and integrated (Olson & Newcombe, 2014). Bauer and Larkina (2014) suggest that childhood amnesia is not caused by a failure to store events, but rather that events are forgotten because the memories are too unstable and contain too few cues to become firmly embedded in memory. The youngest children in their study remembered a great deal for a long time but were unable to clearly position the events in time. The memory structure and cognitive abilities of older children and adults differ to such a degree from those of infants that they are unable to recall events based on the same cues they used for storage at an earlier age, causing them to be forgotten (Bauer, 2015). In addition, the lack of linguistic labels during storage can make it difficult to recall the events (Peterson, D. J. et al., 2016).

Another type of explanation is that infants do not have the mental capacity to deal with perceptions of the world that are in conflict with each other. Therefore it is a functional advantage to forget past conceptions when new ones take their place (Freeman & Lacohée, 1995). This view is corroborated by experiments in which children were shown a Smarties box and asked what they think it contains. Naturally, the children answered *Smarties*. When the box was opened, the children saw that it contained pencils instead of chocolate. When asked what they thought was in the box, children under 3–4 years of age insisted that they themselves had said they thought it was pencils (see Chapter 20, this volume). In the very first years of life, children often encounter events that invalidate their assumptions in a similar, although less clear, way as in the Smarties experiment. Besides, much of what children learn in the first years of their lives is not as useful at a later age and is replaced by new knowledge as part of children's adaptive process (Rovee-Collier & Gerhardstein, 1997). Therefore children rarely remember anything from this time in their lives. It is not an expression of a deficit or failure on the part of the child, but of the functionality of the cognitive system.

False Memories

Recall is a form of re-creation and can occasionally be affected by later acquired knowledge, resulting in incorrect memories. It has been shown that false memories can be grafted onto memory – intentionally or unintentionally – long after an incident allegedly occurred, providing the event is a likely one (Belli, 2012; Howe, 2015). Piaget (1951) recounts that he himself, for 10 years, had distinct memories of having been the subject of a kidnapping attempt as an infant. In reality, it was his nanny who had invented the story. Loftus (1993) describes an experiment in which a (collaborating) adolescent got his 14-year-old brother, Chris, to "remember" that he got lost in a department store at the age of 5 years (Box 10.5). The study demonstrates that it is not easy to distinguish between real and false memories, especially when the false memories are reinforced by a well-known and trusted person.

Intentional inducing of false memories is rare, but the **integration** of earlier and more recent memories, or the filling in of missing event information, can lead to "memory illusions." The **incidence** of spontaneous false memories increases with age, probably because older children have more knowledge than younger children, who are not

Box 10.5 An Experiment of Induced Memory (Loftus, 1993, p. 532)

In this experiment Jim implanted a false memory in his 14-year-old brother, Chris. Jim told his younger brother the following story as if it were true:

It was 1981 or 1982. I remember that Chris was 5. We had gone shopping at the University City shopping mall in Spokane. After some panic, we found Chris being led down the mall by a tall, oldish man (I think he was wearing a flannel shirt). Chris was crying and holding the man's hand. The man explained that he had found Chris walking around crying his eyes out just a few moments before and was trying to help him find his parents.

Just 2 days later, Chris recalled his feelings about being lost:

That day I was so scared that I would never see my family again. I knew that I was in trouble.

On the third day, he recalled a conversation with his mother:

I remember mom telling me never to do that again.

On the fourth day:

I also remember that old man's flannel shirt.

On the fifth day, he started remembering the mall itself:

I sort of remember the stores. I remember the man asking me if I was lost.

A couple of weeks later, Chris described his false memory and he greatly expanded on it.

I was with you guys for a second and I think I went over to look at the toy store, the Kay-bee toy and uh, we got lost and I was looking around and I thought, "Uh-oh. I'm in trouble now." You know. And then I . . . I thought I was never going to see my family again. I was really scared you know. And then this old man, I think he was wearing a blue flannel, came up to me . . . he was kind of old. He was kind of bald on top . . . he had like a ring of gray hair . . . and he had glasses.

When the experiment was completed, Chris was told that his memory of getting lost was false. He replied:

Really? I thought I remembered being lost . . . and looking around for you guys. I do remember that. And then crying. And mom coming up and saying "Where were y ou. Don't you . . . Don't you ever do that again."

able to fill in missing information to the same extent. Studies have furthermore shown that negative false memories result in greater susceptibility to memory illusions than positive memories (Howe, 2015). Claims of recalling memories from a very early age should therefore be treated with scepticism and should not be taken at face value in evaluating a given course of events. In recent years, newspapers and magazines have written about cases in which adults have brought accusations against their parents, claiming that they were sexually abused as infants and toddlers. These memories usually emerged in therapy or under hypnosis. Unfortunately, the abuse of young children occurs all too frequently, but, based on such newly established recollections, it is difficult to distinguish memories of actual experiences from false memories, such as those elicited by leading questions from a psychologist, psychiatrist or other professional (Loftus & Davis, 2006; McNally, 2012).

Memory and Atypical Development

Memory is central to all cognitive and social activity. Therefore, problems related to the functioning of the memory system can be found in many different types of disorders (Peterson, C. et al., 2016). Learning and reading place high demands on the ability to remember. Children's memory thus has a major impact on their academic performance, and measurement of working memory is a better predictor of academic achievement than IQ (DeMarie & López, 2014). Children with ADHD and other attention disorders often have reduced working memory capacity (Martinussen et al., 2005). Limited capacity of working memory and difficulty finding and activating words are considered important underlying factors in language disorders and **dyslexia** (Montgomery et al., 2009; Vulchanova et al., 2014). A relation has also been found between math disorders and working memory (Raghubar et al., 2010).

Children with intellectual disabilities generally have problems storing, organizing and recalling memories. Also, children with severe epilepsy can experience difficulties with working memory and storage in long-term memory (Peterson, C. et al., 2016). Problems with memory are a core characteristic of **childhood dementia** in children and adolescents with juvenile neuronal ceroid lipofuscinosis (see Book 1, *Theoretical Perspectives and Methodology*, Chapter 30). High-functioning children with autism spectrum disorder have more problems with verbal recall than their peers. Their descriptions of past events typically lack both detail and emotional content (Andersen et al., 2013). Children who have been subjected to severe neglect and abuse can be vulnerable to memory impairment (Peterson, C. et al., 2016).

There exist a number of programs for training working memory in children with typical development and with ADHD, autism spectrum disorders and **learning disorders**, and promising results have been reported (Holmes & Gathercole, 2014; Hovik et al., 2013; Klingberg et al., 2002; Wass et al., 2012). However, the results are inconsistent, and larger analyses of working memory training studies indicate that the training produces short-term, specific training effects that do not **generalize** to general problem solving and behavior and thus may have little clinical relevance (Cortese et al., 2015; Melby-Lervåg et al., 2016; Morra & Borella, 2015; Roberts et al., 2016; van der Donk et al., 2015; von Bastian & Oberauer, 2014).

Children as Witnesses

Sometimes it is necessary to gain precise knowledge about a child's experiences. This can involve aspects of the child's daily life, but the need for knowledge about children's ability to relate events they have been involved in arises particularly in connection with possible sexual or other abuse or, sometimes, murder of close relatives (Christianson et al., 2013; McWilliams et al., 2013). In abuse cases, children are usually the only witnesses, and their testimony may be decisive for the outcome (Roberts & Powell, 2001). Many countries have seen dramatic court cases in which the way children were interrogated and how their testimony was interpreted have been a central issue (see Bruck et al., 2006).

Children can be reliable witnesses, sometimes more so than adults. Exactly how much children remember, however, depends on whether they perceived a given event as important and meaningful. Children can also have difficulty keeping events apart (Nelson, 2007b; Roberts, 2002). Information about the time of events often plays an important role in legal proceedings but can be difficult to ascertain, especially from young children (Friedman et al., 2010, 2011; Orbach & Lamb, 2007). In addition, testimony can concern aspects that are difficult for children to understand and relate to, and giving evidence can be a stress factor in itself.

With open questions such as "Tell me what happened," younger children provide less information than older children. They often omit information that adults would consider important, but what they say is generally correct. They tell what they understand and are able to put into words. It is possible to increase the amount of information provided by the child, for example by rephrasing what the child says and encouraging her to tell more about it (Pipe & Salmon, 2009; Qin et al., 1997). Adults provide the most information, but also some inaccuracies. They tend to fill in missing information based on their own experience and knowledge of scripts. Specific questions can take the place of open-ended questions, and also, here, the proportion of correct answers increases with age (Eisen et al., 2002; Pipe & Salmon, 2009).

Younger children are vulnerable to social pressure, such as when adults make claims about persons the child is supposed to talk about, or when they use leading or misleading questions (Peterson, C. et al., 2016). Children are used to reconstructing events with the help of their parents and other adults. They try to find the answer they think the adult is expecting and that they believe to be the correct one. Younger children also tend to agree with leading questions such as "He asked you to come along, right?" This is how adults typically phrase questions when they want children to agree (Bruck et al., 2006). In one study, 3–6-year-olds and adults were presented with 17 neutral questions and four leading questions of the type: "He wore a sweater, right?" There were only minor differences between adults and children on the neutral questions, but the children were more susceptible to the influence of leading questions than the adults (Goodman & Reed, 1986).

Adults often repeat questions to be sure of the child's answer. However, repeating a question the child has already answered can have a leading effect. Typically, it is a signal that the answer was wrong and often leads children to change their response, particularly on *yes/no* questions (Poole & White, 1991). Repeated interviews can refresh children's memory and produce more correct details in later interviews. Similarly, leading questions that are repeated in the course of several interviews can increase the likelihood that children respond in line with the question's bias (Quas et al., 2007). Thus, adults who mistakenly believe they know the sequence of events can – without intending to do so – get children to confirm something that never happened (Ceci et al., 2007; Cronch et al., 2006). The situation in which children find themselves has significance as well. Saywitz and Nathanson (1993) found that 9–10-year-olds remembered less and provided more incorrect answers to leading questions when they were interrogated in a "courtroom" in which the judges, lawyers and spectators were played by actors than when they were interviewed alone at school. Children are used to getting help from adults when reconstructing events. Therefore, any suggestion by an adult about the factual circumstances can affect children's perception and interpretation of an event that has occurred. Children's suggestibility increases when they do not fully understand what they are being asked about, and the information is uncertain or vaguely coded in memory (Warren et al., 1991).

Another important element is the interviewer. Children are more susceptible to influence when questioned by an authority figure such as a parent, teacher or the police (Bruck et al., 2006; Perry & Wrightsman, 1991). In one study, some of the children were interviewed by a "cold" man who did not smile, make eye contact or encourage the children, while the other group met a "warm" interviewer who appeared to be open, smiled and encouraged the children in a friendly way. The children who were interviewed by the "cold" interviewer made more incorrect statements and changed explanation more often than those who had met the "warm" interviewer (Goodman et al., 1991). This suggests that a feeling of safety and emotional support increases the likelihood of children maintaining their version of what they experienced. They are no more susceptible to the influence of adults who appear warm and positive than to persons who provide little support. Studies in which children were exposed to stress – a characteristic feature of many real interrogations – have shown both better and poorer recall (Bruck et al., 2006). A possible explanation for these conflicting results may be that a small amount of stress sharpens the mind, while too much stress leads to insecurity and poor concentration.

A number of aids have been developed for questioning children in connection with abuse and other violations, such as the Cognitive Interview and the National Institute of Child Health and Human Development Investigative Interview, designed to help the child and prevent the interviewer from asking leading questions (Memon et al., 2010; Lamb et al., 2011). These tools are most effective when used with older children as they require strategies that are difficult for lower age groups (Cronch et al., 2006; Memon et al., 1993). The child's age and language and cognitive development are important factors to take into account. Children with **intellectual disability** have less knowledge and can be more susceptible than children of the same age with typical development (Agnew & Powell, 2004; Henry & Gudjonsson, 2003). Children with autism spectrum disorder can be reliable witnesses but may provide less information to open questions and may need questions to help recall (McCrory et al., 2007).

In the past, "**anatomically detailed dolls**" were used in questioning children about sexual abuse, but such dolls seem to increase the likelihood of errors. Younger children can be influenced by the dolls and give false information about the course of events, especially in connection with leading questions (Melinder et al., 2010; Pipe & Salmon, 2009). When 2½–3-year-olds were interviewed about a medical examination, the children pointed at random points on the doll. They seemed not to understand that the dolls were supposed to represent themselves (Bruck et al., 1995b). Infants and preschool children have difficulty representing both their own and the doll's body at the same time, and it may be easier for them to use their own body to demonstrate where they have been touched than to use an anatomically detailed doll (DeLoache & Marzolf, 1995).

Some years ago, testimony from children under the age of 10–14 years was not heard because it was thought to be unreliable. Today, the age limit has been lowered considerably, and the way in which children are questioned has changed somewhat (Cronch et al., 2006; Thoresen et al., 2006, 2009). Even information from preschool children can be relied upon as long as they have adequate knowledge of the topic in question, and the "interrogation" is conducted in a way suitable for children. A child does not remember everything, even if no pressure or misdirection is used. Just as with any other witnesses, testimony must be considered based on children's prerequisites and knowledge. It is especially important to take into account what children at different ages can respond to with relative certainty, and what types of questions may be difficult for them and lead to inconsistent answers, such as questions about time and the sequence of events (Ceci et al., 2007; Peterson, 2002).

11

Executive Functions

In the first years of life, children act spontaneously based on what they have learned and what they perceive to be prominent in a situation. They can suddenly take hold of a toy and do things without considering whether it fits the situation. With age, children become more aware and selective in their actions and get better at planning and performing complex actions in different environments. They do not merely act, but consider the context and adapt their actions to the situation. They choose a target for their action and a sequence of sub-actions, such as putting on their socks before their shoes, monitor their actions and evaluate their effectiveness based on the objective. The executive functions are a foundation for children's planning and mastery of everyday tasks in general, as well as for learning and school work (Blair, 2016; Carlson et al., 2013).

Executive functions consist of several elements, including attention and working memory. Attention to one's own voluntary actions is sometimes referred to as "executive attention." As executive functions are not automated, they require more of the child's cognitive resources than actions that more easily can be carried out on "automatic pilot" (Diamond, 2013). It is common to distinguish between "hot" and "cold" functions. Cold executive functions include cognitive processes, while hot executive functions involve emotional and motivational factors. It is difficult for children (and adults) to plan and make good decisions when motivation and emotional involvement are high. Even toddlers perform better when choosing a reward for adults rather than for themselves. Executive functions largely develop during preschool age, but their development continues throughout childhood and adolescence (Best et al., 2009).

A particular focus has been on children's ability to inhibit action impulses, change solution strategy and plan in advance. *Inhibitory control*

DOI: 10.4324/9781003292500-14

is the ability not to let oneself be distracted and to inhibit thought and action impulses. It is important for replacing previously learned actions with new ones, as well as maintaining concentration on a given task, resisting temptation and distractions, and postponing pleasurable actions. In experiments on inhibitory control, children can typically choose between a smaller immediate reward and a larger delayed reward. In a classical experiment, the child could eat the one marshmallow placed in front of him or her on the table or wait and eat two marshmallows when the experimenter returned after 15 minutes. The 3-year-olds typically chose immediate gratification, whereas the 5-year-olds waited for the larger, delayed reward (Mischel et al., 1989). However, another study showed that how long the child waited was not only dependent on the child's self-control but also on how reliable the child believed the promise to be. If the experimenter had "forgotten" something in an earlier situation, more older children ate the marshmallow instead of waiting for the larger reward (all the children got three marshmallows, whether they had eaten the one or not) (Kidd et al., 2013).

Another type of task to measure inhibitory control is to ask children to point to something they do not want in order to get what they want, or to say "day" when shown a picture of the moon and "night" when shown a picture of the sun. Children's performance on these types of tasks shows a marked change between the age of 3 and 4 years. By the time children start school, they have become less inattentive, impulsive and distractible. It is an important aspect of children's school-readiness and becoming able to master progressively more complex and cognitively challenging situations on their way to adolescence and adulthood (Best et al., 2009; Shaul & Schwartz, 2014). However, adolescence seems to be a period with increased impulsivity and impatience, possibly related to both brain development and physiological changes related to puberty (Steinberg & Chein, 2015; van den Bos et al., 2015).

The ability to inhibit thoughts and actions contributes to *cognitive flexibility*. This helps children pursue complex tasks and find novel solutions, adapted to changing demands (Ionescu, 2012). This ability is often measured by using tasks in which children have to switch from one sorting dimension to another, for example when sorting cards with images of different shapes and colors. Three-year-olds have no problem sorting the cards by image shape *or* color but experience difficulties when they have to switch to sorting by shape after having sorted by color, or by color after they have sorted by shape. Four-year-olds have no trouble switching from one sorting dimension to another (Carlson et al., 2013). Nevertheless, younger children have greater difficulty switching when more categories are introduced, such as size in addition to shape and color. Children's efficiency and speed on this type of task increase throughout childhood and adolescence.

Planning is necessary in order to solve more intricate tasks and perform complex actions. Early planning ability may be observed in how children put on their clothes, build with blocks, make a drawing or play a game. Studies often make use of simple or more complex versions of the Tower of London or Hanoi. Children have to copy a pattern by moving a number of discs or orbs from one peg to another according to certain rules. The task must be solved in as few moves as possible, and planning becomes more difficult and time-consuming the more moves it requires. At the age of 3 years, children get better at correcting themselves when their attempts do not lead to results. Younger children continue to try the same solution, even if it leads nowhere. Four-year-olds handle tasks with two moves equally well as adults, but tasks with three or more moves take time to master. Between the ages of 7 and 13 years, a gradual development takes place with regard to how quickly and correctly children solve this type of task (Best et al., 2009; Carlson et al., 2013).

Young children find it difficult to resist taking the marshmallow

The development of executive functions is believed to be related to neurological development in general and the development of the brain's frontal lobe in particular (Barrasso-Catanzaro & Eslinger, 2016). There are however also cultural developmental differences. Children and adolescents in Hong Kong develop executive functions earlier than in the UK, whereas among adults there is no difference (Ellefson et al., 2017). Children's participation in different social contexts as well as their schoolwork helps develop these functions, while at the same time placing new demands on their executive abilities (Rueda & Cómbita, 2013). A relationship has been found between late or inadequate development of executive functions and both social functioning and academic performance at school (see also below).

Executive Functions and Atypical Development

Children's executive functions affect all areas of their lives. A reduction in executive functioning is associated with disorders such as Tourette syndrome, epilepsy and **fetal alcohol syndrome**, as well as malnutrition and severe deprivation (Carlson et al., 2013). As executive functions include attention and working memory, many – but not all – children with difficulties in these areas will show a reduction in executive functioning. Many children with ADHD, autism spectrum disorders or learning disorders have difficulty planning, monitoring and performing actions in a flexible way (Crippa et al., 2015; Goldstein & Naglieri, 2014; Tillman et al., 2009). Math disorders are linked to cold executive functions and distractibility (Miller et al., 2013; Raghubar et al., 2010), while inattention, overactivity and behavioral problems are primarily linked to hot executive functions (Zelazo, 2015). Children who have social problems in interaction with their peers often score lower on executive functions than other children (Holmes et al., 2016). The important role of executive functions in learning and social adaptation is also reflected in the statistical **correlation** between early executive function disorders and difficulties coping with adult life, criminal behavior and mental problems (Carlson et al., 2013).

The importance of executive function for learning and adaptation has led to a search for interventions that can improve functioning in children and adolescents with executive problems. As working memory is also part of executive functions, many of the same training programs are applied for problems with working memory and executive functions (Rapport et al., 2013). Research indicates that executive functions are influenced by the environment and can be improved at all age levels, but it is not clear how much they can be improved and whether improvements will be maintained (Diamond & Lee, 2011; Diamond & Ling, 2016). A review of executive function training in children with ADHD shows limited efficacy (Rapport et al., 2013).

Summary to Part II

1   Attention is an active, alert state that affects children's perception and priorities in the here-and-now. During the first year of life, children become more alert and better at orienting themselves, filtering stimulation and shifting as well as sustaining attention. Throughout childhood, attention is increasingly directed at what is relevant in a situation, but children can also develop a tendency to take particular notice of either positive or negative emotional cues. Atypical attention processes are a key element in attention disorders and many other neurodevelopmental disorders. Results for attention training are modest. Medication may help some but not all children and is controversial. Interventions directed at behavior disorder in children with attention problems are often useful.

2   Memory is the mental representation and recognition or recall of experiences. *Short-term memory* can store material for a few seconds or minutes. *Working memory* stores and processes and is used when an individual tries to remember something for a short period of time or works on a problem. *Long-term memory* is the relatively permanent storage of experiences. *Autobiographical memory* includes personally experienced events that are meaningful to the individual.

3   Memory is functional even before birth, but initially the capacity of working memory is severely limited. Through childhood and adolescence, it increases with the formation of concepts, the ability to process larger units and improved *memory strategies*.

4   Early long-term memory is limited and depends on perfect uniformity – infants quickly forget once the circumstances or the situation changes. *Refreshment* in the form of full or partial repetition increases the length of time for which children remember,

DOI: 10.4324/9781003292500-15

provided it takes place within a certain *time window*. The extent of what children remember, and for how long, increases with age. The recall of action sequences depends on their meaningfulness, the relationship between the actions and how many times the child has seen them. With age, memory can be refreshed by partial repetition, images or language.

5   In toddlers, expressive language at the time of the experience affects their ability to recount the event at a later age, but not their ability to imitate the action that took place. It is difficult for children to "translate" pre-linguistic memories into verbal form.

6   A *script* is a mental representation of something that usually happens in a given context. Children start to form scripts at an early age and, with time, they accumulate a large supply of scripts that make up an important part of their social and cultural knowledge.

7   *Autobiographical memory* consists of temporal sequences of significant personal events and forms the basis for the development of the self. It begins at the age of 3–4 and continues to develop throughout life. The elaboration style of the parents affects what children remember. Also, cultural differences affect children's autobiographical memory. Some children experience dramatic and traumatic events; exactly how they remember and recall these events is related to the types of events they were exposed to, how often they occurred, how much stress they caused, the child's past experiences and how parents and others talk about the events.

8   *Childhood amnesia* is the phenomenon that older children and adults rarely recall events from before the age of three. The reason may be that the neurological structures involved in storing memories undergo significant development during the first 2 years of life, and that the organization of memory material differs so much between adults and children that adults are unable to activate memories of events that were coded when they were young children. In addition, much of the knowledge of infants and younger children is replaced by new knowledge.

9   *False memories* can occur as the result of intentional or unintentional influence by other people and can be difficult for a person to distinguish from actual memories.

10   Learning and reading place high demands on the ability to remember, and memory problems may be found in many developmental disorders, including attention disorders, language disorders, learning disorders and autism spectrum disorder. Also, children who

have been subjected to severe neglect and abuse can be vulnerable to memory impairment.

11 Children can be reliable *witnesses*, but younger children often provide fewer details and are more *susceptible* to influence from adults. They are used to reconstructing events together with adults and are vulnerable to leading questions, especially about things they do not fully understand and when questioned by an authority figure.

12 *Executive functions* have to do with the planning, execution and monitoring of voluntary actions. "Cold" executive functions are associated with cognitive processes, and "hot" executive functions with emotional and motivational factors. *Inhibitory control* shows a marked increase in preschool age but continues to develop all the way to adolescence and adulthood. The ability to inhibit thoughts and actions contributes to the development of *cognitive flexibility*, which characterizes adolescence and adulthood. *Planning* is necessary to solve intricate tasks and perform complex actions. A reduction in executive functioning is associated with many disorders. The development of executive functions is influenced by experience, but results of training are modest.

13 Relations have been found between delayed or inadequate development of executive functions and social functioning and academic performance at school. An early reduction in executive functioning is associated with many developmental disorders, later criminal behavior, difficulty coping with adult life and mental problems.

Core Issues

• Medical and behavioral treatment of attention disorders.
• The relationship between memory and language.
• Effects of training of working memory and executive functions.

Suggestions for Further Reading

Barrasso-Catanzaro, C., & Eslinger, P. J. (2016). Neurobiological bases of executive function and social-emotional development: Typical and atypical brain changes. *Family Relations*, *65*, 108–119.

Kidd, C., Palmeri, H., & Aslin, R. N. (2013). Rational snacking: Young children's decision-making on the marshmallow task is moderated by beliefs about environmental reliability. *Cognition*, *126*, 109–114.

Ristic, J., & Enns, J. T. (2015). The changing face of attentional development. *Current Directions in Psychological Science*, *24*, 24–31.

Rovee-Collier, C., & Cuevas, K. (2009a). Multiple memory systems are unnecessary to account for infant memory development: An ecological model. *Developmental Psychology*, *45*, 160–174.

Waters, A. M., Lipp, O., & Spence, S. H. (2008). Visual search for animal fear-relevant stimuli in children. *Australian Journal of Psychology*, *60*, 112–125.

Part III

Conceptual Development and Reasoning

Concepts and Reasoning

Children develop an understanding of the world as structured and meaningful. Impressions from the senses are organized, arranged and mentally processed in different ways depending on the child's cognitive abilities, personal and cultural experiences and knowledge. Children notice similarities and differences that form the basis for their categorizations and conceptual development. They create categories based on their own experiences, and their concepts differ in various ways from those of adults. A 6-year-old who invites children to a birthday party, even though it is not her birthday but because she wants to get presents, has understood one of the central elements in the concept "birthday party" (getting presents) but lacks another element (celebrating the day of one's birth). However, the "mistakes" children make in forming concepts do not necessarily reflect an inadequate ability to categorize, but rather that they use this ability.

Reasoning is a form of thinking or mental problem solving that involves drawing conclusions about imagined situations, including both *actual* ones (what is) and *counterfactual* ones (what could be, but isn't). Children show an early ability to reason. They might say that apes have a heart because people have a heart, and apes are similar to people. "If humans were four meters tall, doorways would be five meters high" is an example of a counterfactual statement. Children's understanding of conditional promises such as, "if it's sunny, we'll go for a swim" also depends on reasoning. In addition, reasoning forms the basis for scientific thinking. The question is how children develop the abilities to draw inferences and to reason.

DOI: 10.4324/9781003292500-17

Early Conceptions of Space, Time and Causality

Three factors are basic to an understanding of the physical world: it has a *spatial dimension* and a *temporal dimension* and it includes *causal relationships*.

Space

Spatial perception is necessary to orient oneself and remember where events took place (Moser & Moser, 2016). It allows children to know where they are and to locate people, things and events. The perceptual field is structured by spatial concepts, including relative positions such as "behind," "above," "below" and "between." An understanding of physical space as permanent is also an important element in spatial cognition.

Object Permanence

Piaget was the first to discuss the development of object permanence – the understanding that objects continue to exist and have a physical location even when they cannot be experienced directly. He observed that children aged 7–8 months stopped looking for a toy when a screen was placed between them and the toy so the toy could no longer be seen. In some cases, children showed disappointment, but did nothing to try to find the toy. Piaget interpreted this as a lack of object permanence in children at this age – objects do not exist for them when they cannot experience them with their senses. Children who were 2 months older searched for the toy and tried to get behind the screen to get hold of it (Piaget, 1950).

Others maintain that young infants' failure to search is related not to the fact that they do not remember an object, but to the fact that they do not know how to get hold of it. Using a method that places low

DOI: 10.4324/9781003292500-18

demands on motor skills, Baillargeon (1987) found that 3½-month-olds reacted differently to two events in a way that implied that they had object permanence and remembered the location of objects in space even if they did not see them, far earlier than Piaget found (Box 13.1).

Box 13.1   Early Object Permanence (Baillargeon, 1987)

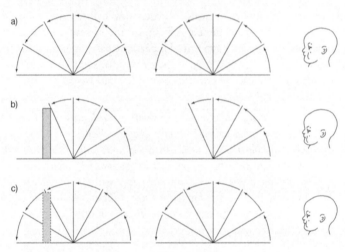

Infants aged 3½ months watched a plate moving in a half-circle from one side to the other (Image a) until they lost interest and looked at it less (habituation). While the children watched, a box was placed in the path of the moving plate in such a way that the children could not see the box when the plate was moving. Following this, each child was shown one of two possible scenarios: either a *possible* action in which the plate stopped moving and returned to where the box most likely was located (Image b), or an *impossible* action in which the plate seemed to continue along its former path as if there were no box to prevent its movement (Image c). The infants looked longer at the impossible (c) than the possible (b) action. This was interpreted as surprise that the plate did not stop, implying that the infants were aware of the presence of the box even though they could not see it and thus had object permanence (Baillargeon, 1987, p. 191. Reprinted with permission from Excerpta Medica Inc.).

There are, however, important differences between Piaget's and Baillargeon's experiments. Baillargeon based her experiment on where the infants *looked*, while Piaget observed how children *acted* when interesting objects disappeared. Baillargeon's method may be suitable to demonstrate children's emerging understanding of space and the objects in it, while Piaget's method reflects a more advanced understanding that also includes knowledge of how to get hold of things that cannot be directly perceived with the senses (Cohen & Cashon, 2006; Gómez, 2005). This is supported by observations showing that children continue to have difficulty locating objects they cannot see, even after developing object permanence. An important observation was that, when infants repeatedly have found a particular toy in one place, they will look in the same spot, even if they have just seen an adult hiding the toy somewhere else, like in this example from Piaget (1950, p. 52):

> *Lucienne is seated on a sofa and plays with a plush duck. I put it on her lap and place a small red cushion on top of the duck (this is position A); Lucienne immediately raises the cushion and takes hold of the duck. I then place the duck next to her on the sofa in [position] B, and cover it with another cushion, a yellow one. Lucienne has watched all my moves, but as soon as the duck is hidden she returns to the little cushion A on her lap, raises it and searches. An expression of disappointment; she turns it over in every direction and gives up.*

A number of studies have since confirmed that infants make the same type of error as Lucienne. It is called **"A-not-B error"** because children search in position A (where they have previously found the object) rather than in position B (where they saw the object being hidden). The error is not caused by motor limitations as it is no more difficult to look in position B than A. Instead, it reflects how complex a task it is for infants of this age to look in a different place than they are used to, leading them to repeat actions that previously have been successful. It is first around the age of 1 year that insight prevails over habit – until then, children always start by looking where they last saw the object disappear. Somewhat older children will also continue to search if they cannot find the toy where they believe it to be. Thus, it takes time for children to integrate new knowledge about an object's location in space with earlier experiences of getting hold of the object. This is contrary to Spelke and Kinzler's (2007) assumption that object localization has its basis in an innate geometry module.

Further Development of Spatial Perception

Children mainly use two types of cues to orient themselves in space. Geometric cues include surface, direction, distance, angle and the like and depend on the viewer's perspective. **Landmarks** include characteristics such as wall color and placement of windows, doors and objects (Ferrara & Landau, 2015). Children use both types of cues. Clear geometric cues and landmarks are important to children's early development, and it takes some time before they are able to take advantage of less prominent physical details to orient themselves (Newcombe et al., 2013). Sometimes children have to take a physical perspective not based on their own body to locate an object (Vasilyeva & Lourenco, 2012).

In an experiment with 12-month-old children, a toy was hidden underneath one of 58 pillows scattered on the floor. The pillows were blue, but sometimes the pillow with a toy under it would have a different color and thus serve as a landmark. The children found the toy when it was lying under a pillow with a different color or under a pillow between two pillows with a different color and succeeded less often when the toy was hidden under a blue pillow near a pillow with a different color (indirect landmark) (Bushnell et al., 1995). Another study found that children under the age of 22 months used geometric cues and made little use of landmarks when they attempted to find a toy they had observed being hidden in a sandbox and had to move around the sandbox. Somewhat older children (22–36 months) did better on these tasks when they also had access to landmarks (Newcombe et al., 1998). This indicates a change in children's use of spatial cues around the age of 21 months and an improvement in their use of directional cues (beacons) from the age of 2 to 4 years (Sutton, 2006).

Children gradually orient themselves better in both larger and smaller spaces but are well into their second year before they are able to take alternative "routes" between two objects, such as moving around an obstacle to reach a target. When children try to find a hidden object, they can remember its location in relation to themselves (egocentric cue), a particular landmark (external cue) or based on where a target is in relation to a hidden object (internal cue), for example if the object is located in a table drawer and the table has been moved. Three-year-olds can take advantage of the first two cues, but children are 5–6 years old before they are able to use internal cues (Negen & Nardini, 2015). In one experiment, children aged 3–6 years hid a toy duck in a corner together with the experimenter. The task of the child was to find the duck after having been blindfolded and slowly turned around. The youngest children used landmarks in large spaces and geometric cues in small spaces, but geometric cues were of limited use in finding the duck because their relative position and perspective changed when they were turned around. Six-year-olds used landmarks in both types of spaces (Learmonth et al., 2008). Children's ability to remember where events take place improves considerably between the ages of 4 and 8 years (Bauer et al., 2012).

With age, children learn to use maps and other aids to orient themselves. Toddlers can use simple maps to find something in a small space (see Book 3, *Perceptual and Motor Development*, Chapter 3). One study found that 5-year-old children had an emerging understanding of maps as a representation of a wider geographical area. When asked to make a map of their daily route from home to school, the map consisted of a single straight line. Slightly older children included landmarks in their maps, but many of these, such as flowers and friends, were of no help in finding the target. The maps produced by 8-year-olds were more functional, and over half of them included intersecting roads and clearly identifiable buildings (Thommen et al., 2010). Children who are 6–8 years old have difficulty finding their way based on a map without landmarks, whereas 10-year-olds can find their way without landmarks (Lingwood et al., 2015). Although children learn

Children gradually become able to use maps to find the way

to measure distances at an early school age (Nunes & Bryant, 2015), the map reading skills of 9–12-year-olds remain limited, with large individual variations (Hemmer et al., 2015).

Individual Differences in Spatial Cognition

The development of spatial cognition shows major individual differences. Some children develop abilities that are suitable for a career as an engineer or a pilot. Boys generally do better than girls on spatial tasks, and differences widen around puberty (Reilly et al., 2017). Others show atypical development. Children with **Turner syndrome** (Vicario et al., 2013) and **Williams syndrome** (Landau & Ferrara, 2013), among others, have special problems with spatial perception and orienting themselves in space. Blind children need more time to explore and form mental representations of space based on their experiences with locomotion, non-visual strategies and landmarks, and this may have consequences for their development of exploration and independence (Gibson & Schmuckler, 1989; McAllister & Gray, 2007).

Time

There are two main approaches to time: either as a dimension of events themselves or as a "framework" in which events can be located on a timeline from past to future (McCormack, 2015).

Time in Events

Piaget (1969a, 1970) was primarily concerned with the development of children's concept of time as a dimension of the physical world, inspired by a question Albert Einstein asked him in 1928 about when children form a concept of time and speed. According to Piaget, this concept of time is based on three operations: the temporal ordering of events, the coherence of event durations and the intervals between them, and the partitioning of time in a way analogous to spatial units (seconds, minutes, etc.). A number of experiments conducted by Piaget and others included two toy trains that rode on parallel tracks. The children's task was to determine which train had moved the furthest, the fastest or for the longest time. The results showed that preschool children understood the individual concepts but failed to integrate time, speed and distance and infer one of the variables (such as time) based on knowledge of the other two (speed and distance). Many of them answered that the train that had travelled furthest also had the greatest speed or had been moving for the longest time, as they only took into account one variable at a time. Slightly older children were able to include two variables at a time, and. from the age of 9 years, many children consistently solved this type of task correctly (Matsuda, 2001; Piaget, 1970).

However, when they used a stopwatch to measure time, 7-year-old children, and some 5-year-olds, were able to solve tasks in which cars travelling at different speeds started and stopped in different places. Without the stopwatch, the children first managed these tasks at 8–9 years of age (Nelson, 1996). Six-year-olds were able to integrate the duration of different events after having been taught to use counting as a strategy (Wilkening et al., 1987). This shows that children need to manage cultural "tools" (counting or stopwatch) to master these types of tasks before their concept of time is sufficiently internalized. However, 5–7-year-olds often count unevenly, and their time estimates can be inaccurate even if they use a counting strategy. This type of task is easier when it does not involve movement and thus has one less dimension. Five-year-olds for example are able to determine which of two dolls has slept the longest when one of the dolls went to sleep earlier than the other, and both woke up at the same time (Levin, 1977, 1989).

Events in Time

Children's earliest understanding of events in time is based on their own experiences, especially their participation in events with a fixed order and schedule (Nelson, 2007a). Children's conversations with parents about past and future events are also important for the development of temporal understanding. Quite early on, parents introduce expressions such as *early, late, morning, evening* and *bedtime* in conversations with their children (Lucariello & Nelson, 1987). Some children use words such as *before, after, today* and *yesterday* at an early age, but most children do not show a conventional understanding of these words before the age of 4 (Harner, 1975). They have some understanding of time based on temporal distance and are able to say whether Christmas or their birthday was "most recent" if one of them occurred during the last 60 days and the other before that. Until the age of around 9 years, children are usually unable to tell which of two events occurred last if both occurred in the past 60 days (Friedman et al., 1995).

Time is perceived both forward and backward from the present. It is easier for preschool children to judge the temporal relationship between two events that have already occurred than between events that will occur, even in cases of recurring events such as Christmas or their birthday (McCormack & Hanley, 2011). Children also continue to have problems placing events earlier or later on a timeline, for example whether Wednesday or Thursday comes first when they go backward or forward in time (Friedman, 2005).

Acquiring the temporal concepts of one's own culture is the result of formal and informal training in dividing up time and arranging events temporally. Learning to read a clock is an important part of this process. When 3–5-year-old children were asked "When do you get up?", the answers were linked to routines such as "When Mom wakes me up." Seven-year-olds answered either "In the morning" or specified a certain time, but many of them did not know the correct time for their routine activities (Nelson, 1996). This shows that development is characterized by the gradual transition from an event-based concept of time to a temporal understanding related to formal divisions of the day into larger (morning, evening, etc.) and smaller units (hours, minutes, etc.). The temporal arrangement of events into weeks and months gradually becomes more precise all the way to adolescence (Friedman, 2014). Children's script knowledge and autobiographical memory are important elements in the development of this ability (see Chapter 10, this volume).

Causality

An understanding of cause and effect, the relationship between events that necessitate one another, is fundamental to gaining an overview and control of the environment and thus an essential part of cognition (Corrigan & Denton, 1996). **Causality** cannot be observed directly but is a concept related to the perception of relationships between events (Saxe & Carey, 2006).

Early Understanding of Physical Causality

A number of innovative studies have attempted to map infants' understanding of how objects behave and interact. They typically consist in showing children physically *possible* and (apparently) *impossible* events. When the children spend more time observing one event than another, it is interpreted to mean that they perceive them to be different, for example that one is expected and the other unexpected. That objects fall when they lack support and that colliding objects affect each other's movement are prototypical examples of causal relationships. These types of events have therefore been widely used in studies on infants' understanding of **physical causality**. Many studies are based on the assumption that infants will look longer at events that violate their expectations than at events that do not (Baillargeon, 2004).

In a classic study, 3-month-olds looked longer at a wooden block placed by a hand into thin air in front of a larger block (without falling down) than when it was placed on the larger block (Box 13.2).

Box 13.2   Studies on Physical Causality: Falling Objects (Baillargeon et al., 1995, p. 82)

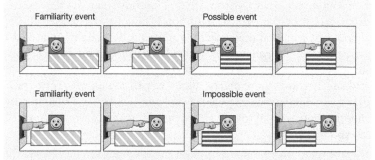

Three-month-old infants were first familiarized with the situation where a smaller block was moved along a larger block. Then they were shown a block that was pushed with a hand (a) along a large block without losing support (possible event) or (b) equally long along a shorter block and into thin air without falling (impossible event). The children looked longer at the block hanging in thin air than at the possible event. The interpretation of Baillargeon and associates is that infants look longer at what is unexpected, and that the longer look indicated that the infants had an emerging understanding of physical causality that made them expect objects to fall if not supported from below.

Another core aspect of physical causation is what happens when a moving object collides with an object at rest. In one study, 2½-month-old children spent less time looking when a ball hit a small toy animal and pushed it forward a little (possible event) than when the toy animal moved forward even though an obstacle stopped the ball before it reached the toy animal (impossible event). Baillargeon and colleagues (1995) suggest that this indicates that the children had formed an expectation that stationary objects move when they are hit by an object in motion, and that they remain stationary when they are not hit. Another study found that 6½-month-old children looked longer when a small rather than a large ball pushed an object forward, while 9-month-olds also reacted differently depending on the width of the object being hit. This is interpreted as a gradual development: children first develop a concept about the difference between a collision and a non-collision and later integrate the properties of the objects involved in the collision event (Wang et al., 2003).

Explanations of how children begin to understand cause and effect vary with regard to the specific innate characteristics they build on. The standard nativist argument of Newman and colleagues (2008) is that this type of understanding is too complex for infants to acquire on their own, and that they must have an innate module capable of perceiving causality. Similarly, Spelke and Kinzler (2007) suggest that infants are born with basic assumptions about how objects move in space, and that this *core knowledge* forms the basis for children's further development of a naive theory of physical laws, which in turn relies on experience (see Book 1, *Theoretical Perspectives and Methodology*, Chapter 15).

In contrast to these hypotheses, Baillargeon (2008) maintains that the development of physical causality is governed by a more general and innate *principle of persistence*: things have a continuous existence in time and space and retain their physical properties (this also includes object permanence). Over time, infants form concepts about the relationships between objects and spaces, objects and surface support, objects and barriers, and so on. They discover different types of causal relations between objects, such as "occlusion phenomena," "passing-through phenomena," "support phenomena" and "unveiling phenomena," and show astonishment when things behave in ways that violate their expectations. It is an experience-based development that changes in line with children's motor development, among other things. For example, children gain new knowledge about what happens when objects collide once they begin to develop hand–eye coordination at 4 months of age and interact more consciously with objects (Book 3, *Perceptual and Motor Development*, Chapter 10). As adults rarely let objects collide in such a way that children can observe the process "systematically," their experience is not primarily based on watching others. Baillargeon's theory suggests that the acquisition of causal relationships is a rapid process rather than a realization of innate knowledge. An understanding of individual physical events is integrated much later, together with a more general understanding of physical causality and the forces that affect the movement of objects (Baillargeon, 1994, 2008; Baillargeon et al., 2009).

Oakes (1994) explains this development from an information-processing perspective, arguing that children notice events that occur together and gradually form a causal understanding based on what happens when objects collide and similar events.

Further Development of Causal Cognition

Infants' early understanding of cause and effect is *implicit* and does not involve the *sense of causal necessity* that a conceptual understanding of physical causality implies (Baillargeon et al., 2009; Piaget & Inhelder, 1975). It is not enough for children to discover that certain events tend to occur together; a conscious understanding of causality requires that they *comprehend* the connection between the events, and this develops slowly. Around the age of 3, children become very interested in causality and begin to ask "why?" about many things, such as why water is shiny. Their questions are often impossible to answer and demonstrate children's limited understanding of cause and effect in many areas.

An emerging understanding of causality does not mean that children immediately understand the mechanism of cause and effect in a given area; this depends on relevant knowledge and experience. Children may show an understanding of causes in some areas and lack the necessary knowledge in others. In a study, half of the 4½–6-year-olds answered "yes" to the question whether a toothache can be contagious and be passed from one child to another. A similar number thought they could get a toothache by playing with a forbidden pair of scissors (Siegal, 1991). As the children responded yes and no equally often, it seemed as if they were simply guessing. In a somewhat older group of children (7½–8½ years), 90 percent ruled out both possibilities. On the other hand, 22 of 24 children between the ages of 4½ and 5½ years knew that a knee wound is not infectious. Thus, the study shows that children gradually develop a deeper and more conscious understanding of cause and effect, based on greater insight into specific areas of knowledge.

14

Object Concepts

Conceptual development also includes children's perception and categorization of people, animals and objects and their characteristics. The **extension** of a concept consists of all the exemplars that fall under the concept: poodles and bulldogs for example belong to the concept "dog." The **intension** of a concept is its meaning or content, the set of distinguishing characteristics that are encompassed by the concept, for example that most exemplars of "dog" have four legs, fur and a shorter or longer tail that can wag.

> One of the most basic functions of living creatures is to categorize, that is to treat distinguishable objects and events as equivalent. Humans live in a categorized world; from household items to emotions to gender to democracy, objects and events, although unique, are acted toward as members of classes. Some theories would say that without this ability it would be impossible to learn from experience and thus that categorization is one of the basic functions of life.
>
> (Rosch, 1999, p. 61)

Children develop concepts gradually, and their conceptual extensions and intensions tend to vary somewhat from those of adults. Some concepts largely reflect the physical characteristics and sensory apparatus of human beings and are relatively similar across cultures. Others are defined by the culture and communicated through language. Children must learn how the culture they grow up in categorizes people, animals, objects and other things.

DOI: 10.4324/9781003292500-19

Theories of Object Categorization

There are two main approaches to object concept formation: feature-based theories and **prototype** theories. Both include different views on *how* children form concepts.

Feature-Based Theories

According to feature-based theories, categorization relies on specific traits or characteristics. These can be physical (such as the fact that a ball is usually round) or functional (a ball can be thrown or kicked). For every category, there is a set of common features that are necessary and sufficient for that category alone and therefore can be used to determine whether an object should be included in the concept. Conceptual development comes about by collecting different traits into categories and getting to know the particular traits that characterize a given category.

One main hypothesis is that children's earliest categorizations are based on *perceptually prominent characteristics* of objects, in particular their shape (Clark, 1973). To begin with, children are attentive to certain features and create categories based on these: the concept "ball" for example can be based on the property "round" and include balls, the moon, oranges, dinner plates and so on (see Figure 14.1, top). As children gain more experience, they create more concepts by dividing up larger categories and adding more features. Their concepts become more differentiated and gradually more similar to those of adults. The features that are added are not exclusively perceptual, however. With the exception of geometric forms, external physical characteristics alone are not enough to lend meaning to a concept.

Functional features have to do with what objects do and what they can be used for, such as sitting on them or riding on them (Figure 14.1, bottom). During early conceptual development, children are aware of only a few features that form the *core* of a concept, such as what they can do with an object, how it moves and so on. "Ball" for example can be categorized as "something that can be thrown and bounced around." As children gain more experience with objects, functional features become more differentiated, their division more complex, and the number of concepts increases (Nelson, 1996, 2007a).

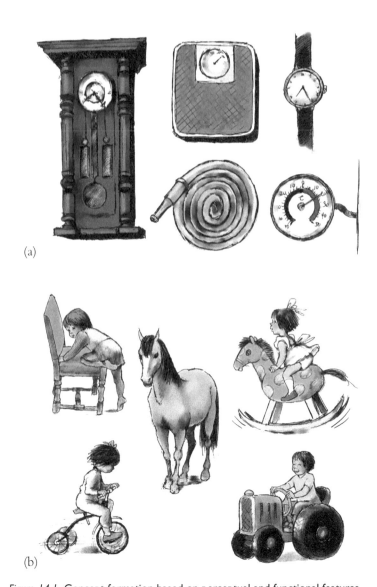

Figure 14.1 Concept formation based on perceptual and functional features.

The objects in the top image (a) represent a category based on perceptually prominent features. The objects in the bottom image (b) are categorized according to functional similarity.

Although Nelson suggested that perceptual traits are too abstract in relation to the cognitive abilities of toddlers, the physical appearance of things is important nevertheless. External features are clues to internal characteristics or usage and help children identify things that belong to different concepts. For example children assume that something that looks like an animal must have a heart, blood and other qualities they associate with animals (see p. 125).

Mandler (2004, 2010) integrates perceptual and functional features. According to her, children form concepts by experiencing the perceptible world and have an innate ability to create *perceptual categories* of how things look, sound and the like. Perceptual categorization allows children to remember people and things in the earliest stage of life. As perceptual categories often are extremely detailed, children will react to subtle differences. The perceptual categories are determined by the design of the human sensory apparatus and result from children's nearly passive registration of sensory impressions, an implicit or non-conscious registration of the perceptual similarity between things. As a next step, children use *perceptual meaning analysis* to categorize things according to different characteristics, such as the way in which they move, whether they can contain or enclose anything or whether anything can rest on them. These features form the basis for prelinguistic concepts. As they represent global features, children's early concepts are global as well, such as "animal" and "vehicle" rather than "dog" and "car." Mandler suggests for example that infants use "self-initiated movement" to distinguish the category "animal" from "inanimate objects."

Mandler (2008, 2012) suggests that there are two parallel systems that handle information from the sensory systems. The first generates purely perceptual categories without conceptual content; the second creates categories based on the function and spatial behavior of objects. These two systems begin to be integrated as early as 3 months of age but are far from complete at 18 months. Language helps children divide the world into smaller global categories and thus serves a crucial function in the formation of concepts. As an example, Mandler mentions children's prelinguistic global concept "living being" (animals). From a purely perceptual point of view, however, children are able to distinguish between dogs and cats and learn that some animals say *meow* and others say *woof*. When children hear other people call these animals by different names, it tells them that the differences are significant, and that dogs and cats belong to different categories.

Prototype Theories

One fundamental objection to feature theories is the difficulty of describing enough necessary and sufficient features to define even simple categories such as "table" or "chair." Possible features for "table" might include "has a flat surface," "things can be put on top," "has legs" and so on. But even after listing these three features one runs into problems, as some tables have a solid base, and the feature "legs" no longer represents a common property. When it comes to "flat surface" and "things can be put on top," it is difficult to include all tables while at the same time excluding benches, planks and trays.

Prototype theories are therefore an alternative to the feature-based theories (Lakoff, 1987; Rosch, 1999). Rather than grouping by common features, children assign different categories to people, animals, objects and so on. The category "bird" for example may initially contain only sparrow and crow. They represent the prototype. As time goes by, hen and penguin are added to the category as well. Studies show that children, when asked to determine whether a picture shows a bird, take a longer time to respond to more peripheral exemplars such as hen and duck than when the picture shows a swallow or a thrush. According to feature-based theories, it should take the same amount of time, as all category members share the same traits (Rosch, 1973).

Mervis and Rosch (1981) describe three conceptual levels: a superordinate level (animal, furniture), a basic level (dog, chair) and a subordinate level (poodle, rocking chair). According to Mervis and Rosch, objects belonging to the basic level are easier to perceive as perceptual units and physically more similar than objects at the superordinate level. At the same time, they are not as similar as objects at the subordinate level, which can be difficult to keep apart. Although a chow chow and a German shepherd are quite different, dogs are nevertheless more alike than a dog, a horse and an elephant. Therefore, children naturally begin by forming concepts of objects at the basic level, rather than broad superordinate concepts or narrow subordinate concepts. When forming a **prototype category**, the first exemplars the child meets will constitute the prototype.

Elaborating on this theory, Quinn (2002) describes early conceptual development as proceeding from collections of individual exemplars to the creation of prototypes, which in turn give rise to "magnets" that form the core of categories and attract new exemplars (Figure 14.2). For instance, children first form a prototype "chair" based on their

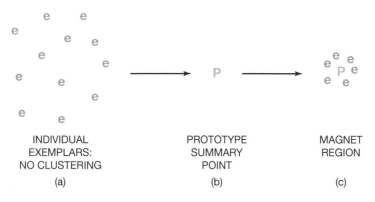

INDIVIDUAL   PROTOTYPE   MAGNET
EXEMPLARS: SUMMARY   REGION
NO CLUSTERING   POINT

(a)   (b)   (c)

Figure 14.2 Quinn's model of early categorization and concept formation.
(a) Children begin by grouping a number of exemplars that seem to belong together based on perceptual similarity. (b) The sum of these exemplars forms the basis for a prototype. (c) Categories are developed by the addition of new exemplars that are attracted to the prototype like a "magnet" (based on Quinn, 2002, p. 186).

concrete experiences with chairs, maybe also the word *chair*. An unfamiliar object is perceived as a "chair" and included in the concept to the extent that the child perceives it to resemble the prototype. Whether the resemblance is perceptual or functional is not a decisive factor.

According to Quinn, the earliest categories are based on perceptual information but, instead of traits, they build on summary-level representations or prototypes. "Dog" for example is initially defined by all the visual characteristics of animals the child perceives to belong to the category "dog," such as four legs, a snout and a tail. Quinn disagrees with Mandler's division between perceptual and conceptual characteristics, maintaining that there is **continuity** in conceptual development despite the fact that concepts change, new ones appear and categories are split up and combined in increasingly complex ways. The characteristics children initially use can make it difficult to assign exemplars to the correct concept. Many animals have four legs, a snout and a tail. When the visual prototype "dog" is augmented with the knowledge that dogs bark, eat bones, are called *dog* and so on, the content of the concept will change but still maintain the perceptual characteristics that were included in its initial formation and that contribute to the recognition of exemplars belonging to the concept (Quinn, 2002, 2008).

The theories presented here illustrate the range of different views and at the same time reflect the continuing lack of agreement on the processes underlying the formation of concepts.

Early Categorization of Objects

Researchers have designed innovative experiments to find an answer to the question of what types of categories children begin with. As infants are not yet able to talk or are in their earliest language development, researchers have to use non-verbal methods. Studies based on preferential looking (see Book 1, *Theoretical Perspectives and Methodology*, Chapter 25) suggest that 3-month-olds are able to distinguish between cats and horses, tigers and cats and lions and cats, but not between horses and zebras or horses and giraffes (Eimas & Quinn, 1994). Because 3–6-month-olds have no understanding of the types of "beings" cats, horses, tigers, lions and elephants are (living creatures, mammals and so on), Eimas and Quinn suggest that children at this age distinguish between them based on visual features alone and still have to develop broader conceptual categories (see Figure 14.2).

The study in Box 14.1 illustrates how the breadth of children's experiences influences what is included in their conceptual categories. The perceptual differences are usually greater between dogs than between cats, and children therefore tend to develop broader dog concepts and narrower cat concepts. This may explain why children more often call cats *woof-woof* than they call dogs *kitty*.

Another method is based on the fact that studies have found that 18-month-old children touch the objects in a certain pattern, and according to Mandler this pattern is motivated by their interest and therefore reflects their conceptual system. Objects from different categories are placed in front of children without leading them to do anything specific with them. If the objects for example include toy animals and vehicles, and the child consecutively touches the toy animals more often than chance would suggest, Mandler interprets this to mean that the child has formed a category "animals" as distinct from "vehicles." By using this method, Mandler found that 18-month-olds distinguished between exemplars of the categories "bird" and "airplane," even though birds and airplanes are perceptually quite similar, as well as between "bird" and "animal." At the age of 2½ years, they first differentiated consistently between exemplars

Box 14.1   Asymmetries in Categorization of Dogs and Cats (Quinn, 2002; Quinn et al., 1993)

In an experiment based on preference looking, 3–4-month-olds were first shown a set of photographs of either different cats *or* different dogs, two at a time. By observing the photographs, the children developed either a "dog" category or a "cat" category. Then, all the children were shown a pair of photographs with a new dog and a new cat. The infants who had been shown different cats looked longer at the picture of the dog than that of the cat (**novelty preference**), while the other group, which had been shown different dogs, looked equally long at the dog and the cat.

One explanation for this difference may be that cats resemble each other more than dogs. The children who were shown pictures of different cats therefore formed a relatively narrow category "cat." They looked longest at the dog, perceiving it as new compared with the cat, which in turn they perceived to belong to the category to which they had habituated. The dogs in the pictures were so different, however, that the children who were shown dogs formed a category broad enough to also include cats and therefore did not assign the cat to a different category than the new dog.

This explanation is supported by an analysis of ten surface measurements on the photographs of the dogs and cats that showed that half of the cats perceptually fit into the dog category, while only two of 18 dogs fit into the cat category. When the dog category was narrowed down by removing the most atypical dogs and the experiment was repeated, the children showed novelty preference for the image of the cat after having habituated to the narrower range of dogs.

from different basic-level concepts, such as "hare" and "dog" (Mandler et al., 1991).

Early concepts also include functions, what things do and what one usually does with them. Mandler and McDonough (1996) began by observing what 14-month-old children spontaneously did with different animals and vehicles that were put in front of them. Then the children were shown a normal play action with one of the items, such as feeding an animal with a small spoon or opening the door of a toy car with a key (Figure 14.3). When the children got to play with an animal and a vehicle shortly after, they imitated the action with the object that belonged to the same higher-level category, although it was quite unlike the one they had observed (such as a dog and a fish). Only rarely did they imitate actions that did not fit with the item. They did not feed the plane or open the bird with a key, even when they were only given a single toy after watching the experimenter demonstrate the action. Mandler explains the results by inferring that the children's categorizations were based more on knowledge about animals and vehicles than on visual similarity.

Mandler's results suggest a development from global to more specific categories, but other studies have not supported this conclusion. For example, in one study, 3-year-olds were able to find two objects that belonged together when two of them belonged to the same basic-level concept and a third belonged to a different superordinate category (for example two cats and a car). When the objects belonged to different basic-level categories (car, motorcycle, cat), the children seemed to make random selections (Rosch et al., 1976). The results suggest that children at this age do not have a clear understanding of things that belong to the same superordinate category, the opposite of Mandler's findings.

Rakison (2003) explains the conflicting results by proposing that young children do not have global concepts such as "animal" or "vehicle" and only appear to categorize objects based on global traits because they focus on one or two prominent features (Box 14.2). Rakison's results suggest that children initially are aware of one or a few prominent features, but that the object as a whole is important as well. Somewhat older children had difficulties forming categories when things appeared to violate the object's familiar integrity as a whole. Rakison suggests that children have an innate tendency to pay attention to parts of objects and a general ability to form **associations**. Over time, children associate the objects' parts with movement and other functions and form concepts of complex feature patterns that usually are connected. This leads to a continuous development from infants' earliest categorizations based on one or two features to the complex concepts of adults.

Exactly how children begin to categorize things and form concepts is one of the fundamental questions of developmental

Dissimilar test

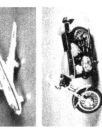

Similar test

Exemplar for
modeling

Figure 14.3 Photographs of animals and vehicles used in Mandler and McDonough's study (1996).

Box 14.2   Categorization of Blends of Animals and Vehicles (Rakison, 2003)

The study included children aged 14, 18 and 22 months. Rakison (2003) observed how they behaved when there were:

(a)   different exemplars of "animals" (cow, dog, goose and walrus) and "vehicles" (terrain vehicles, trains, buses and motorcycles)
(b)   different animals without legs and vehicles without wheels
(c)   animals and vehicles with either legs only or wheels only
(d)   animals and vehicles with wheels or legs.

He found that the children touched the typical exemplars in line with common categories, as other studies have found as well. However, the children did not seem to form two separate categories for animals without legs and vehicles without wheels, or when both animals and vehicles had either legs or wheels. When the parts were mixed, that is, animals with wheels and legs and vehicles with wheels and legs, the 14- and 18-month-olds categorized the toys based on their functional parts independent of the body – "things with legs" and "things with wheels" – while the oldest children (22 months) showed no systematic categorization (Rakison & Butterworth, 1998).

In a similar study with objects at the basic level (cows and cars), 18- and 22-month-old children distinguished between cows and cars when they had no legs or wheels. Children aged 14 and 18 months did not seem to form any categories when all the objects had either wheels or legs. The oldest children distinguished between cows and cars on all the tasks (Rakison & Cohen, 1999). (Thanks to David Rakison for photographs.)

psychology, but the results are ambiguous and partly seem to contradict one another. Mandler interprets her findings to mean that children form global concepts before they begin to categorize at the basic level. Quinn and Eimas's studies show that infants are able to distinguish between animals at the basic level based on perceptual analysis alone. The question is why children do not seem to use this ability. Mandler's explanation is that they represent different levels of categorization, while Eimas and Quinn's studies merely show a simple form of perceptual categorization. Eimas and Quinn disagree with this view. They consider the formation of perceptual prototypes to be an early stage in conceptual development as such. Rakison argues that the results are consistent with the view that children form concepts from prominent perceptual and functional features by means of *associative learning*, grouping together characteristics that tend to occur together. This is similar to Quinn and Eimas's explanation, except that children start with a few perceptual characteristics instead of single exemplars, which in turn form the basis for later prototypes and broader categories. Both explanations involve a continuous process by which concepts constantly become more specific and varied.

These different explanations illustrate how difficult it can be to interpret the results of infant studies (see Kagan, 2008a). Perhaps the results of these experiments say more about how infants perceive a collection of things shown to them than the types of categories they form in the course of early development. This is important knowledge, but it is possible that children use other characteristics to create functional categories in a world where many objects appear together with constantly new things and in different situations (Walker-Andrews, 2008). Children most likely form concepts in more than one way, and variations in culture determine which of them they use the most. Both similarities and differences between objects determine the distinguishing characteristics for their categorization. Among a group of different objects, any similarity will stand out. If for example some triangles and rectangles are blue, it will be their shape that distinguishes them and be the property that stands out the most. If two identical triangles have different colors, their color will be more salient than their shape and receive more attentional weight (Sloutsky, 2003). And, although children's earliest concepts do not involve object categories alone, it is these categories that have been studied the most (Nelson, 2011).

Conceptual Development in Childhood and Adolescence

Through development, children's physical and social environment expands, and they take part in more varied activities. These activities play an important role in concept development. Over time, children develop a complex conceptual structure with greater internal consistency and structural relationship between concepts. At preschool age, many of their concepts are based on the role things have in activities and events. Lucariello and Nelson (1985) call these concepts slot-fillers because they involve things that can fulfill the same role in an event or activity, such as putting on X (pants, shirt, socks) in the morning or eating X (cheese, jam, salami) for breakfast. Therefore, a slot-filler category for food at this age is not a global concept such as "all edible things" but rather "what is eaten during a particular activity," for example at lunch or breakfast. Evidence for such concepts is provided by a study of preschool children who were able to list more items when asked for examples of "breakfast foods" or "snacks" than of "food." School-age children listed more items when asked about "food" (Lucariello, 1998). The fact that things are exchangeable at a certain point in a daily activity or routine helps children see similarities and group them together.

The number of slot-fillers decreases with age, and many of them are later reorganized into **hierarchical structures** (Nelson, 1988). Between the ages of 5 and 7 years, a conceptual shift seems to take place whereby hierarchical or scientific concepts become more prominent (Nguyen & Murphy, 2003; Perraudin & Mounoud, 2009). These are related to each other in a hierarchy that includes more wide-ranging concepts with many subordinate concepts, as well as others that are more narrowly defined. Some are superordinate to others in the sense that all members of one category are members of the other but not vice versa. For example, all cats are animals, but not all animals are cats. "Dog" and "cat" are different categories but belong to the same superordinate category "animal" (Sloutsky, 2015).

The relationship between two classes or categories in which one class is part of another is called class inclusion. As this involves the coordination of many concepts, an understanding of class inclusion is considered an important milestone in conceptual development, and there are differing views on when children pass this milestone. Inhelder and Piaget (1964) performed a series of experiments showing that class inclusion – such as the inclusion of "rose" in the category "flower" in Figure 12.4 – was difficult to understand for children before they had reached the concrete operational stage at around 7 years of age (see also Part I, Chapter 3, this volume). Other studies however have found class inclusion in younger children. In a much-cited study, children were shown a teddy bear that was supposed to walk up a staircase with four red and two white steps to reach a table. The children were asked whether there were more red steps or steps. Children as young as 4 years old answered correctly, far earlier than what Piaget and Inhelder had found (McGarrigle et al., 1978). The results are interpreted to suggest that class inclusion develops more gradually and at an earlier age when it concerns toys and other areas that are familiar to children (see Chapter 3, this volume). However, others have pointed out that this task may not measure class inclusion, and that the children instead solve it by comparing two lengths (Halford & Andrews, 2006).

From an early age, language becomes increasingly important in the formation of concepts. Words are referents to meanings that contribute both to the formation of new concepts and the reorganization of preexisting ones (Lupyan, 2016). Words lead the attention to important events and situational characteristics, and the words children hear people use about different objects in the environment tell them what does and does not belong together according to their culture. It is not certain that toddlers would place cats and dogs in different categories if adults' use of language had not led them to do so. Words can also draw children's attention to various forms of categorization. When an adult uses a noun to refer to a toy such as *teddy bear* or *doll*, the word is likely to be the name of the toy. If the adult uses an adjective such as *soft* or *raggedy*, it tells the child that the toy has characteristics that place it in a

Figure 14.4 Class inclusion.
Each child was shown a collection of 11 flowers – seven roses and four white flowers – and asked: *Are there more roses or more flowers?* Children who had not yet reached the concrete operational stage answered *roses*, while older children answered *flowers*. The youngest children were able to tell that some of the flowers were roses and that the others were a different type of flower. They did not understand, however, that roses are flowers as well and must be included when counting "flowers" (Inhelder & Piaget, 1964).

group with other soft and raggedy things (Waxman & Gelman, 2009). The importance of conceptual knowledge also shows up in the fact that 4-year-old children remember the name of a greater number of new objects when they are told how they work, and younger children themselves often ask how a thing works when they are told the name of a new object (Nelson et al., 2008). In addition, language is a prerequisite for forming abstract concepts such as "politics" or "democracy."

As children's use of words also reflects their concepts, many studies of conceptual development have focused on how children use language. Children under the age of 2½ years rarely use words that refer to global concepts; when they do, their understanding and use of them usually differ from those of adults (Griffiths, 1986). Neither are the global categories of a culture necessarily identical with those formed by children early on. In a certain sense, "vehicle," "furniture" and "animal" are cultural constructs and do not exist in the real world. Children learn such categories when they turn up during conversation. Macnamara (1982) found that 2–3-year-olds seemed to follow a prototype strategy in acquiring global concepts whereby new members are gradually assigned to a concept. Initially, the children used the word *animals* only for a group of different animals and objected strongly when Macnamara held up a toy horse and asked whether it was an animal. Observations showed that children's understanding of *animals* was related to the way their parents used the word in conversation with their children. They only used the word *animal* when they talked about several different types of animals. A herd of horses, for example, was called *horses* by the parents, not *animals*. Gradually, children learn that dogs are "animals," cats are "animals," horses are "animals" and so on. The point at which animals are assigned to this category will depend on the animals children encounter during play and in reality. In more exotic parts of the world, elephants and giraffes may be among the earliest members of children's "animal" category.

The research of Carey (1985) gives insight into other aspects of concept development. She asked children aged 4–10 years about the characteristics of real animals and of dolls. The 4-year-olds differentiated between real animals and dolls and attributed a number of relevant characteristics to animals, such as internal organs. None of the 4–7-year-olds commented that all animals and plants are living things or that "dead" things are not alive. The children who said that dead things are dead also said the same thing about plants. The children's answers seemed to reflect a prototype rather than a feature-based strategy: the characteristics they attributed to animals were based on how similar they were to people. Four-year-olds attributed characteristics to new animals only if they were told that people also had these characteristics and did not generalize in the same way from other animals. Nor did they transfer knowledge of people to things, even if the same rules could be applied, such as the weight of rocks and people. The 7-year-olds generalized both ways (Heyman et al., 2003). In addition, the younger children's categories were *asymmetrical*: animals are more like people than people are like animals.

Gradually, the children transferred more human characteristics to other living beings. The more familiar they were with the animals, the more human qualities they attributed to them. Carey concludes that children's early biological understanding is based on their perception of *similarities* between individual species rather than the taxonomic categorization used by older children and adults. Not until the age of 10 did the children consider plants to be living things, and they then appeared to be using the term "living" in a way similar to adults. They understood that the body represents a whole, and that the body's organs cooperate. The asymmetry typical of younger children's understanding was largely absent among the 10-year-olds. The children's answers thus reflected the general principle that children make use of their previous knowledge when learning something new. Because human characteristics are so prominent in children's experiences, assumptions about these characteristics often form the basis for younger children's exploration of animal characteristics.

The transition from non-hierarchical to hierarchical categorization is important for the formation of new structures and coherence in children's conceptual network. The studies conducted by Nelson and Carey suggest that children do not form larger hierarchical structures before entering school age. Education exerts a systematic and profound influence on children's conceptual structure by supplementing their "spontaneously" formed concepts through participation in various activities (Wells, 2008). A lot of schoolwork implies categorization – much time is spent for example on reviewing and clarifying the biological taxonomy (Wertsch, 1991). It is at school that children learn that whales are mammals rather than fish, the way children tend to classify them spontaneously. Nevertheless, not all concepts undergo this type of reorganization. Many adolescent and adult concepts are non-hierarchical or associated with certain situations as well (Perraudin & Mounoud, 2009). Conceptual metaphors often form a cluster or chain-like structure, such as the concept "mother," which includes biological mother, foster mother, surrogate mother, stepmother and so on. Some cultures do not base their biological categories on a taxonomy of species, genus, family, order and class. The Australian Dyirbal tribe for example assigns women, dogs, some snakes, some fish, the sun, the moon, shields, some spears, some trees and many things associated with water and fire to the same category *balan* (Lakoff, 1987). A group of farmers in Central Asia seemed to form concepts not based on hierarchy, but rather on their association with different activities. *Axe*, *saw* and *log* for example were considered part of the same conceptual category as they belonged to the same activity: cutting down trees and chopping them up for firewood (Luria, 1976).

Adolescents have developed a better understanding of the boundaries between different knowledge domains but also an increasing ability to see similarities or correspondences between them. Nonetheless, conceptual development is not an unfinished jigsaw puzzle to which missing pieces are added and the totality reorganized to create a conceptual hierarchy. Most domains undergo extensive minor and major reorganization before a large and varied conceptual structure is established – a structure that continues to be impacted by experience and changes in society.

15

Reasoning

The most common forms of reasoning are analogy, induction and deduction. All three are important in everyday thinking and scientific work and also, hence, how they develop (Kuhn, 2013). *Analogical reasoning* means that children apply a familiar solution to a new "task," such as when toddlers are aware of the fact that humans have a heart and deduce that apes have a heart as well. **Inductive reasoning** involves making a general assumption on the basis of one or a few cases, such as an assumption that all swans are white because every swan one has ever seen has been white. Induction leads to more or less probable assumptions depending on the observations they are based on (Hayes et al., 2010). **Deductive reasoning** moves from a general rule to a specific conclusion that must be true if the rule is correct. If the rule says that all swans are white, the swans in the park must be white. Thus, deduction is a "top–down" process whose logical conclusion *must* be true. Observations that do not conform to the rule require the rule to be rejected. If a single black swan is observed, the rule that all swans are white must be incorrect (Johnson-Laird, 1999). Reasoning is a resource-efficient way of solving problems because it allows one to arrive at decisions about what to do without first having to try out several scenarios. More advanced forms of reasoning include *metacognitive* skills – thinking about thinking.

The reasoning of children and adolescents undergoes age-related changes. However, both children and adults occasionally draw wrong conclusions, and their errors reflect the knowledge they have (and don't have) as well as how they analyze tasks and choose solution strategies. In addition, reasoning can take place individually or in collaboration with others.

Analogical Reasoning

Analogy is a kind of similarity (Holyoak, 2005). The earliest reasoning is based on observations of perceptual or functional similarities. Young

DOI: 10.4324/9781003292500-20

children may notice a similarity in the relationship between things and properties, such as between "wide–narrow" and "high–low" (Bulloch & Opfer, 2009). When a 2-year-old uses a rake to get hold of a toy after having seen an adult use a candy cane for the same purpose, a form of analogical reasoning tells the child that using the rake can be another way of achieving the same goal. Children do not choose a shorter candy cane that more closely resembles the cane used by the adult but is too short to reach the target (Brown, 1989).

Goswami (1992) maintains that the ability to notice similarities is innate, and that children can perceive similarities between relations as early as the first months of life. The basic mechanism is thus in place, but children's reasoning depends on sufficient relevant knowledge and analogical relations that are not too abstract. When children first begin to use analogies depends on the context and the child's experience in each domain. A 3-year-old who says "Gasoline is milk for the car" bases his knowledge on the milk he himself drinks to explain why cars need to be refueled. Five-year-old Ross was at the cemetery together with his mother, asking her whether the big tombstones were meant for kings. He applied his knowledge of the relationship between "kings" and "ordinary people" to "large tombstones" and "small tombstones" (DeLoache et al., 1998). In another study, children were asked: "Food is to body as rain is to . . .?" (ground). To respond correctly, the children had to know that food nurtures the body and rain nurtures the ground. The children who did not have this knowledge gave associative answers related to rain, such as "water", "storm" and "coat" (Goswami, 1992). A lack of knowledge makes younger children feel more insecure and easily leads them to change the correct answer. One girl chose "eyes" on the pairing task "Radio–ears, television–?" but quickly changed "eyes" to "plug" at the experimenter's suggestion.

The task complexity increases as the number of relational items grows. The pairing task "Horse–foal, dog–?" (puppy), for example, consists of two binary relationships. Two-year-olds are able to manage this task, but only if there are distinct similarities (Singer-Freeman & Bauer, 2008). The task "Peter is fairer than Tom, John is fairer than Peter; who is fairer – John or Tom?" includes three binary relations: Peter–Tom, John–Peter and John–Tom. Five-year-olds are usually able to solve this type of task. Younger children can easily be distracted by irrelevant information, especially when tasks are complex; it is not until the age of 9–11 years that they are able to cope with both complexity and distraction (Richland et al., 2006).

Older children have more knowledge, are more aware of the relationships between things and hold on to their own answers to a greater degree. Adolescents give more correct answers, justify their answers based on relational similarity and resist counter-suggestions. Even so, it is not difficult to create analogies that many adults are unable to work out because they lack knowledge in the domains from which the analogy is taken.

According to Halford (1992), analogical thinking arises from the ability to form **mental models**. As children's cognitive capacity increases, they form new and more advanced mental models and become capable of mastering more complex and abstract analogical relationships. While early analogical thinking is implicit, children become more aware of their own thinking with age (**meta-knowledge**). Younger children often make use of the first model that comes to mind. If the model is wrong, the answer will be wrong as well. Older children can keep several models in mind and consider them at the same time (Halford & Andrews, 2004).

Explanations based on analogy are a key element in all teaching. Students' ability to reason by analogy is therefore of great importance for how they manage their schoolwork, and teachers need to ensure that the students understand the analogies they use in teaching (Vendetti et al., 2015).

Logical and Pragmatic Reasoning

In **logical reasoning**, all inferences are restricted to the rules of logic. It is the logic of reasoning itself, rather than its content, that is of importance. Whether a deductive inference is correct does not depend on whether a condition actually is or may be a certain way, but on the agreement between a set of premises and a conclusion. Given two premises – (a) there are more eggs in basket X than in basket Y and (b) there are more eggs in basket Y than in basket Z – more eggs must be in basket X than in Z by *necessity*. Anything else would be impossible. If basket Z actually contained more eggs than basket X, it would be *incompatible* with the two premises. One of them would have to be wrong. If the premises are correct, the conclusion *must* also be correct (Johnson-Laird, 1999).

In logic, a *syllogism* is a statement about the relation between two objects or conditions based on two independent statements about the relation between them (Johnson-Laird, 1999). According to Donaldson (1978), even toddlers are able to draw (implicit) syllogistic inferences based on their – often limited – know ledge, as in the following example (DeLoache et al., 1998):

Three-year-old Laura takes an opened can of soda from the refrigerator and says to her mother: "Whose is this? It's not yours, cause it doesn't have lipstick".

Laura's reasoning can formally be described as follows:

(a) Her mother's soda can always has lipstick marks after she has drunk from it.
(b) The opened soda can has no lipstick marks.
(c) The soda can is not her mother's.

Expressed more generally, the logic behind this example is: If *p*, then *q*. *Not q*, therefore *not p* (no lipstick, therefore not her mother's can). Logic is a mental tool that makes it possible to disregard issues involving content and experience and to ensure internal consistency between a premise and a conclusion. But there is little reason to ascribe an understanding of logic to a 3-year-old. It is more likely that Laura's conclusion was based on her observations of soda cans her mother had drunk from. With clear instructions, 4-year-olds can learn how to pick one of four flowers that gets a monkey to sneeze when observing the monkey's reaction to different flower combinations (Schulz & Gopnik, 2004). But, without clear guidance, younger children's reasoning is intuitive and unsystematic. Their answers – like Laura's – are based on their experience and knowledge of circumstances without considering the necessity inherent in logic (Kuhn, 2013).

A qualitative change in reasoning across knowledge areas seems to take place around the age of 11 or 12 (Marini & Case, 1994; Richland et al., 2006). Children become more attentive to logical connections, and, around 13 years of age, adolescents improve at solving problems based on internal logical consistency (Markovits et al., 1989).

This is not to say that logic takes over reasoning completely. The reasoning of adolescents and adults is not exclusively based on logic, but equally much on experience and knowledge of what usually is true. Wason (1977) and other researchers have shown that adolescents and adults often reason in a similar way as children when the material is new and unfamiliar. They manage tasks involving areas they have experience with better than more abstract tasks. In tasks like the first in Box 15.1, people tend to search for *positive evidence*: if a vowel is opposite a blue square, and a blue square is opposite a vowel, the hypothesis is confirmed. If a consonant is opposite a blue square, it has no bearing on the evaluation of the rule as the rule says nothing about it. The

Box 15.1   Logical and Pragmatic Reasoning (based on Wason, 1977)

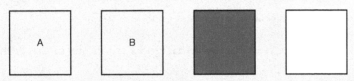

Problem 1 (Logical)

The participant was shown the cards above and given the following rule: "If there is a vowel on one side of the card, there is always a blue square on the other side." The task was to find out which of the four cards need to be turned to determine whether the rule is true.

The typical answer was A only, or A and the blue square. The correct answer is A and the white square. The rule can only be rejected if a white square is opposite a vowel or a vowel is opposite a white square. Only about 10 percent of the participants gave the correct answer to this task.

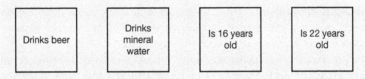

Problem 2 (Pragmatic)

The participant was shown the cards above and asked to imagine a policeman who checks whether a restaurant adheres to the following rule for serving alcohol: "Only those above the age of 18 years are allowed to drink beer." The cards included information about four restaurant guests. One side listed their age, the other what they were drinking. The task was to find out which of the four cards needed to be turned to determine whether the rule for serving alcohol had been broken.

About 75 percent of the participants answered this task correctly: they checked the card of the person drinking beer and the card of the 16-year-old. The task has precisely the same logical structure as Problem 1 but relates to an area the subjects had

concrete experience with. When they were familiar with the
situation, the participants also understood the need for negative
evidence.

tasks must be solved by looking for *negative evidence* (such as 3-year-
old Laura did to determine whether the soda can belonged to her
mother). Only a white square opposite a vowel and a vowel opposite a
white square would invalidate the rule that there must be a blue square
opposite a vowel. The need for negative evidence seemed clearer to
the participants in the second task. The percentage of correct answers
increased dramatically for a task with a corresponding logical structure
but related to an activity that the participants were familiar with.

Cheng and Holyoak (1985) explain these results by proposing
that both children and adults make use of *pragmatic reasoning schemas* instead of logic. These schemas are abstracted from past experience, and the answers depend on the individual's ability to associate
a given problem with experience from earlier tasks and situations
with a similar goal. Children are able solve this type of task if they
have the relevant experience and can base their reasoning on related
mental models (Halford & Andrews, 2004; Chen & Klahr, 2008). For
example, in a study, children aged 3–4 years were told the rule "If
Sally wants to play outside, she must put her coat on." When asked
to point out where Sally is being naughty and not doing what her
mom told her, most of the children pointed to the picture of a girl
playing outside without wearing a coat (Harris & Núñez, 1996). The
presentation of this task is not entirely comparable to the tasks in
Box 15.1, but 6–7-year-olds are able to solve this type of task when
the material is familiar and meaningful to them, such as breaking
a rule about when trucks are allowed to drive into town (Girotto
et al., 1988; Light et al., 1990). Younger children however have difficulty generalizing and applying their knowledge to new situations
and begin to reason all over again in the next situation (Kuhn, 2013).
The variation in children's reasoning demonstrates that they do not
develop the ability for formal reasoning in a vacuum: logical knowledge must operate on and in the context of the child's knowledge of
the world (Overton et al., 1987).

Some types of tasks cannot be solved through **pragmatic reasoning** and require logical knowledge. Children and adults most likely use
both logical and pragmatic rules in their reasoning. Pragmatic schemas

have their origin in children's individual experiences, which are largely shaped by cultural activities. Cultural differences suggest that the application of logical rules depends on the introduction to formal reasoning as part of the regular school curriculum in industrialized countries (Richland et al., 2010). It is also likely that dialectical reasoning is important for the ability to reach beyond one's own experiential rationale (see below). Logic thus becomes a cultural tool in the Vygotskian sense rather than an individual trait as described by Piaget's theory. Furthermore, it is a tool that different cultures have developed in different ways and to varying degrees (Nisbett & Norenzayan, 2002).

Dialectical Reasoning

Dialectical reasoning is a form of shared problem solving involving two or more people who argue on behalf of their individual views. Taking a social constructivist perspective, Salmon and Zeitz (1995) describe dialectical reasoning as a fundamentally social process. The individual child's capacity for this type of reasoning and reflection is the result of internalized social processes that in turn affect the child's dialectical reasoning in social contexts. Therefore conscious reasoning is not merely the product of joint reflection, but also forms the basis for renewed social and individual dialectical reasoning and cognitive development. However, younger children have difficulty maintaining attention on both their own opinion and that of others. Dialectical reasoning is therefore mostly relevant to older children and adolescents (Kuhn, 2013). Dialectical reasoning and argumentation in the classroom may support the development of scientific and critical reasoning (Osborne, 2010).

16

Atypical Development

The research presented in this chapter shows that children, adolescents and adults do not think and reason in any one particular way but approach problems from different angles, depending on the situation and the knowledge and strategies they have acquired through personal experience and informal and formal training. Disorders that affect children's cognitive functioning can also affect their reasoning, including intellectual disability (Harris & Greenspan, 2016). One study showed that children with specific learning disorders who scored within the normal range on intelligence tests had greater problems with analogical reasoning than children without learning disorders; this was particularly true of children who struggled with math at school (Schiff et al., 2009). Other studies have found that children with autism spectrum disorders have difficulty drawing inferences (Grant et al., 2004; Leevers & Harris, 2000). At the same time, it is important to map the types of tasks children with different forms of atypical development do *not* have particular difficulties with. Some studies for example have found that children with autism spectrum disorder are able to master analogical reasoning as well as their peers but that they do not always make use of this ability, even in areas they are quite familiar with. They need explicit instructions to understand the nature of the problem (Green et al., 2014).

DOI: 10.4324/9781003292500-21

Summary of Part III

1 Children's developing understanding of the world includes a *spatial dimension*, a *temporal dimension* and *causal relationships*. From an early age, children perceive that objects exist and have a physical location even when they cannot be experienced directly (*object permanence*). "A-not-B error" means that children search where they recently found an object rather than where they last saw it being hidden. With age, children make increasingly precise use of *geometric cues* and *landmarks*. Independent locomotion and exploration of the physical environment are important elements in this development.

2 Children in preschool age understand time, speed and distance as separate entities. Closer to school age, children are able to manage two dimensions at a time, and three by the age of 9. By counting, using a stopwatch or other "timing aid," children are able to manage this type of task earlier.

3 Children's initial understanding of time comes from their own experiences with routines and schedules. Conversations with parents and other adults help children organize days and events on a timeline between past and future. Formal and informal training are important for a cultural understanding of time.

4 *Physical causality* has to do with the physical behavior of objects and how they interact. Studies have found an emerging understanding of physical causality in 3-month-olds, but children are much older before the concept of causality includes a sense of physical *necessity*. According to a nativist view, it is an understanding too complex to be acquired and must therefore be innate. In contrast to this, Baillargeon suggests that the development of physical causality is based on an innate *principle of persistence*. Children's early understanding of individual events is later transformed

DOI: 10.4324/9781003292500-22

into a general understanding of physical causality. From an *information-processing* perspective, children are assumed to notice events that occur simultaneously and gradually form an understanding of physical causality, for example what happens when objects collide.

5   According to *feature-based theories*, children's earliest object categorizations are based on the *perceptual* or *functional* properties of objects. Mandler describes a development that moves from *perceptual* to *conceptual categories* by way of *perceptual meaning*. Features and categories are initially global and gradually become more differentiated.

6   From the perspective of *prototype theory*, Rosch suggests that people, animals, things and so forth are assigned to three conceptual levels – superordinate, basic and subordinate – and that children develop basic-level categories first. Quinn describes a development from collections of individual exemplars to the creation of prototypes that form conceptual "magnets." New objects are assigned to concepts that are perceived to have important similarities with the prototype. Prototypes are summary-level representations; traits are perceived in context.

7   Mandler interprets her results to mean that children acquire global categories before categories at the basic level. Quinn and Eimas's findings suggest that children's early differentiations mainly occur at the basic level. According to Rakison, children initially become aware of one or two perceptually prominent features. Gradually, they form overall categories with complex patterns of perceptual and functional traits. Early categorization is affected by the characteristics of the things children are aware of in the moment.

8   Nelson describes *slot-filler categories* in children's transition from "spontaneous" to "scientific" concepts. Slot-fillers are linked to a particular situation and do not form hierarchies based on their own function but consist of things that can fill the same place in an event or activity. *Class inclusion* is a necessary property in any hierarchical system.

9   Beginning in early childhood, language becomes increasingly important for children's categorizations. Words are cues to meaning and contribute to both the formation of new concepts and the reorganization of previously established concepts. Children under the age of 2½ years rarely use superordinate terms generally in the same way as adults but use them in the way their parents use them in conversation with the child.

10 *Analogical reasoning* is based on relational similarity. Goswami suggests children have an innate ability to notice such similarities, and that relations continue to become more complex with age. Others believe development to be the result of an age-related increase in cognitive capacity. Compared with younger children, older children are able to keep several models in mind and consider them at the same time. Analogy is a key element in all teaching, and the development of analogical reasoning is of importance for children's schoolwork.

11 Younger children are able to draw *deductive* inferences, but their reasoning is mostly based on experience rather than logic. Adolescents and adults make more use of logic, but studies based on *selection tasks* and similar problems show that adults also are able to master reasoning tasks better when they can relate them to events they have experience with. One explanation is that children and adults use *pragmatic reasoning schemas* abstracted from past experience. Another explanation is that reasoning has a basis in mental models formed in connection with certain situations, and that it is easier to activate mental models that lie closer to the individual's own experiences. Children are able to solve reasoning tasks that are not too complex and for which they have the relevant mental models. Pragmatic schemas underline the importance of activities for children's knowledge about the world.

12 *Dialectical reasoning* sets the perspectives of two or more persons against each other. Children's ability to reason and reflect is the result of internalized dialectical social processes.

13 *Cognitive disorders* can affect children's concept formation and reasoning, including children with learning disorders, intellectual disability and autism spectrum disorders.

Core Issues

* The development of physical causality.
* Features and prototypes in object concepts.
* Logic and pragmatics in reasoning.

Suggestions for Further Reading

Baillargeon, R. (2008). Innate ideas revisited: For a principle of persistence in infants' physical reasoning. *Perspectives on Psychological Science, 3,* 2–13.

Friedman, W. J. (2005). Developmental and cognitive perspectives on humans' sense of the times of past and future events. *Learning and Motivation, 36*, 145–158.

Learmonth, A. E., Newcombe, N. S., Sheridan, N., & Jones, M. (2008). Why size counts: Children's spatial reorientation in large and small enclosures. *Developmental Science, 11*, 414–426.

Rosch, E. (1999). Reclaiming concepts. *Journal of Consciousness Studies, 6*, 61–77.

Schulz, L. E., & Gopnik, A. (2004). Causal learning across domains. *Developmental Psychology, 40*, 162–176.

Part IV

Mind Understanding

The Human Mind

Humans seem to have a *species-specific* ability to understand and reason about people, a *social cognitive* ability that other species lack. It forms the basis for human interaction and understanding of one another's actions, intentions, desires, thoughts and feelings, for **sympathy** and empathy, but also for deceiving or misleading, as well as exposing trickery and deceit.

Thus, children develop a **mind understanding**, an understanding that they themselves and others perceive the world around them and form mental representations of people, things and events. The ability to perceive that others see something represents an emergent understanding of other people's minds, and gradually also of *what* they see. This includes an understanding of the fact that others may lack knowledge or have knowledge different from one's own, and that this knowledge will determine how the other person reasons and acts. Because the mind cannot be observed directly, an understanding of other people's minds requires the child to draw inferences about their perceptions, thoughts, desires and emotions beyond what she can observe directly. Therefore, this type of understanding is sometimes referred to as "theory of mind" (Premack & Woodruff, 1978). It is also referred to as **mentalizing**, defined as the interpretation of one's own and others' behavior as an expression of mental states, desires, feelings, beliefs and so on. In a broader sense, mentalizing is described as a process that involves all thinking about relations, human interaction and psychological processes in human beings (Allen, 2003; Fonagy et al., 2004). Others talk about the development of "commonsense psychology," "mindreading" or "social understanding" (Carpendale & Lewis, 2015). I have chosen to use the term "mind understanding" because it is concise and theoretically neutral.

DOI: 10.4324/9781003292500-24

Visual Perspective

In the second half of their first year, most children become increasingly attentive to others looking at them and to what others are looking at and follow their gaze to look in the same direction as the other person (see Book 5, *Communication and Language Development*, Chapter 2). One-year-olds show a nascent ability to take the perspective of others when they leave their mother's lap and crawl to see what an adult is looking at behind a wall that prevents the child from seeing what is there (Moll & Tomasello, 2004). When they are a little older, they also understand that the adult may see something different than they do (Flavell, 2004).

Two Levels of Visual Perspective-Taking

Flavell (1992, 2004) describes two levels of **visual perspective** knowledge. At *Level 1*, children understand that other people see the world around them, while *Level 2* involves an understanding of *what* they see, the fact that the same thing can appear differently depending on the viewpoint, and that people may see things in different ways.

Children who perceive the visual perspective of others on Level 1 know that they themselves and others do not necessarily see the same thing. With sufficient cues, they can infer what others do and do not see. A development in the ability to assume someone else's visual perspective seems to take place between the ages of 2 and 3 years. In a study of 2–3-year-olds, even the youngest children were able to place a toy in such a way that the experimenter *could see it*, even when this meant that the children had to place the toy out of their own line of sight. The 2-year-olds however had difficulty hiding a toy so the experimenter on the other side of a screen *could not see it*. Some of the children hid the toy behind the screen so the experimenter could see

DOI: 10.4324/9781003292500-25

the toy, while they themselves could not see it. The 3-year-olds had no problems with this task. After hiding the toy correctly, several of them went to the experimenter's side of the screen to make sure that it was not visible from that side (Gopnik & Meltzoff, 1997).

In another study, children aged 2–5 years were shown a card with a picture of a cat on one side and a dog on the other. The 3-year-olds had no difficulty saying that the experimenter saw the cat while they saw the dog when the card was held between them (Masangkay et al., 1974). The same study also included a picture of a turtle that could be positioned so the turtle seemed to be standing on its legs when viewed from one side of the table, while it seemed to be upside-down from the other. In this case, most of the 3-year-olds were unable to say what the experimenter was seeing, even when they could go around the table and view the picture from the other side. They lacked the cognitive skills of Level 2 perspective-taking, which this task requires. Almost all of the 4–5-year-olds managed this task.

According to Flavell, Levels 1 and 2 require the same skills and knowledge, but children at Level 2 additionally know that things can look different from different viewpoints. If given sufficient cues, they can infer approximately how things look from another visual angle. Four-year-olds rarely fail on any of the previously mentioned tasks.

The Three Mountain Task

In a classic experiment, Piaget and Inhelder (1956) found that children below the age of 7 had difficulties taking a visual perspective different from their own (Box 18.1). Their explanation of these results is that children below this age are **egocentric** and unable to take the perspective of others in addition to their own. Donaldson (1978) disagrees with the assumption that children are egocentric and suggested that much younger children have the necessary skills to solve this type of task, which requires perspective-taking skills at Level 2. She maintained that the mountain task was only difficult because the children lacked the relevant experience. Therefore, she conducted a similar experiment using a model of a house with several rooms and a boy doll and a policeman doll placed in different parts of the house (Box 18.2). Like in Piaget's experiment, the child was sitting in one place, and nearly all of the youngest children accomplished this task. Donaldson explains these results by the fact that her task – unlike the mountain task – represented a meaningful context for the children. Children at this age have been playing hide and seek and know that the police can look for someone who is hiding, while they have little experience working out how mountains look from different sides.

Box 18.1   The Three Mountain Task (Piaget & Inhelder, 1956)

Children aged 4–11 years were first allowed to examine a model of three mountains from all sides. Then they were seated in front of the model at one of its sides. A doll was placed on a chair at one of the other sides. The children were then shown photographs taken from all sides and asked to identify the photograph of the mountain as the doll was seeing it.

Children below the age of 7 years had difficulty saying which of the photographs showed the mountains from the doll's point of view, while older children accomplished these tasks.

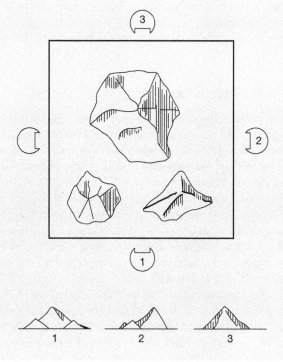

Box 18.2   The Dollhouse Experiment (from Donaldson, 1978)

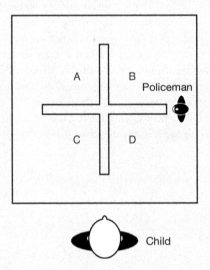

Thirty children aged 3½–5 years participated in the study. The child was sitting in front of a dollhouse and was told that a police doll was trying to catch a boy doll, and that he or she was supposed to help the boy doll hide so the police doll could not find him. The child sat in one place, while the police doll was moved around. The child's task was to say where the boy had to hide from the police in order not to be seen. Nearly 90 percent of a group of the youngest children, with an average age of 3;9 years, were able to tell correctly where the boy doll should hide.

Another possible explanation for children's problems with the mountain task is that they lacked clear cues for the mountains' placements. When Newcombe and Huttenlocher (1992) placed various stickers on the sides of the mountains in the model, children as young as 3 years succeeded in the task. The stickers functioned as "landmarks" for where the doll was looking (see also Part III, Chapter 13). In effect, Donaldson's visual cues were simpler as well: all sides were equal, and the children only needed to look at the location of the police doll in relation to the walls to solve the task.

Whatever the reason for younger children's difficulties with the mountain task may be, these studies show that their difficulties are hardly caused by an egocentric worldview, as Piaget claims. Also, more recent studies have found that children under the age of 7 have problems when the task is presented according to Piaget's model. In one study, children aged 4–8 years were shown two dolls photographing a scene with a pyramid, a cylinder and a cube from different sides. Most of the youngest children were unable to say which of the dolls had taken the pictures, while a majority of the 8-year-olds managed to do so well above the level of chance (Frick et al., 2014). Children are not egocentric but find it difficult to take multiple perspectives in unfamiliar situations with indistinct cues.

19

Private Speech

When listening to conversations between toddlers, one can occasionally wonder whether they are talking about the same subject or with each other at all. Often, children do not convey enough information for a listener to be able to understand what they are talking about. They may begin by describing an event without giving any background information such as where it happened, who was involved and so on. Or they may refer to *him* without having mentioned a male person. Children also talk when they are engaged in something without anyone else being present.

There are many contradictory explanations for these forms of language use. Piaget (1959) associates this type of **private speech** with *egocentricity*, an inability to take the perspective of others. According to Piaget, 50 percent of preschool children's speech is egocentric in the sense that it does not lead to effective communication and consists of what he calls **collective monologues**. Vygotsky (1962) offers a different explanation: private speech shows that children often speak not to communicate something to others but to solve problems and to plan and regulate their own actions. Such use of language may *seem* egocentric but, as it is not intended to be communicative, it is not egocentric. Instead, it is part of children's internalization of conversations with others, a step on the way to *internal speech*, a transition from solving problems in conversation with others to solving them independently without talking aloud (Alderson-Day & Fernyhough, 2015).

The difference between Piaget's individual **constructivism** and Vygotsky's social constructivism becomes clear in the context of this debate (see Book 1, *Theoretical Perspectives and Methodology*, Part II, and Part I, this volume). Piaget's theory claims that cognitive knowledge comes from within. Toddlers talk side by side rather than with each other because they are not yet able to communicate in a way that takes

DOI: 10.4324/9781003292500-26

into account other people's perspective. Their speech is egocentric and will be replaced by rational and social speech once they become aware that they need to adapt their speech to the listener and have acquired the cognitive tools for doing so. According to Vygotsky's theory, cognitive skills are formed through interaction with other people. Language is culturally imparted knowledge. It comes from outside and needs to be not socialized but internalized. Private speech disappears once language has become fully internalized as a tool for thinking.

In line with Piaget's theory, there are many examples of children not taking sufficient account of the other person's knowledge in situations where they seem to try to communicate with someone, as in this telephone conversation between 3-year-old Alice (A) and her grandmother (G) (Warren & Tate, 1992, p. 258):

A: *I got a green one* [opening topic].
G: *You got a what?*
A: *A green one.*
G: *A green one . . .*
A: *There's a baby out there* [points out window].
G: *There is . . .*
A: *Is a baby out there.*
G: *My goodness.*

Piaget's explanation that children lack the cognitive skills to take the perspective of others is also supported by a study in which children from second through eighth grade were to teach a new game to a group of adults. Half of the adults were blindfolded, while the other half could see. Children in the lowest grade did not take into account whether the adult could see, but gave the same description in both situations. Eighth-graders used many more words when describing the game to the blindfolded adults (Flavell et al., 1968).

Vygotsky's theory, on the other hand, is supported by the fact that younger children often talk while doing something else. Their speech does not seem to be directed at anyone, and often no one else is present (McGonigle-Chalmers et al., 2014). Sound recordings made of toddlers before falling asleep show that they may lie in bed and talk to themselves about the day's events and what will happen the next day, as in this monologue of 24-month-old Emily (Nelson, 2015, p. 174):

> *That Daddy brings down basement washing, I can hold Emmy, so,*
> *Daddy brings down the,*

the washing on the basement,
washing,
so my can.

Similarly, while most **gestures** used by toddlers have a clear communicative intent, toddlers also point without such an intent – *private pointing* – in connection with memory and problem solving in situations in which there is no one to communicate with (Delgado et al., 2009, 2011). Deaf children use *private* **sign language** similar to how hearing children use private speech (Winsler, 2009). The incidence of private speech or sign increases when children have to solve complex tasks, resist temptations, experience difficulties or become frustrated and use language to regulate both their actions and their feelings (Bono & Bizri, 2014; Luria, 1961; Manfra et al., 2014).

Research thus lends a certain amount of support to both Vygotsky and Piaget, and a practical differentiation between their theories is not entirely unproblematic in this context. A possible explanation could be that children at this age are egocentric in the sense that they lack the necessary insight to take sufficient account of the person they are talking to, *as well as* using gestures and language "privately" in noncommunicative contexts to manage *executive functions* that regulate attention, actions and emotions (see Chapter 11, this volume).

The proportion of children who talk while engaged in tasks and other activities steadily decreases from preschool age to adolescence, from nearly half of all 5-year-olds to 10 percent of 17-year-olds. Children with **attention deficit disorder** (ADD) and behavioral problems use speech to control attention, actions and emotions in a similar way as other children but continue to use overt private speech for somewhat longer. They seem to benefit from regulating themselves through speech, and it may be useful to encourage them to use speech as a self-regulatory strategy, even if they talk out loud because their speech has yet to be internalized (Winsler, 2009).

Private speech after childhood also occurs in typical development – adolescents speak quietly when working out problems, and many of them report that they use inner speech while solving difficult tasks (Winsler & Naglieri, 2003). Even adults sometimes talk to themselves when faced with a difficult task or making plans (Duncan & Tarulli, 2009).

20

Early Understanding of Desires and Beliefs

Mind understanding is about subjective experience, the fact that other people are thinking beings who reason and act according to their own desires and perception of a situation (Doherty, 2009).

Desires

Children become aware of other people's desires early on. Unlike 14-month-olds, 18-month-old children understand that people can desire different things, and that others can have wishes the same as or different from their own, for example that an adult wants broccoli while they prefer a cracker (Repacholi & Gopnik, 1997). They expect other people to act according to their own desires, for example that an adult will choose the same thing she usually chooses. At the end of their second year, children often speak with their parents about desiring or wanting something, but it is not until the age of 2½ that they understand that people can have conflicting desires about something, for example that Peter wants ice cream and Mary doesn't (Poulin-Dubois et al., 2009). Three-year-olds have difficulty separating a person's action goals – their *intention* – from the action as such. Four-year-olds have a better understanding of the mental and subjective aspects of desires, the fact that someone could wish to do something and try without succeeding, for example that a person can end up somewhere else than where he intended to travel (Feinfield et al., 1999).

Beliefs

Understanding the minds of others involves recognizing that the mental world can differ from the real world, and that people can have false beliefs about something – such as Little Red Riding Hood who *thinks*

DOI: 10.4324/9781003292500-27

it is her grandma lying in bed – and that they will act based on their *beliefs* about the world rather than how it actually is. The question is at what point in their development children acquire this type of understanding. The standard test for assessing the development of mind understanding is based on tasks showing whether children understand that other people act according to their own perception, especially tasks involving false beliefs. These are often called theory-of-mind tasks and deal with two types of events: unexpected transfer and unexpected content.

Unexpected Transfer

In this kind of task, something is moved unknown to a person. In Wimmer and Perner's (1983) original experiment, children were told a story about Maxi's chocolate, which was moved without his knowledge (Box 20.1).

When asked where Maxi will look for the chocolate, the youngest children answered that Maxi will look in the place where the chocolate was moved, while over half the children between 4 and 6 years and most of the older children answered that he will look where he put the chocolate before leaving, in other words where he *thinks* it is. Wimmer and Perner interpreted their findings to mean that children under the age of 4–5 years lack the cognitive skills to understand that other people will act based on their perception of the situation, even when it contradicts the facts. Therefore, they understand the question of where Maxi will look as a question about where the chocolate is and base their response on that. Many subsequent studies with different variations on the Maxi task have shown that children usually begin to master this type of task around the age of 3–5 (Wellman et al., 2001).

Some researchers have pointed out that children's responses do not necessarily reflect a lack of mind understanding, but that limited language comprehension can lead children to misunderstand the question. Therefore, researchers have varied the verbal instructions and implementation in trying to identify the factors that are decisive for children's ability to solve the problem. For example, when Siegal and Beattie (1991) changed the question to "Where will Maxi first look for his chocolate when he comes back?" twice as many 3–4-year-olds were able to answer correctly. Including "first" in the question seemed to make them aware of the possibility that Maxi would look in several places, and that he looks in the wrong place before looking

Box 20.1   The First Maxi Experiment
(Wimmer & Perner, 1983)

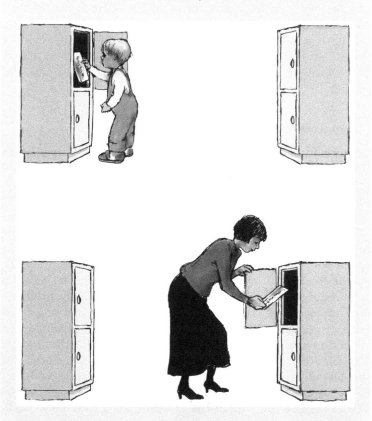

Children between the ages of 3 and 9 years were told and
shown a story in which a boy named Maxi put his chocolate
in a gray cupboard before going out to play. While outside,
his mother moves the chocolate to a blue cupboard. Then the
children were asked: "Where will Maxi look for the chocolate when he comes back?" The 3–4-year-olds replied that
he would look in the blue cupboard where the chocolate,
unknown to Maxi, was moved. Fifty-seven percent of children
aged 4–6 years and 86 percent of children 6 years and older
correctly answered that Maxi would look in the gray cupboard, where he believed it to be.

where the chocolate is actually located. This interpretation is supported by a relation between children's ability to retell stories and their answers to tasks of the Maxi type, independent of age (Lewis et al., 1994).

Unexpected Content

The second type of experiment deals with children's understanding of having acted on a false belief *themselves*. These studies typically are based on asking children about the content of a box that is clearly labeled, for example with a brand of chocolate. Then they get to see that it contains something completely different and are asked what they thought was in the box (Box 20.2). Children under the age of 4 years usually answer that it was the actual content of the box, rather than what they previously said it contained.

Children generally like to do well and give the right answers. One possible explanation for why the younger children in the experiment answered *pencils* when asked what they had thought was in the Smarties box may be that they were embarrassed to have given the wrong answer and did not want to say so. Therefore, Wimmer and Hartl (1991) conducted a similar experiment with "Kasperl," a puppet most Austrian children know from children's television. Kasperl is notorious for making mistakes, so it would not be strange if he had a false belief about something. It turned out, however, that it made no difference whether the children were asked what Kasperl had thought was in the box or whether they were asked what they themselves had thought.

A significant change in mind understanding thus seems to occur around the age of 4. Wimmer and Hartl (1991) suggest that 3-year-olds have yet to form a notion of what it means to assume or believe something and therefore do not distinguish between assumption and reality. It seemed as if the children in the study understood the question "When you first saw the box, what did you think was in it?" to mean "When you first saw the box, what was in it?" Winner and Hartl therefore conducted a new experiment in which the children could observe the contents of the box being replaced. The children were asked about the contents of the Smarties box and could see that it contained Smarties. These were taken out of the box and exchanged with pencils while the children watched. This time, when the children were asked what they had first thought, twice as many answered correctly: 87 instead of 43 percent when the box contained pencils when they opened it. Wimmer and Hartl interpret the higher number of

Box 20.2   Smarties Experiment (Astington & Gopnik, 1988; Gopnik & Astington, 1988)

Children aged 3;6–6;3 years were shown a Smarties box and asked what they thought was in the box. Even the youngest children were familiar with the box and answered *Smarties*. The experimenters opened the box so the children could see that it contained pencils instead of Smarties. When the children were asked what the box contained, all of them answered *pencils*.

Then the box was closed again, and the children were asked what they themselves had thought was in the box before it was opened. The following dialogue between the experimenter (E) and a child (C) aged 3; 8 years is a typical protocol for children under the age of 4 years:

E: *Look. Here's a box.*
C: *Smarties!*
E: *Let's look inside.*
C: *Okay.*
E: *Let's open it and look inside.*
C: *Oh . . . holy moly . . . pencils!*
E: *Now I'm going to put them back and close it up again* [does so].
E: *Now . . . When you first saw the box, before we opened it, what did you think was inside it?*
C: *Pencils.*
E: *Nicky* [friend of the subject] *hasn't seen inside this box. When Nicky comes in and sees it . . . When Nicky sees the box, what will he think is inside it?*
B: *Pencils.*

About half of the youngest children (3;0–4;0 years) and most of the older children (4;1–6;3 years) gave the correct answer, saying they had thought the box contained Smarties.

correct answers to indicate that the children understood the question as, "When you first saw the box, what was in it?" Thus, they did not reply to a question about what they thought, but about the contents of the box. In the standard task, the children did not get to see the pencils in the box throughout the experiment and therefore answered incorrectly.

Freeman and Lacohée (1995) view these results in connection with *childhood amnesia*, the fact that older children and adults do not remember what happened early in life (see Chapter 10, this volume). They believe that toddlers have a limited mental capacity, and that the results of the Smarties experiments reflect a cognitive mechanism that prevents children from incorporating all of their previous misconceptions. As only the most recent belief is preserved, and everything contradicting it is forgotten, children form consistent beliefs. False beliefs are preserved as well, but only as long as no new beliefs are formed that run contrary to the old ones. This is why children are unable to reconcile their initial belief that the box contains Smarties with the fact that they know there are no Smarties in it. Freeman and Lacohée thus view younger children's failure to remember earlier beliefs as an expression of a *positive* developmental mechanism.

Over the past 30 years, thousands of studies have been conducted with preschool-age children and tasks of the Maxi and Smarties type. Although the results vary depending on language instructions and implementation, most studies have found that, by around 4 years of age, children have developed a mind understanding that younger children do not have. They understand that people may lack knowledge or believe something that does not correspond to reality, and that this determines how people act in a given situation (Schaafsma et al., 2015; Wellman et al., 2001). A number of studies involving much younger children, however, have raised doubts about this conclusion (Baillargeon et al., 2010).

Very Early Understanding of Others' Beliefs

A number of studies have been founded on the assumption that the traditional theory-of-mind tasks require cognitive and linguistic skills that go beyond the ability to perceive what others know (Caron, 2009). Researchers have therefore tried to find new methods capable of revealing an *implicit* mind understanding, that is, an understanding that does not require children to formulate their responses explicitly (through language or by pointing). Instead of questioning the children, their spontaneous reactions to events are observed, similar to studies of early spatial concepts (see Chapter 13, this volume).

The first study involved an *unexpected transfer* of a toy watermelon slice from one box to another and a woman who either sees it or does not see it (Box 20.3). Onishi and Baillargeon (2005) interpret

Box 20.3   Maxi Experiment with 15-Month-Olds (based on Onishi & Baillargeon, 2005)

Fifty-six children aged around 15 months participated in the experiment. Each child was seated in front of a small puppet theater stage. (a) In order to familiarize the children with the material, they first watched a woman play with a toy watermelon slice for a few seconds and hide it inside a green or yellow box, always the same for each child. The woman wore a visor so the children could not use her eyes as a cue. (b) The following two trials ended with the woman putting her hand into the box with the watermelon, but without removing it, and holding it in place until a curtain was lowered and the trial ended. Then the children were shown two different events that were to provide them with a basis for assumptions about where the woman would believe the watermelon to be. (c) Someone moves the watermelon without the woman seeing it, or the woman sees someone move the watermelon to the other box. (d) The woman reaches into the yellow or the green box. On some occasions, she reaches inside the box into which she had seen the watermelon being moved, or into the box that contained the watermelon before it was moved without her seeing it. Her actions are consistent with what she was able to know. At other times, she reaches inside the box to which the watermelon has been moved without her seeing it, or into the box from which she has seen the watermelon being moved. Both actions are in conflict with her knowledge of the watermelon's location. The children looked a little longer at the woman when she put her hand into the empty box after having seen the watermelon being moved, or into the box that contained the watermelon when she had not seen it being moved. This is interpreted as caused by the woman acting in a way not expected by the children.

the results as indicating that the children were able to understand that the woman believed the watermelon to be where it was when she left and not where it actually was, and that she therefore had a false belief about the location of the watermelon. Other studies involving unexpected transfer have used children's *gaze direction* – where they look – based on the assumption that children have an implicit tendency to anticipate the actions they expect others to perform. One example of this is a study in which a woman was supposed to find a ball in one of two boxes. She saw the ball being placed inside the box, but in some of the trials it was moved while she appeared to be distracted by a ringing telephone. As she did not see what happened, she formed a false belief about where the ball was located. Seventeen out of 20 children aged 25 months first looked at the box in which the woman had to believe the ball to be, based on what she had seen. They did not look at the box in which the ball was actually hidden, but anticipated where the woman would look *based on her own knowledge* (Southgate et al., 2007a). Another study using measurements of brain activity found similar differences in response patterns as early as 6 months of age (Southgate & Vernetti, 2014).

Studies based on gaze direction assume that children at this age have acquired a certain degree of mind understanding but are unable to apply it in practice. Buttelmann and associates (2009) use a method that builds on children's general tendency to help adults. Together with a helper, children aged 16 and 18 months saw a man put a toy caterpillar in either a yellow or a green box. The box lids had a special locking mechanism, and the helper had shown the children how to open and close the boxes. Then the helper moved the caterpillar to the other box, either while the man was watching or while he was away for a short while (with the pretext of picking up his keys). Afterwards, the man tried to open the now empty box (where the caterpillar had been), but without succeeding. He sat down right between the boxes and behaved as if he was at a loss about what to do. The children either took initiative to help the man themselves or were encouraged to do so by the helper, more often when he had been away than when he had seen the caterpillar being moved. A greater percentage of children tried to tell him where the caterpillar was located when it had been moved without his knowledge than when the man had been present when the caterpillar was moved. Therefore, it seems the children assumed that the man was looking for the caterpillar when he had not seen it being moved, and for something else when he tried to open the box after having seen it being moved. The difference was most pronounced among the 18-month-olds (Buttelmann et al., 2009). In similar experiments with *unexpected content*, 18-month-old children also seemed to use their knowledge of what another person could know, based on what they had seen (Buttelmann et al., 2014).

Ever since Onishi and Baillargeon's first experiment, many studies have been conducted with similar results. They show that children to some extent are able to implicitly infer other people's knowledge earlier than previously thought. But there is no disagreement about the fact that children aged 3 years or younger consistently fail in tasks of the Maxi type when they *explicitly* need to describe or show what people or dolls will do based on the knowledge these can have and how a particular situation is shown and described. There is however wide disagreement on what children actually understand and how the results should be interpreted (Low & Perner, 2012; Rakoczy, 2017).

Theoretical Explanations

Any theory of the development of mind understanding must be able to explain both the fact that toddlers seem to react to the knowledge others have about something *and* the problems much older children have in solving tasks that require mind understanding (Caron, 2009; Rakoczy, 2012, 2017). These theories mainly deal with very early and early mind understanding. Most of them assume a certain innate basis but vary considerably with regard to the particular innate mechanisms at play and the importance of experience (Baillargeon et al., 2016; Carpendale & Lewis, 2015).

From a nativist point of view, Leslie suggests that human beings have a neurological module with a *theory-of-mind mechanism* that is functional by the age of 18 months. When children fail on Maxi and Smarties tasks before the age of 4, it is not owing to a lack of mind understanding but because it takes too many cognitive resources for children to inhibit the tendency to respond based on their own knowledge and formulate a correct answer (Leslie, 2005; Leslie et al., 2004). Expanding on this view, Baron-Cohen (1995) assumes that human beings have an *intentionality detector*, an *eye direction detector* and a *shared-attention mechanism*. These modules are independent and together make up what he calls a *mindreading system*. The two detectors are functional in early infancy, while the shared-attention mechanism becomes operative at the end of the first year. The theory-of-mind mechanism is functional by the age of 18–24 months.

The *theory-theory* asserts that children are born with certain assumptions or "theories" about the world that they use to analyze statistical and other "data" from different domains (see Chapter 5, this volume). These innate "theories" only represent a starting point, however, and change in line with development in other areas and children's specific experiences (Gopnik and Bonawitz, 2015). According to Wellman, *theory of mind* is one such domain-specific theory. It represents a kind of "commonsense psychology," a system of assumptions used by children and adults to explain and predict the actions of others. Children start with a theory of other people's desires and motives, but it first develops into a full theory of mind once it also includes other people's beliefs. This happens around the age of 4–5 years and leads to qualitatively new insights into other people's thoughts that 3-year-olds lack. Wellman thus considers the age of 4 to mark the beginning of a new stage in social cognition (Rhodes & Wellman, 2013; Wellman, 1990).

The *simulation theory* represents a slightly different approach (Goldman & Mason, 2007; Gordon, 1986; Harris, P. L., 1992). The understanding of other people's minds is based on children's knowledge of their own mind. An innate mechanism enables infants to take part in activities with shared emotions and joint attention (see Book 6, *Emotions, Temperament, Personality, Moral, Prosocial and Antisocial Development*, Chapter 6). Based on their experiences with these activities, they become aware of other people's **intentionality**, discover that perceptions and feelings are directed at specific goals and begin to *simulate* such relationships between intention and goal – what others believe and feel about particular things – using memories of their own former mental states. A parallel development takes place in children's imagination that allows them to reach beyond their own experiences and conceive of the mental state of others. Children simulate their own beliefs and feelings while imagining what they assume to be other people's desires and beliefs. Their continued development is the result of more complex thoughts and correspondingly more powerful simulations. Experiences with language play a significant role. One objection to the simulation theory is its implicit assumption about children's understanding of their own mental state. However, children do not seem to have any more insight into their own misconceptions than into those of others. This is not only demonstrated by the Smarties experiments, but it is altogether difficult to understand how children should be able to simulate their own mental states (Hala & Carpendale, 1997). A criticism of the theory-theory and simulation theory is that it has proven difficult to design experiments that distinguish between them (Apperly, 2008).

Several theories address the paradox of very early mind understanding and difficulties with mind understanding in toddler age by suggesting that children have two social cognitive systems – often based on Flavell's two levels of visual perspective-taking (see Chapter 18, this volume). Baillargeon and her colleagues (2010, 2013) describe two innate and independent social cognitive conceptual systems. *System 1* is intuitive and allows children to immediately grasp what others see and thus know, and to ascribe motives to them. This system deals with children's perception of reality. *System 2* enables children to understand that others may have a belief about something that differs from reality, and to predict and explain others' actions based on the knowledge they seem to have. It is this system that enables children to correctly answer Maxi tasks.

Apperly (2011) proposes that children initially develop a system that allows for *minimal* mind understanding. System 1 is a distinct modular system that includes processes capable of quickly registering people's actions and their perception of reality. The system needs few cognitive resources but is also correspondingly inflexible. System 2 is more flexible and requires more cognitive resources. System 1 is innate and develops in the course of the first year, while System 2 emerges more gradually, depending on experience. According to Apperly's model, children need System 2 to solve tasks of the Maxi type. However, if two such systems exist, it is uncertain whether System 1 is replaced by System 2, whether System 2 is a continuation and expansion of System 1, or whether both systems continue to function in parallel (Rakoczy, 2017). These systems also share similarities with the two modes of thinking described by Kahneman (2011). In his model, System 1 is fast, instinctive and emotional, while System 2 is slow and reflective.

Social constructivist theories of mind understanding argue against innate modules, theory-theories and simulations, which all build on internal characteristics as a primary basis. They maintain that the mind is not an innate container capable of holding thoughts, desires and feelings, and that mind understanding is not a theoretical but a social construct with a basis in social processes. Social constructivists thus do not base their ideas on individually predetermined knowledge. Although not rejecting the presence of parallel neurological maturation, they believe it only offers a limited explanation of the differences in children's performance on various tasks. Mind understanding is viewed in the context of developing cultural awareness, a mentally shared world that arises from **joint attention**, the experiences children form through conversations with adults about past and future in various events and activities, and their **role** as members of a "society of minds" (Carpendale & Lewis, 2004; Nelson, 2007a). Increasing language skills and gradually more complex conversations with adults about situations involving the human mind allow children to realize that people can believe different things, and that these differences are related to the experiences of each individual (Carpendale et al., 2009; Turnbull et al., 2009). Like Harris, they emphasize language and conversation, but their basic theoretical assumptions about the underlying processes differ considerably.

The psychoanalytic tradition views the ability to mentalize – including mind understanding – as the result of **attachment** and early relational experiences. Mentalizing (also called "reflective function") is the primary developmental goal of the attachment process. Secure attachment is a prerequisite for mature mind understanding, while insecure attachment will lead to inadequate mentalizing or understanding of one's own mind and others' minds (Fonagy et al., 2002). This view differs radically from both other theories of mind and theories of attachment (see Book 7, *Social Relations, Self-awareness and Identity*, Chapter 2). A number of studies have found a relation between children's early attachment and their later performance on traditional tasks of the Maxi and Smarties type, but this can be explained by coexisting factors such as language skills, **parenting style** and parental **sensitivity** and mind-mindedness. Most studies find no connection between the developmental paths of attachment and mind understanding, and research generally provides little support for Fonagy's theory. Critics argue that, as attachment has to do with security and mind understanding has to do with social insight, they do not share the same motivational basis (Cortina & Liotti, 2010; Symons, 2004).

This brief presentation illustrates the complexity of mind understanding and its theories. There is agreement about the fact that children show some degree of mind understanding early in life, but researchers disagree on how to interpret children's gaze patterns and actions, the types of processes and knowledge actually involved in early mind understanding, and the relationship between early and later, more advanced mind understanding. However, a two-level theory of mind understanding seems best to explain the paradox of early mind understanding and later problems with theory of mind tasks.

Pretense and Lies

Many theorists presume there is a connection between mind understanding and the ability to pretend, *to make believe*, as pretense involves performing a targeted action on another person in a make-believe way. The ability to understand that someone is pretending also involves insight into the *intention* behind the action. It is the intention that turns a banana into a phone when someone talks while holding a banana to their ear and mouth. Correspondingly, a child playing with a wooden block as if it were a car must have a mental representation of the car represented by the block (Lillard, 2001). Studies have found a relation between children's **pretend play** with peers and their mind understanding (Dunn & Cutting, 1999; LaBlonde & Chandler, 1995). Sometimes, the goal of pretense is to create a wrong perception in someone else's mind, such as when one person tries to get another to believe he has not done something when he actually has. In verbal form, this type of pretense is generally called "lying" (Lee, 2013). Deliberate lying therefore requires mind understanding.

Pretense

The earliest form of what might be called *make-believe* is when children at the end of their first year hold out an object and withdraw their hand when an adult reaches for it (Reddy, 1991). Piaget (1951) describes how his 15-month-old daughter Jacqueline used a piece of cloth as a pillow, laughing and saying "no-no." (It was clear that she had not simply made a mistake, but actually pretended the cloth was a pillow.) Around 18 months, pretend play becomes common, and children begin to understand when others are "kidding around," an understanding that rapidly develops. One study found that 21-month-olds had few problems when asked to use a yellow wooden block as a piece of soap while pretending to wash a teddy bear. But only half of a group of 28-month-olds were able to shift from make-believe soap to make-believe bread by pretending that the same block was a piece of bread when they were told to feed the teddy bear right after (Harris, 1994).

This early understanding of pretense means that younger children have some understanding of the difference between what is real and what is make-believe, but not of the full implications of pretense. This is illustrated by a study of 4–5-year-olds who were told a story about Moe, a troll who jumped like a hare although he had never heard of hares. Most of the 4-year-olds thought that Moe pretended to be a hare, even though they had been told that he had never heard of hares and therefore could not know how a hare jumps. Twice as many 5-year-olds answered that Moe did not pretend to be a hare, but one-third nevertheless responded that he did pretend (Lillard, 1993, 2001). The results suggest that many 4–5-year-olds perceive pretense as an action, while older children perceive it more as a mental function. Lillard explains this development as the result of better language skills and of children eventually coming to view *pretend* as a mental verb rather than as an action verb.

Lying

It is uncertain when children start to be able to tell lies. Studies have shown that children as young as 2 years of age lie about things they have done, but at this point they probably do not understand that lying affects someone else's knowledge and instead perceive it as a way of avoiding the consequences of a prohibited action, such as being scolded or losing a privilege. In one study, the experimenter told 3-year-old children that a play zoo was hidden behind a curtain and that they would get to see it in a little while. The experimenter then made an excuse to leave the room, and the children were left by themselves. Only four of 33 children resisted the temptation to peek. Among the 29 children who peeked, 11 later answered "true" when asked whether they had looked. Seven of them lied, and 11 did not answer the question (Lewis et al., 1989). Relatively few of the children thus told a direct lie. Similar studies have found that a third of all 3-year-olds lied, while a majority of 4–7-year-olds and almost all 6–11-year-olds did so in the same situation (Talwar et al., 2007; Talwar & Lee, 2002). In one study, 4–8-year-olds were asked not to look at a toy while the experimenter was away for 1 minute. About two-thirds of the children peeked at the toy. When the experimenter returned, some of the children were told that they might be punished for lying, others were told it was right to tell the truth, and some did not receive any such appeal. More than 80 percent of the children in the no-appeal group and slightly fewer in the **punishment** group lied about peeking. Only the positive appeal reduced lying significantly (Talwar et al., 2015).

Another study investigated the use of lying among 3–4-year-olds to prevent a "villain" from getting a reward that otherwise would be given to themselves (Box 20.4). The children enthusiastically locked the box containing the reward, and some spontaneously tried to prevent the villain from opening it when it was not locked. However, the younger children honestly told the villain where the reward was hidden, while many of the 4-year-olds pointed at the wrong box to fool the villain. The 3-year-olds did not seem to understand that they could prevent the villain by giving him faulty information and use mind knowledge in addition to action knowledge (Sodian, 1994). In a similar study, children could choose a toy, but the study was set up in such a way that there was always another child who wanted exactly the same toy and he was the one to choose first. However, the children could secure the toy for themselves by saying that they wanted a different toy than the one they actually wanted, as this meant that the other child would choose that toy. More than 80 percent of the 5-year-olds used this strategy, compared with less than 20 percent of the 3-year-olds (Peskin, 1992).

Lying is not only for concealing mischief or obtaining something; lying may also be a positive expression of politeness. Even 3-year-olds lied and said that they liked a gift they did not like, for example that they really needed the piece of soap they got. Older children were more likely to tell such white lies, and they were also better at explaining why they did so (Lee, 2013; Talwar et al., 2007).

These studies on pretense and lying suggest that a development takes place from using action understanding to using mind understanding

Box 20.4   Strategic Lying (Sodian, 1994)

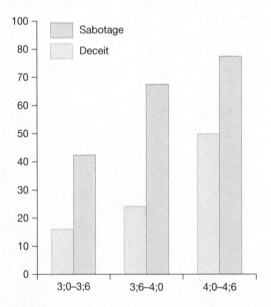

Children aged 3–4;6 years were told they would receive a reward contained in one of two cardboard boxes. The other box was empty. They were also told that there was a villain who would try to take the reward for himself and a friend with whom they should share the reward. They were told that they could prevent the villain from taking the reward by locking the box containing the reward (sabotage), or by pointing to the empty box (deceit). Similarly, they were told that they could lock the empty box and point to the one with the reward when their friend came. Nearly half the children aged 3;0–3;6 years and over 60 percent of the older children locked the box with the reward when the villain came and the empty box when their friend came. Approximately half the 4-year-olds also quickly pointed to the wrong box to trick the villain, while 85 percent of the 3;0–3;6-year-olds honestly answered the villain's question about which box contained the reward.

between the ages of 3 and 5. This agrees well with other studies of mind understanding in children of this age. Studies have also found a relationship between the development of mind understanding and lying (Ding et al., 2015). Telling a lie to hide one's knowledge of something or portray one's thoughts in a more positive light requires second-order understanding (see below), as it involves a deliberate attempt to influence what another person thinks about one's own thoughts (Miller, 2009).

21

Further Development of Mind Understanding

In the studies cited previously, children make **first-order belief attributions**. They solve explicit tasks involving what another person thinks, such as the Maxi tasks. **Second-order belief attribution** requires an understanding of what a person thinks about someone else's thoughts. This is often studied by using the following type of story (slightly abbreviated):

> *Mary and John have gone to the park together, where an ice cream vendor is standing with his van. Mary wants to buy an ice cream, but has left her wallet at home. The ice cream vendor tells her that he will also be there in the afternoon, and she goes home. After a while, the ice cream vendor tells John that he will be selling ice cream near the church, because more people are buying ice cream there. He drives off. On his way to the church, the ice cream vendor passes Mary's house. She sees his van and goes out to ask him where he is going. He tells her that he will be selling ice cream near the church. John does not know that Mary talked to the ice cream vendor. A little later, John goes to visit Mary. Her mother opens the door and tells him that Mary has gone out to buy ice cream.*

Children aged 5–10 years were told the story and then asked where John will go to look for Mary. Most of the 5-year-olds answered incorrectly (to the church), while many of the 6-year-olds and a majority of the older children responded correctly that John will go to the park, at least after being reminded that John did not know that Mary had talked to the ice cream vendor. Thus, they understood the consequence of John's belief – that he did not know Mary had met the ice cream vendor and believed that she believed the ice cream vendor was still in the park (Perner & Wimmer, 1985).

DOI: 10.4324/9781003292500-28

Second-order belief attribution involves a greater degree of awareness (Nelson, 2007a). Children who manage this type of task are usually able to explain why they responded the way they did, what knowledge or beliefs the people in the story have and why they acted the way they did (Miller, 2009). It is uncertain however whether 5-year-olds have an incomplete mind understanding or whether second-order belief attribution tasks simply are more complex. A larger percentage of children answer correctly when the stories are shorter and involve fewer people and events, and when the language is simpler and they are given more reminders (Coull et al., 2006; Sullivan et al., 1994). Similarly, children are older before they are able to solve more complex first-order tasks, such as including emotional or moral content (Lagattuta et al., 2015).

With age, children also become better at understanding the wider implications of holding a certain belief. An understanding of the relationship between belief and feeling (what someone with a particular belief will feel) develops somewhat later than that of the relationship between belief and action (how someone with a particular belief will act) (Lagattuta et al., 2015). In a study with tasks of the Smarties type, most 5–7-year-olds correctly answered questions about a belief they had, but only a few of them were also able to describe the feelings related to this belief. The results were interpreted to mean that it is easier for children to suppress what they see in the moment and activate memories of a past situation than to suppress what they feel in the moment and reconstruct a past emotion. There was little difference between the youngest and the oldest children, and it made little difference whether the situation dealt with their own or someone else's past **emotion** (de Rosnay et al., 2004).

The combination of pretense and false belief is difficult for children below school age. In one study, 5–6-years-olds managed common tasks of the Maxi and Smarties type, but had trouble with tasks in which someone had a false belief about an object because it looked like something other than it actually was, such as an eraser that looks like a die. Although the children were told that the puppet Heinz believed the object was only a die, many of them answered that Heinz will look in the box with the die/eraser when he needs an eraser (Apperly, 2011).

Around the age of 7–8, children develop a more flexible mind understanding. They begin to understand that human beings have **interpretative minds**, meaning that they can perceive the same information in different ways and react differently to the same situation (Lagattuta et al., 2015). The spectators at a football match, for example, might disagree with the judgment call of the referee, depending on which team they are rooting for. Compared with 5-year-olds, 9-year-olds are better able to accept that people can have different beliefs that are equally valid, but this also depends on the topic. Both 5- and 9-year-olds are more absolute – believing that only one point of view can be correct – when it comes to moral issues than issues concerning facts or taste (Carpendale & Chandler, 1996; Wainryb et al., 2004). Adolescents show more advanced mind understanding in positive than in negative relations (O'Connor & Hirsch, 1999). Activities that can be important to later development of mind understanding include jokes and other forms of humor, conversations about causality and internal states, parents' handling of conflicts, and **moral reasoning**. Thus, mind understanding is not a general ability that emerges fully formed during childhood, but continues to evolve all the way into adulthood (Hay, 2014).

22

Individual and Cultural Differences

The development of mind understanding is affected by both individual and environmental factors, including cultural issues. Twin studies suggest that genetic differences generally do not contribute to individual differences in this area (Hughes & Devine, 2015), but some disorders associated with mind understanding problems have a high degree of heritability (see below).

Individual Differences

The social environment contributes to individual differences in mind understanding. Studies have found a relationship between parental behavior and children's mind understanding (Pavarini et al., 2013). In one study, 33-month-old children whose mothers talked about mental states when explaining the actions of others showed better insight into such states 6 months later (Brown & Dunn, 1991; Dunn et al., 1991). In another study, how much mothers talked about cognitive states to 2-year-old children was related to the children's mind understanding measures at 6 and 10 years of age (Ensor et al., 2014). In a third study, 4-year-olds who often referred to the mental states of others when talking with their friends mastered tasks requiring mind understanding better after 12 months than children who did not talk about mental states as often (Hughes & Dunn, 1998). The relationship between language and mind understanding seems to be reciprocal. There is a relationship between early language skills and later performance on tasks involving mind understanding, but also between early mind understanding and later language development (Milligan et al., 2007).

Studies have furthermore found a relationship between parents' early *mind-mindedness*, the proclivity to treat their child as an individual with a mind, and children's later mind understanding (Meins &

DOI: 10.4324/9781003292500-29

Fernyhough, 1999). In one study, maternal mind-mindedness when the child was 6 months old correlated significantly with the child's mind understanding at 4 years of age. Mind-mindedness is reflected in the way mothers speak with their children, but, at the age of 6 months, children could not possibly have understood what their mother was saying. The mother's language therefore did not communicate knowledge but rather reflected her attitude toward her child (Meins et al., 2003). Shy children typically show mind understanding earlier than other children, possibly reflecting a particular sensitivity to other people's intentions and actions (Mink et al., 2014).

Other studies have found that children with siblings develop mind understanding somewhat earlier than only children (Perner et al., 1994). The daily interactions between siblings promote an understanding that children can have different beliefs, for example about where something is located, and that only one of these can be correct. After all, it is quite common for siblings to argue about where they have put things (McAlister & Peterson, 2007; Randell & Peterson, 2009). It is also likely that parents with more than one child talk about the different needs and abilities of their children more often than parents with only a single child and thus add to the siblings' own experiences.

Cultural Differences

Cultures differ in their language, activities and way of interacting, and this may influence children's development of mind understanding. Studies generally show consistent age agreement across cultures, but also a certain age variation in the ability to solve Maxi and Smarties tasks (Callaghan et al., 2005; Wellman et al., 2001). Avis and Harris (1991) designed a Maxi task adapted to Baka children, a group of pygmies living in the rainforests of southeast Cameroon. The children saw the experimenter move mango kernels from a pot to a hiding place while the adult who was cooking the mango was away. They found that most of the children above the age of 5 years said that the adult would look for the mango in the pot when he came back.

On the other hand, many studies have found cultural differences in age. British children scored slightly higher than Italian children on tasks that measure mind understanding (Lecce & Hughes, 2010). Children in Samoa manage unexpected transfer tasks considerably later than in the classic studies, but it is not clear why they pass these tasks later (Mayer & Träuble, 2013). In another study, children from Cameroon who had attended school showed better mind understanding than those who had not gone to school (Vinden, 2002). In line with this, British children did better on theory of mind tasks than children in Hong Kong, but only those who attended Chinese schools. Children who attended international schools did as well as the British children (Wang et al., 2016). Education thus seems more important than the general culture. However, it has also been suggested that fewer opportunities for play may contribute to the delay in mind understanding (Wang et al., 2017). Moreover, the British mothers were also more **mind-oriented** than the mothers in Hong Kong, and both in the UK and in Hong Kong there was a significant association between the mother's mind-mindedness and the children's performance on theory of mind tasks (Hughes et al., 2017). The results of these studies emphasize that many aspects of cultural practice may influence the developmental course of mind understanding.

23

Atypical Development of Mind Understanding

Problems with social understanding and interaction are a characteristic of people with autism spectrum disorders, and a large number of studies have investigated mind understanding in this group. However, children with different disorders seem to have social cognitive problems that also include mind understanding.

Autism Spectrum Disorders

The diagnostic criteria for autism spectrum disorder require impaired social cognitive skills (see Book 1, *Theoretical Perspectives and Methodology*, Chapter 32), and studies have shown that children with this diagnosis have greater problems with tasks involving mind understanding than other children. In one of the earliest studies, children with autism spectrum disorder, **Down syndrome** and typical development were told and shown a story about unexpected transfer (Box 23.1A), and, although the children with autism spectrum disorder scored higher on **assessment** of language and intelligence, they had far greater difficulties with this task than the children with Down syndrome and typical development (Baron-Cohen et al., 1985). In a related study, the same children were asked to arrange three sets of picture cards in the right order to create meaningful stories (Box 23.1B). One of the story sets required mechanical insight, another behavioral and the third mind understanding. The children with autism spectrum did well on the two first sets compared with the two other groups but much poorer on the story that required mind understanding (Baron-Cohen et al., 1986).

DOI: 10.4324/9781003292500-30

Box 23.1A   Mind Understanding in Children with Autism Spectrum Disorder

Unexpected Transfer

A study with unexpected transfer tasks included 20 children with autism spectrum disorder aged 6;1–16;6 years, 14 children with Down syndrome aged 6;3–17 years, and 27 children with typical development aged 3;5–5;9 years. The children with autism spectrum disorder scored slightly higher on assessments of intelligence and language than the children with Down syndrome and typical development. The children were told and shown a story about two dolls, Sally and Anne. Sally puts a marble into a basket and leaves, and Anne moves the marble somewhere else while Sally is away. Then Sally returns, and the children are asked: "Where will Sally look for her marble?"

Figure 23.1 shows that approximately 20 percent of the children with autism spectrum disorder and over 80 percent of the other children answered correctly (Baron-Cohen et al., 1985).

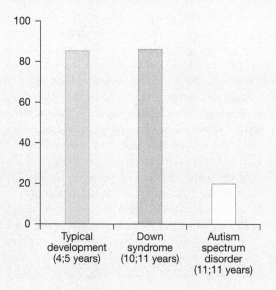

Figure 23.1

Box 23.1B   Mind Understanding in Children with Autism Spectrum Disorder

Stories

In a follow-up study, the same children were given three sets of picture cards and asked to arrange each of them in the right order to create meaningful stories. In Figure 23.2, Sequence a is mechanical, Sequence b is behavioral, and Sequence c is a mind story. Arranging the pictures in the mechanical stories requires an understanding of physical conditions; the behavioral stories require an understanding of the actions being carried out, while the mind stories require the ability to attribute mental states to the people in the pictures.

Figure 23.2

Figure 23.3 shows the number of correct answers for each of the three groups. The children with Down syndrome performed equally well on all three types of stories, while the children with typical development did best on stories that required behavioral knowledge and mind understanding. The children with autism spectrum disorder did best on the mechanical stories, where they almost achieved full scores, and poorly on the story that required mind understanding. The results show that the children with autism spectrum disorder had particular difficulties understanding the context of actions if this means they have to infer the thoughts of the people in the pictures (Baron-Cohen et al., 1986).

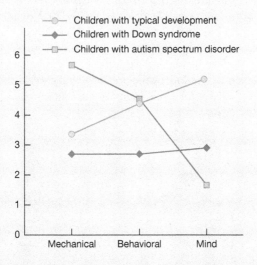

Figure 23.3

Following these early studies, a large number of studies have demonstrated that children with autism spectrum disorder do not develop mind understanding in the same way as other children, but there is no generally accepted explanation of these difficulties (Hoogenhout & Malcolm-Smith, 2014). This is a heterogeneous group with frequent problems in other areas, including perception and emotion understanding and regulation. They have restricted interests and depend on regular routines (Happé & Ronald, 2008). Most likely, their problems are caused by impairment in perceptual, communicative and cognitive processes and the interaction between them, rather than impairment in a particular module, as Leslie and Baron-Cohen suggest. Moreover, as about 20 percent among this group are able to solve theory-of-mind tasks (Hamilton, 2009; Happé, 1994), performance on these tasks alone cannot be used to include or exclude a diagnosis of autism spectrum disorder (Belmonte, 2009; Charman, 2000), although problems with such tasks may indicate the level of severity of the disorder (Hoogenhout & Malcolm-Smith, 2017). Moreover, most children in this group manage to solve tasks requiring first-order understanding, but they may be 9 years or older before they are capable of tasks that other children usually master around the age of 4 years. Some adults with autism spectrum disorder are able to solve tasks requiring second-order understanding, but children with typical development do so as early as 6–7 years of age (see Chapter 20, this volume). Practical training in mind understanding has shown mixed results, and they are often not generalized to everyday situations (Fletcher-Watson et al., 2014; Kimhi, 2014).

Thirty years of studying mind understanding in individuals with autism spectrum disorders have been extremely important for an understanding of the types of problems they face, but also for the understanding of human mind understanding in general (Happé & Conway, 2016). Without such studies, the scope of this research as well as the insights it provides would have been much the poorer. The study of mind understanding in children and adolescents with autism spectrum disorder is therefore a good example of how atypical development can lead to insights that are important for the understanding of typical development.

Other Disorders

Many types of disorders can affect social cognitive development. Most research is based on visual tasks and interpretations of why children see what they see, but the development of mind understanding is not dependent on vision alone. Lack of visual experiences may make the acquisition of mind understanding more difficult, but most blind children develop mind understanding and manage to solve Maxi and Smarties tasks (tailored to their visual impairment), although somewhat later than sighted children (Brambring & Asbrock, 2010; Green et al., 2004). They also seem to catch up with sighted peers (Pijnacker et al., 2012). Studies of children with language disorders support the assumption of a relationship between language and mind understanding. Children with specific language disorders have a delayed mind understanding (Miller, 2001; Nilsson & de López, 2016), performing similar to children at the same language level (Andrés-Roqueta et al., 2013). The differences to peers may persist into school age (Spanoudis, 2016). Also, children with severe motor impairments and speech disorders are delayed in mind understanding (Dahlgren et al., 2010). Deaf children with hearing parents have a delayed development in both language and mind understanding. Deaf children with deaf parents and a good sign language environment at home, and who are taught sign language at school, show a development similar to children with normal hearing. Deaf children with deaf parents who attend a school without a sign language environment do not develop as well. This may partly be owing to fewer opportunities for play and conversations with peers in a predominantly speech-oriented environment (Peterson, 2009, 2016).

Consequences of Problems with Mind Understanding

Experimental studies using the types of tasks discussed previously lend important insights into the development of mind understanding and also point to possible causes of problems in everyday life. Although inadequate social skills lead to major problems in the daily life of children with autism spectrum disorders, studies have not found a relationship between mind understanding and empathy in this group (Peterson, 2014). Many high-functioning children with autism spectrum disorder are sensitive to criticism, and anxiety and depression, as well as **behavioral disorders**, are extremely common (Joshi et al., 2010). These disorders may be related to confusion originating in the children's lack of mind understanding and general cognitive problems. By facilitating positive social interaction with other children, this group can be supported in the development of social skills and learning in general (Conn, 2014).

Studies show that good mind understanding is associated with positive friendships (Fink et al., 2015). Deaf children with higher scores on mind understanding have better peer relations and are more popular in class than deaf children with lower scores (Peterson, C. et al., 2016). A great deal of schoolwork concerns psychological causes and motives (Wellman & Lagattuta, 2004), and mind understanding generally makes it easier to handle criticism from teachers (Lecce et al., 2017). Good insight into other people's thinking is not always an advantage however. Some children with good mind understanding are sensitive to criticism from teachers and others (Cutting & Dunn, 2002). Spitefulness is associated with difficulties in mind understanding (Ewing et al., 2016). Some imprisoned juvenile offenders have inadequate social insight and have profited from measures to promote mind understanding and social problem solving (Noel & Westby, 2014).

Summary of Part IV

1   *Mind understanding* is people's understanding of each other's per-
    ceptions, thoughts, attitudes and feelings. As the mind is not directly
    observable, children must be able to make inferences beyond what
    they can observe directly and become "mind readers."
2   *Visual perspective-taking* at *Level 1* involves the understanding
    that other people see the world around them. *Level 2* addition-
    ally involves the understanding that something can appear differ-
    ent from various viewpoints. According to Piaget and Inhelder,
    younger children are egocentric and unable to take a *visual perspec-
    tive* other than their own. Donaldson and others have found that
    children are able to solve perspective-taking tasks earlier when
    they include more familiar situations and distinctive *landmarks*.
3   According to Piaget, toddlers use *private speech* because they are
    egocentric. Vygotsky points to the fact that younger children talk
    aloud to solve problems and to plan and regulate their own actions.
    Their speech is private but not egocentric. Both may be true to a
    certain extent – children may be a little egocentric *and* use speech
    for **self-regulation** in non-communicative contexts. Children
    with ADHD and behavioral disorders use overt private speech
    longer than other children.
4   Children become aware of others' *desires* early on. Eighteen-
    month-olds understand that people's desires affect their actions;
    at 2½ years, they understand that people can have conflicting
    opinions about the same thing. Three-year-olds have difficulty
    distinguishing between intention and action, whereas 4-year-
    olds understand that a person can try to do something without
    succeeding.
5   Children develop an understanding of the fact that people can
    have a *false belief* about a situation. Most children begin to solve

DOI: 10.4324/9781003292500-31

theory-of-mind tasks involving *unexpected transfer* and *content* between the ages of 3 and 5 years. Studies based on non-verbal tasks suggest that children in as early as their second year of life have an implicit understanding of what others know. Theories must be able to explain early mind understanding as well as problems with explicit mind understanding in early childhood.

6   One explanation is that mind understanding is rooted in an innate neurological module for *meta-representation* or a *theory-of-mind mechanism.* According to the *theory-theory,* children form a domain-specific *commonsense theory* about other people's minds that they use to explain and predict the actions of others. According to the simulation theory, children use their understanding of their own mind to *simulate* the relationship between other people's feelings and beliefs about particular things. Several researchers suggest that there are two social cognitive systems: *System 1* is intuitive and allows children to immediately grasp what others see, and thus know, and to ascribe motives to them. *System 2* enables children to understand that others may have a belief about something that differs from reality. From a *social constructivist* point of view, mind understanding is a **social construction** of a mentally shared world that arises from the experiences children form in conversation with adults about situations involving the human mind. They discover that people can believe different things, and that these differences are related to the experiences of each individual. From a psychoanalytic perspective, *mentalizing* is seen as the primary developmental objective of the attachment process.

7   The earliest forms of *make-believe* suggest that young children have an understanding of the difference between what is real and what is pretense. Toddlers do not seem to understand that pretense does not have to involve an external action, while children aged 4–5 years perceive it more as a mental function.

8   Relatively few 3-year-olds tell outright *lies,* whereas 5-year-olds are able to use lying as a strategy to prevent someone else from getting hold of something desirable. Telling a lie to hide one's own knowledge of something or portray one's thoughts in a more positive light involves a deliberate attempt to influence what others think about one's own thoughts and thus requires second-order mind understanding.

9   Children show *second-order belief attribution* once they understand what a person thinks about what another person is thinking. It develops 1–2 years after first-order understanding and somewhat

earlier if simpler stories and language are used. At around 7–8 years of age, children begin to understand that the mind is *interpretative*. Development of mind understanding in later childhood and adolescence also involves the ability to infer how a particular belief affects another person emotionally, and the understanding that different people can perceive the same event in different ways.

10 The development of mind understanding is affected by many environmental factors. There is a relationship between children's mind understanding and their language skills, their parents' *mindmindedness* and how the parents talk with their children about mental states. Children with siblings develop mind understanding earlier than only children. Also, the effects of practical training have shown that experience is of importance in the development of mind understanding.

11 Although the development of mind understanding appears relatively consistent across cultures, there are also a number of age differences in the development of children from different cultures.

12 Children with autism spectrum disorders have difficulty with mind understanding, but there is considerable variation in the group. Some never develop second-order understanding, and there are different theories about the underlying mechanisms. Their problems are most likely caused by an interaction between basic deficiencies in perceptual, linguistic and cognitive processes, rather than damage to a particular module for mind understanding. The studies of mind understanding have been extremely important to gain insight into the problems faced by children with autism spectrum disorder, as well as for a general understanding of human mind understanding.

13 Blind children develop mind understanding somewhat later than sighted children as their lack of visual experience makes its acquisition more difficult. Compared with their peers, children with specific language disorders have a delayed mind understanding; this also applies to children with severe motor impairment and speech disorders. Deaf children with hearing parents show a later development in both language and mind understanding, while deaf children with deaf parents and a good sign language environment show a development similar to children with normal hearing.

14 A slow or deficient development of mind understanding may create problems in the daily life of children with autism spectrum disorders. Sensitivity to criticism, anxiety, depression and behavioral

disorders may be related to confusion originating in the children's problems with mind understanding and general cognitive problems. By facilitating positive social interaction with other children, this group can be supported in the development of social skills and learning in general. Results from training mind understanding are mixed.

15   Good mind understanding is associated with good peer relations, friendship and popularity in class. Good mind understanding can make it easier to deal with criticism from teachers but can also involve greater sensitivity to criticism from teachers and others. Spitefulness is associated with deficits in mind understanding. Some juvenile offenders have inadequate social skills and have profited from measures to promote mind understanding and social problem solving.

Core Issues

- The functions of private speech.
- The biological bases of mind understanding.
- The connection between implicit early mind understanding and later explicit abilities.

Suggestions for Further Reading

Buttelmann, D., Carpenter, M., & Tomasello, M. (2009). Eighteen-month-old infants show false belief understanding in an active helping paradigm. *Cognition, 112*, 337–342.

Grant, C. M., Grayson, A., & Boucher, J. (2001). Using tests of false belief with children with autism: How valid and reliable are they? *Autism, 5*, 135–145.

Lillard, A. S. (1993). Pretend play skills and the child's theory of mind. *Child Development, 64*, 348–371.

Low, J., & Perner, J. (Eds) (2012). Special issue: Implicit and explicit theory of mind. *British Journal of Developmental Psychology, 30*, 1–223.

Talwar, V., Murphy, S. M., & Lee, K. (2007). White lie-telling in children for politeness purposes. *International Journal of Behavioral Development, 31* (*1*), 1–11.

Wellman, H. M., Cross, D., & Watson, J. (2001). Meta-analysis of theory of mind development: The truth about false belief. *Child Development, 72*, 655–684.

Part V

Intelligence

The Concept of Intelligence

Currently, there is no widely accepted definition of intelligence (Goldstein, 2015; Nisbett et al. 2012). It is generally agreed that intelligence involves reasoning and problem solving, but, aside from this, definitions vary considerably. Some view intelligence as a general ability to solve problems, while others see it as the sum of many different abilities. Some believe there are multiple forms of intelligence. It is not easy to define, but this description seems to catch the essence: "The ability to understand complex ideas, to adapt effectively to the environment, to learn from experience, to engage in various forms of reasoning, to overcome obstacles by taking thought" (Neisser et al., 1996, p. 77).

Intelligence is about individual differences and is closely related to testing. The development of tests has shaped the concept of intelligence as it is generally used today (van der Maas et al., 2014), and intelligence tests have been of major importance in assessing children's learning and development. When Binet and Simon designed the first intelligence test for children in 1905, some special classes had just been established, and their aim was to find a way to identify children who needed remedial education (Binet, 1975). Today as well, the most common reason for testing children is to reveal skills and abilities that can affect academic achievement, as well as other areas.

DOI: 10.4324/9781003292500-33

Theories of Intelligence

Theories of intelligence deal with the foundation and structure of intelligence. One of the key questions is whether there is one or several forms of intelligence. Spearman (1927) suggested that humans have a domain-general ability, the *g-factor*, as well as some more specific abilities, *s-factors*. The *g* is the common factor in all subtests on intelligence tests, and Spearman maintains that the *g-factor* is the most important one to assess. Some researchers associate *g* with IQ and intelligence as a general ability measured by intelligence tests; others distinguish intelligence through factor analysis of tests results, emphasizing that intelligence is more than a psychometric concept (Neisser et al., 1996; Nisbett et al., 2012) – for example, a central processing capacity, an abstract reasoning ability or processing speed (Neisser et al., 1996). A different view is that intelligence consists of many domain-specific components. Guilford (1988) describes 180 different factors.

An important distinction is between crystallized and fluid intelligence (Cattell, 1963). **Fluid intelligence** may be defined as the ability to solve problems in unfamiliar domains, using inductive and deductive reasoning (Kyllonen & Kell, 2017). It is predominantly biologically determined and includes basic skills such as memory and spatial perception. It shows especially in problem solving requiring adaptation to new situations, where crystallized skills are of no particular advantage. **Crystallized intelligence** consists of experience-based cultural and personal knowledge, such as vocabulary and factual knowledge, and reflects schooling and learning. The name comes from the notion that "skilled judgment habits have become crystallized" (Cattell, 1963, pp. 2–3). The different views on intelligence also determine how it is measured (Conway & Kovacs, 2015).

DOI: 10.4324/9781003292500-34

A Triarchic Model

More recent theories emphasize the role of intelligence in adapting, learning, using skills and coping in a particular environment. Sternberg's (1997, 2015) model of intelligence comprises three parts, or sub theories: process, experience and adaptation, which is why it is called **triarchic**. *Process* involves the mental processes that form the basis for all intelligent action and includes a number of components. *Metacomponents*, or *executive processes*, consist of a limited number of higher-order processes that detect and define problems, choose strategies, plan what to do, distribute cognitive resources, monitor things as they are being done and evaluate results. *Performance components* are lower-order processes that carry out the instructions dictated by the metaprocesses. There are a great number of these, and many are specific to a particular type of task. The *knowledge-acquisition components* consist of processes used to learn which tasks the metacomponents and performance components are meant to carry out. They include, among other things, selective attention, shift of attention and choice of certain types of information above others.

The *experiential sub theory* (also *facet* or *aspect*) of Sternberg's model deals with applying these processes in the outer world. The various components always come into play in situations the individual has some prior experience with, and their function is closely linked to individual experience. How well the components serve as a measure of intelligence depends on the experiences of the person being tested. Intelligence is best measured by tasks that are relatively novel but not altogether unfamiliar to the child (Raaheim, 1969). Performing a task that lies too far below or above the child's level of experience will not yield any insight into the child's intelligence. A simple addition problem that allows plenty of time is as ineffectual in measuring a sixth-grader's intelligence as an equation with three variables. The first type of task is too easy; the second is too difficult. The experiential sub theory also includes usage-based automation. Children who have not automated the basic reading process, for example, have fewer cognitive resources to interpret the content of what they are reading and will perform worse on tasks requiring reading comprehension.

The basis for the *contextual sub theory*, sometimes called the *practical sub theory*, is that intelligent behavior is not accidental but has a purpose or a goal and must be seen in the context of the child's situation. According to Sternberg, the goal of intelligent thought is to adapt the individual's actions to the environment, change the environment or choose an environment to suit the individual's needs and possibilities. The content of these goals will depend on the culture and the child's situation. Knowledge that is important to a child growing up in Paris is not necessarily helpful to a child growing up in New York or in Tonga, but the same underlying components contribute to intelligent behavior in all cultures. Differences in intelligence are the result of differences in how effectively processes can be applied in the child's culture. What may be intelligent **adaptive behavior** in one culture is not necessarily so in another.

Despite its division into three sub theories of intelligence, each with its own components and processes, the triarchic model constitutes a whole, and any assessment of a child's intelligence must take into account all three aspects. According to Sternberg's theory, it would be insufficient and have little meaning to measure processes not related to a purpose and a cultural context. Intelligent behavior must always be assessed based on the child's culture and specific situation. It is necessary to take this into consideration when making a cognitive assessment of a child who is seeking asylum and has limited experience with the country where the family is seeking asylum (Whitaker, 2017).

Multiple Intelligences

Gardner (1993, 2006) refutes the notion of a *g-factor*. In his theory, human intelligence is not a unitary construct or ability but consists of several functionally independent intelligences, which may work together. They include linguistic, spatial (spatial perception and recognition of visual patterns), logical-mathematical, interpersonal (cooperation and understanding of others' intentions, motives, needs and desires), intrapersonal (self-understanding), naturalistic (recognition and categorization of living organisms and objects), bodily kinesthetic (use of body and movement) and musical intelligence. Each intelligence has a computational capacity to process a certain kind of information that originates in human biology and human psychology and is assumed to reside in a module with its basis in evolution and with separate neurological processes and individual developmental histories (see Chapter 2, this volume). Each intelligence implies problem-solving skills that allow the individual to approach a situation in which a goal is to be obtained and to locate the appropriate route to that goal. According to Gardner, intelligences must be universal, but he also emphasizes social and cultural contexts, and that an intelligence should enable the person to solve problems or create products that are valued in one or more cultural contexts or communities. Moreover, according to Gardner, an intelligence must also be susceptible to encoding in a symbol system – a culturally contrived system of meaning that captures and conveys important forms of information. All humans have all these eight forms of intelligence but have individual strengths or weaknesses. Chen and Gardner (1997) maintain that traditional intelligence tests disfavor many children by focusing on school-oriented linguistic and mathematical intelligence and do not place sufficient emphasis on other abilities valued by culture.

The theory of **multiple intelligences** is controversial (Willingham, 2004). There is no disagreement about the existence of many competencies, for example that some people are more musical or socially adept than others, and that it is important to encourage these types of abilities. Disagreements concern whether the various areas of competence can be considered forms of intelligence. Inasmuch as cognition is the core concept of intelligence, body control, important as it may be to athletes and dancers, is not usually viewed as a cognitive ability. The same goes for musicality, which is generally regarded as an ability independent of intelligence (Willingham, 2004). There is further disagreement on whether Gardner's eight types of intelligence reflect independent biological modules (Almeida et al., 2010; Waterhouse, 2006a). The evidence Gardner (1983, 2006) presents for separate intelligences is similar to other module theorists (see Chapter 2, this volume): that each can be impaired by brain damage without consequence for the other intelligences, the existence of individual variation, including individuals with exceptional abilities, as well as impaired functioning and savants with special abilities in spite of low general abilities. However, critics point out that the evidence Gardner cites does not support his claims or distinguish his theory from others (Waterhouse, 2006a, b; Willingham, 2004).

26

Intelligence Tests

Internationally, there exist a large number of standardized tests that measure intellectual functioning in children and adolescents and rank their performance in relation to their peers. Most of the tests were originally in English and constructed in North America and Western Europe, but many countries also have local tests (Oakland, 2004). The major intelligence tests such as the *Wechsler Intelligence Scale for Children* (WISC; Wechsler, 2014) and the **Stanford–Binet Intelligence Scales** (Roid, 2003) are translated and standardized in several languages.

The major tests include several subscales with different tasks. They provide an overall (full-scale) intelligence quotient (IQ) and a number of sub scores that together give a broad profile of the child's ability structure. Other tests measure only some aspects of intelligence: the *Leiter International Performance Scales* (Roid et al., 2013) and *Raven Progressive Matrices* (Raven et al., 1998) measure non-verbal cognitive abilities, while the *Peabody Picture Vocabulary Test* (Dunn & Dunn, 2007) and *Test of Reception of Grammar* (Bishop, 2005) measure language comprehension. The *Bayley Scales of Infant Development* (Bayley, 2006), *Mullen Scales of Early Learning* (Mullen, 1995) and other tests of development in the early years measure a broader set of abilities than intelligence tests, such as motor skills. They are often called "developmental scales" but essentially fulfill the same function as intelligence tests.

Intelligence cannot be measured directly as an ability in its own right, although some tests aim to measure more basic cognitive processes (Naglieri, 2015). Intelligence tests measure children's performance on knowledge and skill tasks at a particular point in time. Testing is based on the assumptions that (a) the test items are representative of children's abilities, and (b) their performance is an expression of the cognitive ability or abilities called intelligence. Intelligence tests use a

DOI: 10.4324/9781003292500-35

variety of tasks (see Table 26.1), but the tasks are merely "samples." It is not important whether a child knows for example the exact meaning of "comical" or is able to repeat "3, 8, 6" after the tester has said the three digits. It is the correspondence between the knowledge and skills probed by the tests and the child's abilities that makes the tasks useful. If the tasks are not representative of the child's abilities, the test is of little value.

To avoid cultural or other biases, in constructing intelligence tests one tries to use tasks requiring a minimum of specific experience or formal education. However, children's skills and knowledge – and thus their performance on a test – always reflect their education and cultural

Table 26.1 Examples of types of tasks often found in intelligence tests for children and adolescents

None of the questions below are part of an actual test, but they are similar to those found in intelligence tests.

Knowledge	Questions such as: *Where is your left hand? How many grams are there in a kilo?*
Encoding	Mark the correct graphic shapes or digits based on a code key (time limit).
Word understanding	Questions such as: *What is a jacket? What is a saw? What does horizontal mean? What does comical mean?*
Completing pictures	Point at the place in a picture where something is missing (time limit).
Categorizing pictures	Indicate which pictures belong together.
Comparing and finding similarities	Questions such as: *You put on a winter hat and you put on ...? In what way are a cow and a horse similar?*
Searching	Mark pictures of things that belong to a particular category.
Completing patterns	Find a missing picture in an array of several pictures.
Labyrinth	Trace the way out of a maze with a pencil.
Arithmetic	Indicate which object is largest or smallest, greatest or smallest in number; addition and traditional arithmetic problems.
Drawing	Copy a shape.
Copy a pattern	Copy a pattern consisting of blocks or squares of different color (time limit).
Puzzle	Work out a jigsaw puzzle (time limit).
Reasoning	Questions such as: *Why do trains have doors? Why do streets have names?*
Sentence memory	Repeat a sentence read by the tester.
Number memory	Repeat rows of numbers forwards and backwards.

background. If children do not have the education and cultural experience required by a test, this will influence the correspondence between test tasks and child abilities, and hence the test may not measure the children's underlying abilities (intelligence). This will include children who grow up in an environment using a different language and belong to another culture than those for whom the test is **norm-referenced**. In designing test tasks, one therefore tries to make them as culturally "fair" as possible (Shuttleworth-Edwards et al., 2004). Non-verbal test items measuring fluid intelligence, such as Raven's Matrices, usually show smaller differences between ethnic groups than test items measuring crystallized intelligence, which reflect more cultural knowledge (Naglieri, 2015). However, it is important to distinguish between *tests of non-verbal intelligence* and *non-verbal testing*, that is, test administration without complex verbal instruction, such as with the Leiter test. Many of the performance items of standard intelligence tests require that the child understands a lengthy verbal instruction (Franklin, 2017).

Many children and adolescents with disabilities participate less in social activities with peers and other everyday activities. They may therefore have an experience background so different from those of children without disabilities that their performance on a regular test can give a false impression of their intelligence (Bedell et al., 2013; King et al., 2013; Martin, 2014).

Standardization

The standard measure of intelligence is the **intelligence quotient** (IQ). Some developmental scales use a "**developmental quotient**" (DQ) rather than IQ. The **raw scores** of a test are the points the child gets on each subtest. The **age score** or **mental age** is the average age when children obtain a particular raw score. Originally, the IQ was calculated with the formula: IQ = mental age/chronological age × 100. This implies that a mental age of 9 years and a chronological age of 10 would give an IQ of 90. With the same mental age, an 8-year-old would get an IQ of 112.5. The IQ difference of a year in mental age would thus change through development, and, with adolescents and adults, the formula would not make sense.

Today, intelligence tests are standardized or norm-referenced by testing a large **representative sample** of individuals in the age group for which the test is intended. This is based on the assumption that intelligence has a *normal statistical distribution* among the population, and that IQ scores are symmetrically distributed around the mean with a fixed percentage of the population within each **standard deviation** (see Figure 26.1). It is the distribution of raw scores in the **standardization** group that determines the size of the standard deviation and thus the IQ resulting from a particular raw score at different ages. The standard deviation indicates the child's relative placement in relation to the statistical average and the score distribution in the standardization sample, or **norm** group, which should be the same as his peer group. The mean is 100, and the standard deviation is 15 IQ points on most intelligence tests. An IQ within ± 1 standard deviation from the statistical mean (IQ 100 and **standard score** 0) is considered within the typical range of variation. An IQ one standard deviation below the mean for the age group (IQ 85) is a low normal score often used in clinical work as a threshold to identify the need for further assessment. The curve in Figure 26.1 shows that about 68 percent of the population score between 85 and 115, and about 95 percent score between

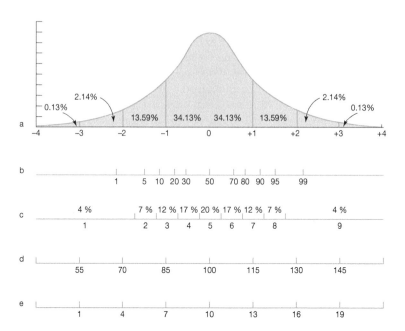

Figure 26.1 Normal distribution curve and intelligence.

The figure shows (a) the normal distribution curve (or Bell curve) with percentages and standard deviation, (b) percentiles, (c) **stanine** scores consisting of nine different scores or test categories and their percentage distribution, (d) IQ based on the Wechsler test and (e) scores for each Wechsler subtest.

70 and 130. Only 2.3 percent score two standard deviations or more above the mean, or IQ 130 and above. An equal number score lower than minus two standard deviations, or 70 and below.

Many children show a relatively even performance across subscales, while others have more pronounced strengths and weaknesses in cognitive functioning. Some are quick at solving puzzles; others are strong in language or particularly fast at mental arithmetic. To understand a child's functioning, it is necessary to assess his **cognitive profile**. WISC and other major intelligence tests have a verbal and a performance part. It is also possible to calculate different indexes by adding the scores of different combinations of subtests. WISC includes indexes for "verbal comprehension," "visual spatial," "fluid reasoning," "working memory" and "processing speed." The Stanford–Binet includes "fluid reasoning," "knowledge," "quantitative reasoning," "visual-spatial processing," and "working memory," which have both verbal and nonverbal items. In addition, there are tests made up exclusively of verbal tasks or non-verbal tasks. Raven Matrices are considered a good test of fluid intelligence.

Two children can achieve the same full-scale IQ and still have very different test profiles. In assessing children, emphasis is therefore placed on their profile (Greenspan & Woods, 2014). A child may have a clear language delay, but it is not enough to assess his language skills compared with his peers: his non-verbal cognitive functioning must also be assessed. A language delay may be part of an intellectual disability but may also be a specific language impairment (see Book 1, *Theoretical Perspectives and Methodology*, Chapter 32). In some extreme cases, children show near-normal performance on non-verbal tasks without managing any of the verbal tasks; this is the case for some children with Landau–Kleffner syndrome (Caraballo et al., 2014). A full-scale IQ based on the average scores from the verbal and performance parts would give an overly positive impression of verbal abilities and an overly negative impression of non-verbal intelligence.

Other Observations of Intelligent Action

Cognitive assessments of children never rely on tests alone. Test results must always be collated with observations of how children cope with familiar and unfamiliar everyday situations. With younger children, observing their play may give useful information (Vig, 2007). Chen and Gardner (1997) are sceptical about the use of tests and believe one should identify domain-specific skills by observing preschool children in their normal environment and in familiar contexts. Examples of observations include children's body control during physical play, perception and use of colors and materials in arts and crafts, comprehension and use of words about objects and events in the environment, counting and arithmetic during regular activities, ability to notice physical changes in their surroundings and understanding of other people's social interests and reactions. Such observations can reveal children's practical understanding in a way standardized tests are poorly designed to capture and may be a useful supplement to cognitive assessment. Nonetheless, in the absence of some type of standard, they cannot replace traditional intelligence tests altogether.

27

Stability and Variation in IQ Scores

In most cases, the purpose of using an intelligence test is to find out whether a child needs special training or support in certain areas to ensure optimal future development. Implicit in this objective are the assumptions that the test is able to predict how children will function in the future if their environment is not changed in a significant way, and that the scores will help develop appropriate intervention measures.

Early Prediction

Correlations are generally low between early test scores and later performance on intelligence tests. On average, developmental scores from the first 6 months of life correlate around 0.1 with IQ at 5–7 years of age and 0.06 with IQ between 8 and 18 years. For tests conducted between 12 and 18 months, the correlation is 0.3 with IQ at 5–7 years and 0.2 with IQ at 8–18 years. Scores at 3–4 years of age correlate around 0.3–0.4 with IQ at 10–12 years (Bishop et al., 2003; McCall & Carriger, 1993; Sternberg et al., 2001).

In addition to collating early and later test results, researchers have searched for relationships between more basic and presumably stable information-processing mechanisms and later cognitive functioning (McCall, 1994). Visual processing, attention and memory have been a particular focus of study using tasks based on habituation and novelty preference (see Book 1, *Theoretical Perspectives and Methodology*, Chapter 25). Habituation means that the child is gradually reacting less to the same stimulation. In studies of novel preference, infants are shown two identical pictures for a certain length of time, after which they get to see one of the pictures together with a new picture. Novelty preference is when they spend longer looking at the new picture than the one they saw first (Fagan & Detterman, 1992).

DOI: 10.4324/9781003292500-36

The amount of time it takes children to habituate during their first year of life correlates on average 0.35–0.40 with their IQ between age 1 and 11. The corresponding value for early memory is 0.35 (Kavšek, 2004; McCall & Carriger, 1993). Some studies have found even higher correlations. Slater and colleagues (1989) for example found that the habituation time at the age of 1½–6 months correlated –0.58 with a full-scale WISC IQ when the children were 8½ years old. The negative correlation means that children who needed less time to habituate in infancy tended to achieve higher WISC scores 8 years later. However, the correlation was much higher for the verbal part of the WISC (–0.75) than for the performance part (–0.28). This suggests not that the time infants spend habituating reflects a possible general ability (*g-factor*), but rather that the child's capacity for visual processing and orientation toward novel objects may have an impact on establishing joint attention and thereby on the acquisition of communication and language skills (see Book 5, *Communication and Language Development*). This is supported by another study that found a correlation of 0.26 between novelty preference at 7–12 months and a vocabulary test at 21 years of age (Fagan et al., 2007).

Early Prediction and Transaction

One of the main objectives of clinical developmental psychology is to identify factors of importance to children's development and be able to predict how development will proceed under different conditions. At the same time, it is not the goal of early tests and other observations to predict *too* well. This would imply a deterministic view of children's cognitive functioning and intelligence as something fixed and immutable. To the contrary, interventions are based on the assumption that children's developmental problems and disorders can be mitigated by changes to their environment (training is also a form of environmental influence). In line with a **transactional model** (Sameroff, 2010), innate characteristics and early development of skills lay the foundation for future skills and abilities but do not determine them (see Book 1, *Theoretical Perspectives and Methodology*, Chapter 6).

One reason for the low correlation between very early test scores and later intellectual functioning may be that children at this age still are so "incomplete" that many abilities have yet to develop enough for individual differences to become noticeable. In addition, some genes that are relevant remain inactive and are not expressed until later in life (Briley & Tucker-Drob, 2013). A low statistical relationship can also indicate **discontinuity**, a lack of a direct relationship between skills measured during infancy and children's later cognitive functions. Some early skills reflect infants' unique adaptation to the environment and are only relevant for that age. Other skills form the developmental basis for future skills and therefore show a higher correlation (McCall, 1989; Slater, 1995). A low statistical relationship between infants' habituation time and their concurrent performance on the infant scales suggests that the skills measured by these scales do not necessarily reflect processes that affect future performance on intelligence tests (Berg & Sternberg, 1985), but they may still give important information about the present state of the child. The ability to follow an object with one's eyes or pick up a wooden block at 4 months of age may not be related to the ability to turn the pages of a book or build a tower with three blocks at 12 months, abilities that in turn differ considerably from the broad set of tasks on modern intelligence tests (see Table 26.1).

Prediction of future intelligence based on tasks involving information processing, such as the Fagan test (Fagan & Detterman, 1992), appears to work best when children are between the ages of 2 and 8 months. After that, the correlation with future cognitive functioning declines (McCall & Carriger, 1993). At this early age, children almost can't help but look at the pictures they are shown in such studies. Once they have grown a little older, other activities begin to compete for their attention, even in the relatively unstimulating environment of a research lab. For example, as children usually sit on their parent's lap during the test, they have a familiar partner to communicate and interact with. This can be more attractive than the study material, even if the researcher does her best to attract the attention of the child. Moreover, a study of children with low birth weight found a higher correlation between early socioeconomic background and IQ at age 8 than between novelty preference in the first year of life (Fagan Test of Infant Intelligence) and IQ at age 8 (Smith et al., 2002). Hence, the social background of infants is a better predictor of intelligence than early visual processing.

Some types of early injury or developmental anomalies are so severe that they are decisive for children's further development. In such cases, it is possible to estimate future skills with some confidence. There is also developmental variation in IQ among children with intellectual disability, but developmental processes are slower, and change curves have been found to be longer in young children with Down syndrome

(Smith & von Tetzchner, 1986). It should be noted however that most developmental tests are not designed to measure individual differences among children with IQ scores lower than 50 and are therefore not capable of predicting individual differences in the development of this group of children.

Stability and Variation in Later Childhood

For children above preschool age, test results usually correlate relatively high with test scores at later age levels. Tests from 7 years correlate usually 0.6 or higher with IQ at age 10–12 years (Bishop et al., 2003; Schneider et al. 2014; Sternberg et al., 2001). The higher correlations from school age to late adolescence are partly due to the diminishing time interval up to the age of 18, but statistical correlations increase relatively little between the age of 6–7 and the beginning of adolescence. A unique long-term study showed a correlation of 0.54 in IQ at 11 years and 90 years (Deary et al., 2013).

At the same time, a relatively high correlation does not mean that children's IQ remains stable throughout childhood. In one **longitudinal study**, children's IQ varied on average by a good 28 IQ points between the ages of 2 and 17 years, even though the average for the entire group was well over 100, which is the standard mean (Box 27.1). In another study, 794 children were tested every other year over a 7-year period. Among them was a "labile" group of 107 children whose average IQ varied by 38 points over the entire period. Some of them alternated between an IQ in the typical range and intellectual disability, while others varied between the typical and very high range. Variation was significant even over relatively short time spans, with an average change of 16 IQ points for each 2-year period (Moffitt et al., 1993).

The studies mentioned above do not furnish a basis to establish the cause of variation in IQ with certainty. Genetic and epigenetic factors emerging over time, as well as transactional changes related to age and the environment, can contribute to variation in development. Most studies have not used the same tests at different age levels, and the children's motivation may have varied during testing. As a number of studies show that many children do not perform consistently on intelligence tests over time, it is important that professionals do not rely on earlier test results alone when assessing cognitive development, and that they compare current results and former results.

Box 27.1   IQ Can Vary Considerably over Time (McCall et al., 1973)

Eighty children, 38 boys and 42 girls, were assessed with the Stanford–Binet test at 2½, 3, 3½, 4, 4½, 5, 5½, 6, 7, 8, 9, 10, 11, 12, 14, 15 and 17 years of age. The group average was well above 100, and the average difference between highest and lowest score from 2 to 17 years of age was 28 IQ points. For 21 percent of the children, the difference between their highest and lowest IQ scores from 2 to 17 years was less than 20 IQ points, 43 percent had a difference between 21 and 30 IQ points, and 36 percent had more than 30 points between their highest and lowest IQ. One child had a difference of 74 IQ points.

The figure shows the average variation in IQ over time for five groups, each consisting of children who showed a similar progression. Four of the groups obtained similar results around the age of 17 years, and the differences between them during school age may have been related to conditions in the home. Some of the children may also have developed slightly earlier than others, with a leveling-out during adolescence. Children in Group 2 showed a very different development than the other

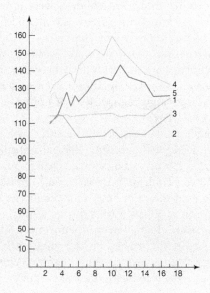

groups. Their IQ initially declined between the ages of 2 and 6 years, after which their scores increased throughout school age and declined once again as they approached the age of 17. It is possible that these children had a difficult situation at home, and that the school contributed positively to their development until they dropped out of school.

28

Nature, Nurture and Intelligence

Intelligence can have major consequences for an individual's prospects and place in society. The debate about nature and nurture has a central position in the study of intelligence. The basic issues are the same as in other discussions about nature and nurture in development (see also Book 2, *Genes, Fetal Development and Early Neurological Development*, Chapter 6).

Genetic Variation

The most common approach to the study of nature and nurture in intelligence has been to compare the correlation between IQ scores among identical and fraternal twins, siblings growing up together and apart, and children and their biological and adoptive parents. Figure 28.1 shows that the correlation increases with the amount of shared genetic material. It is highest for identical twins growing up together and lowest for adopted children and their adoptive parents. Age also matters: in one **twin study**, the **heritability estimate** (see Book 2, *Genes, Fetal Development and Early Neurological Development*, Chapter 6) at 10 months was 2 percent and, at 24 months, 23 percent (Tucker-Drob et al., 2011). Based on several twin studies, the heritability estimate for intelligence seems to increase from 20 percent in infancy to 40 percent in adolescence and 60 percent in adulthood (Plomin & Deary, 2015; Tucker-Drob et al., 2013). The influence of genes thus increases with age.

On the other hand, Figure 28.1 also shows that the IQ of siblings growing up together is closer than that of siblings growing up apart. Furthermore, heredity estimates for intelligence are not consistent but vary with the individuals' socioeconomic background. In one study, the differences in IQ among 7-year-old twins with a low socioeconomic

DOI: 10.4324/9781003292500-37

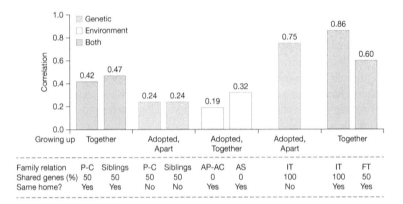

Figure 28.1 Family studies on intelligence.
The figure shows the mean correlations between IQ in persons with varying degrees of genetic and environmental similarity. Identical twins (IT) share twice as many genes (100 percent) as fraternal twins (FT) (50 percent). Biological parents (P) and children (C) also share 50 percent of their genes, while adopted children (AC) and adoptive parents (AP), as well as adoptive siblings (AS), do not share any genes (based on Plomin et al., 1997, p. 140).

background showed little relationship with genes (low heritability), while genes were of great importance among twins with a high socioeconomic background (high heritability) (Turkheimer et al., 2003). These findings may suggest that the genetic influences contribute most when the environment is good enough and differences contribute little to development, or that genetic differences are suppressed by environmental factors, and children from lower socioeconomic backgrounds do not develop their full potential (Nisbett et al, 2012). One implication of this would be that children from a lower socioeconomic background will benefit most from intervention (Hanscombe et al., 2012).

It should be noted that some studies have not found the same influence of socioeconomic background (Hanscombe et al., 2012). One reason may be societal differences in education and provision of social and health services.

Moreover, if the environment does not have the same importance in different socioeconomic groups, the socioeconomic backgrounds of the sample have consequences for the size of the heritability estimate. The influence attributed to genes in heritability estimates is dependent on the environmental variation (see Book 2, *Genes, Fetal Development and Early Neurological Development*, Chapter 6). If there

It is noteworthy that these failures to replicate have predominantly been in northern European nations, where social welfare systems are more comprehensive, whereas most of the positive results have been obtained in the United States, where social class differences in educational opportunity are vast. Socioeconomic disadvantage may not disrupt gene–environment transactions to the same extent in countries that ensure access to adequate medical care and high-quality education.

(Tucker-Drob et al., 2013, p. 353)

is little environmental variation, the differences between individuals must mainly be caused by their genes, and vice versa. It is therefore of relevance that individuals from lower socioeconomic backgrounds are typically underrepresented in behavioral–genetic studies. The consequence will be a narrower range of environmental variation, which will increase the heritability estimate and attribute less importance to environmental factors (Nisbett et al., 2012).

Many hundreds of different genes are believed to be involved in cognitive development. Although thousands of children have been compared with regard to intelligence and genetic makeup, it has been difficult to single out the effects of individual genes, and many of the findings have not been replicable, indicating that they are chance findings (Chabris et al., 2012; Kleefstra et al., 2014). One finding in need of explanation is the fact that culture-dependent skills such as vocabulary knowledge show a higher degree of heritability than skills that are not as culture-dependent, such as memory for digits and the ability to reconstruct a visual pattern (Kan et al., 2013). A possible explanation may be that some of the genes believed to be related to intelligence result in different degrees of environmental susceptibility. This is in line with research showing that children with a high IQ are more susceptible to experience than children with a low IQ (Brant et al., 2013).

Environmental Factors

Studies show that many environmental factors influence the development of intelligence. Nutrition during prenatal development and childhood has an impact on children's intellectual development (Prado & Dewey, 2014). Long-term malnutrition can have permanent consequences, whereas the effect of shorter periods is reversible. However, it is not easy to distinguish the effect of nutrition from other factors: children who suffer from poor nutrition usually have parents who are undernourished themselves, live under difficult conditions and have little energy for interaction and play. The children may receive less stimulation and encouragement to pursue activities that promote intellectual development (Sigman & Whaley, 1998). In industrialized societies, lead and other contaminants are a possible source of cognitive problems (Dapul & Laraque, 2014; Needleman, 2004).

Classical studies of children in overcrowded orphanages with few personnel have clearly demonstrated that **under-stimulation** and lack of social contact lead to low cognitive functioning and, in extreme cases, to death, even if the children were not malnourished (Provence & Lipton, 1962; Spitz, 1946). However, the studies also show that delay due to severe under-stimulation can be reversed. In one study, severely under-stimulated and developmentally delayed 18-month-olds were moved to an institution for women with intellectual disability. After 15 months, during which the children received stimulation and care from the women with intellectual disability and staff, the children showed normal functioning (Skeels & Dye, 1939). Similar results have been found in more recent studies of children who lived under extremely unstimulating conditions in Romanian orphanages. The children showed dramatic progress when they were adopted by British families, and those who were youngest at the time of adoption showed the most cognitive progress. Children who were adopted after the age of 6 months, however, scored 15 IQ points lower at the age of 11 years than children who had been adopted before this age (Beckett et al., 2007).

The impact of environmental factors is also apparent in the relationship between IQ and socioeconomic background, and the effect becomes more apparent with age (Huston & Bentley, 2010). One longitudinal study found an increase in correlation between children's IQ and their **socioeconomic status** from 0.17 at 6 months to 0.51 at 3 years of age (Wilson, 1983). A large study summarizing results from many countries found that children growing up in orphanages scored on average 20 IQ points lower than children reared in foster or biological families (van IJzendoorn et al., 2008). It was not clear what qualities of the orphanages made a difference for the children's development. The statistical effect of the caregiver–child ratio was not significant, but, when the ratio was three children per caregiver or fewer, the children did not show developmental delay compared with children living in families. In addition, some of the children in orphanages were more resilient (see Book 1, *Theoretical Perspectives and Methodology*, Chapter 8) and showed positive development in spite of poor environmental conditions (van IJzendoorn et al., 2011). Another study found significant differences in IQ (112 vs. 100) between children adopted by parents with high and low socioeconomic backgrounds (Capron & Duyme, 1989). The socioeconomic background of the biological parents was of importance as well. Children with biological parents from a higher socioeconomic background scored higher than children with parents from a low socioeconomic background (114 vs. 98).

Exactly how socioeconomic background affects children's intelligence is not entirely clear. Poverty may imply non-optimal nutrition and care even if low socioeconomic status does not always lead to poor cognitive development (and lower IQ). Families with a low socioeconomic status often come from a **minority language** background, have little education, are more often unemployed and have a greater number of psychological problems. The more such factors are present, the greater the **risk** that children will score low on intelligence tests (Figure 28.2). Furthermore, the incidence of environmental risk factors is often the same from preschool age to adolescence – children usually remain in the same environment (Huston & Bentley, 2010; Sameroff et al., 1993).

Many countries have designed programs to improve the developmental opportunities of children growing up under difficult social conditions. In 1965, half a million US children enrolled in **Head Start**, a relatively short-term preschool initiative that was to give children some basic knowledge and skills to get a better start in school. The results of the effort are controversial, partly owing to the inconsistent quality of follow-up studies. There seems to be agreement, however, that children who took part in Head Start showed fewer learning disorders, did better in school and completed middle school to a greater extent than their peers with a similar background who did not participate in the program (Lazar & Darlington, 1982; Zigler & Valentine, 1979). The reason for these differences is not only what children learned through Head Start, but equally the fact that they developed more positive attitudes toward learning from the start, which in turn affected their teachers' expectations of them (see also Rosenthal effect, below). A more recent study of children born between 1995 and 1998 suggests a primary relation between development and environmental risk factors, such as unemployment and low quality of parent–child interaction (Ayoub et al., 2009). Between 1972 and 1977, the *Abecedarian Project* implemented early educational intervention for 111 children

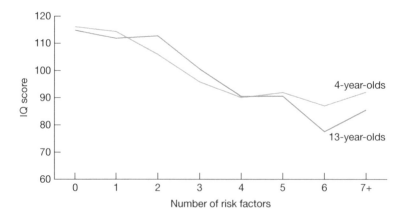

Figure 28.2 IQ in relation to risk factors.

A longitudinal study tested 152 children growing up in high-risk environments, using WPPSI at 4 years and WISC-R at 13 years. The study included a total of ten risk factors: minority background, parental provider with low-status job, mother with low level of education (had not completed US high school), large family (four or more children), single parent (neither father nor stepfather), many stressful life events (e.g., parents lose their jobs, death in the family), parents with main-effect perspective on the importance of child rearing (suggesting that children's fate is determined by a single cause, either constitution or environment), anxious mother, mother with mental health problems, and interaction between mother and child characterized by negative or undifferentiated emotions (based on Sameroff et al., 1993, p. 89).

from birth until the age of 5. The results showed that preschool initiatives were more effective both in terms of IQ and academic performance at school than initiatives introduced during school age. At the same time, the effect of preschool initiatives was strengthened when the education was especially adapted to the children's needs during the first years of school (Campbell & Ramey, 1994; Campbell et al., 2002).

The studies of orphanages and adopted children above show that environmental factors can have positive as well as negative – and sometimes dramatic – consequences for children's intellectual (and emotional) development. The fact that genes are of importance in the development of intelligence does not change this.

Zone of Modifiability

Genes and environment impose both possibilities and constraints on intellectual development (Rinaldi & Karmiloff-Smith, 2017). Gottesman (1963) suggests that genes limit the degree of environmental impact in the form of a **reaction range** within a given developmental domain. Figure 28.3 shows the reaction range for cognitive development based on four different hypothetical **genotypes**, indicating a relationship between intelligence and reaction range. In line with this model, one study found a higher environmental susceptibility in children with high IQs than in those with low IQs, and that development spans a longer period of time in the high-IQ group (Brant et al., 2013). Another study found IQ scores to be stable earlier in a group of children with an average IQ of 93 than in another group with an average IQ of 121 (Schneider et al., 2014).

The notion of a reaction range implies that children's intellectual development is constrained rather than prescribed by genes, and that competence can change over time as a result of environmental influences. According to Ramey and Ramey (1998a), a reaction range represents the child's **zone of modifiability**, which is important to utilize to promote optimal development for the child. They further argue that modifiability may be higher earlier than later in development, and that appropriate preschool programs should be introduced to accelerate cognitive development in children at biological or social risk of developmental delay (Ramey & Ramey, 1998b).

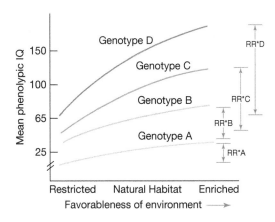

Figure 28.3 Reaction range.

The figure shows the reaction range curves for IQ with four hypothetical genotypes (A–D). The genotype that would result in the lowest intelligence in a normal environment (A) is least susceptible to the environment, both in a positive and a negative sense. The genotype that would result in the highest intelligence in a normal environment (D) has the greatest reaction range. A genotype with a wide reaction range can thus lead to large variations in IQ (Gottesman, 1963, p. 255).

The Rosenthal Effect

Knowledge of how children perform on intelligence tests can be useful but also brings with it certain dangers, as the results are often viewed as a "true" expression of children's abilities. It has been shown for example that this type of knowledge can affect teachers' expectations of children and, in turn, children's performance at school. Rosenthal and Jacobsen (1968) gave a non-verbal IQ test to all the students in an elementary school. The teachers were told that the test could predict which of the children would be "intellectual bloomers" at the end of the school year. They were also given a list of these bloomers, but the children were actually picked at random. When they were tested 8 months later, the scores of the group on the list had increased by comparison with the other children, with the greatest effect among the youngest children. As this group presumably had received more interest and follow-up from the teachers, the "prediction" about a more positive development became a self-fulfilling prophecy. Similar effects have been found in other studies (Rosenthal, 1994; Rubie-Davies, 2006), demonstrating the potential damage negative attitudes among teachers can do to children's cognitive development. It is likely that teachers' positive and negative assumptions about children have a similar impact in non-experimental situations.

29

Gender Differences

The cognitive profiles of boys and girls show some differences. These differences do not involve general intelligence (*g-factor*) but mostly language, mathematics and spatial abilities. Girls are generally better at language and begin to read and write earlier, and fewer girls than boys have reading and writing disorders (Calvin et al., 2010; Kimura, 1999). Furthermore, average differences tend to be greater among the male group than the female group (Arden & Plomin, 2006; Johnson et al., 2008, 2009), and more boys than girls receive special education (Hibel et al., 2010).

When it comes to math abilities, boys on average do better than girls, but the differences change with age. Girls are slightly ahead of boys in early childhood. In elementary school, there is no difference in math skills between boys and girls, but in secondary school boys start to be ahead. Among those starting at university, males perform better in this area than females. This is consistent with the fact that the differences seem to be greater among those with high scores on intelligence tests. Children with more average IQ scores show no clear **gender differences** (Hyde et al., 1990), suggesting that there is no general difference between genders. It seems rather as though males and females with higher education make different choices, probably based on cultural factors, which is also supported by the finding that gender differences in the high-scoring group have been reduced (Wai et al., 2010).

Boys are clearly better than girls at spatial tasks, such as reading maps and imaging three-dimensional objects in their mind, a difference that has also been related to male sex hormones (testosterone). This is not to imply that the difference depends on biology alone, but that hormonal differences between males and females affect brain development and in turn contribute to the differences between them

DOI: 10.4324/9781003292500-38

(Halpern et al., 2007). Girls and boys may also differ in the strategies they apply to such tasks (Lawton, 2010).

When it comes to intelligence, the similarities between males and females are more prominent than the differences. Although consistent, the differences between the groups are too small to have any bearing on the assessment of individuals. Differences are far greater among boys and among girls than between the mean scores of boys and girls as groups (Arden & Plomin, 2006). However, it is still discussed whether these differences are due to evolutionary biological factors or to differences in upbringing (Bleie, 2003; Jones et al., 2003; Kimura, 2004). In this context, it is important to mention that some gender differences gradually seem to disappear in tandem with changes in society. Most likely, the differences are not related to upbringing alone, for example that males and females are encouraged to enroll in different school subjects, but equally to the experiences they gain through the activities in which they participate. Tradition ally, boys are physically more active and play with technically more complex toys. As girls progressively take part in more traditional boy play, and boys in girl play, some of these differences diminish.

Ethnicity and Intelligence

Many studies have found variation in average IQ scores among different ethnic groups, and there is considerable controversy about what the intelligence scores measure and the bases for this variation (Dramé & Ferguson, 2019; Fagan & Holland, 2007; Neisser et al., 1996; Nisbett et al., 2012; Rushton & Jensen, 2010). In the USA, some maintain that genetic differences were the basis for an observed difference of around 15 IQ points between Black and White adults (Herrnstein & Murray, 1994; Jensen, 1985; Rushton & Jensen, 2005, 2010). However, a division into "races" is a socially and not a biologically constructed concept (Sternberg et al., 2005), and there is no reason why the genetic basis of skin color should influence cognitive development. The opposing view is that the difference in average IQ is a consequence of environmental and cultural factors, of differences in the life conditions of Black and White individuals (Nisbett, 2005). To explain such results, Lewontin (1970) uses an analogy about two corn fields planted with seeds that have the same genetic variation but only one is watered and cared for. It is not surprising that the field that is cared for gives a better harvest. However, it is not owing to different genes but to the growth environments of the seeds. Similarly, the differences between the economic and social conditions of the Black and White populations in the USA are so large that they have consequences for the populations' scores on intelligence tests. In line with Lewontin's analogy, and in accordance with an environmental explanation, relatively recent evidence suggests that the difference in IQ has narrowed by around five IQ points (Dickens & Flynn, 2006a, b). A change process is also supported by an even more recent finding that 4-year-old Black children are five points behind their White peers, compared with 17 IQ points among 24-year-olds (Nisbett et al., 2012).

DOI: 10.4324/9781003292500-39

Changing Norms
The Flynn Effect

Average scores on intelligence tests have steadily increased over many years, making it necessary to re-standardize the tests at regular intervals to maintain a **normal distribution** of IQ scores with a mean of 100 (Flynn, 2007). In the USA, the average total score on the Stanford–Binet test and on Wechsler tests has increased by about three IQ points per decade (Baron, 2004). Similar and larger changes have been found in European as well as developing countries (Daley et al., 2003), although the gains vary somewhat between countries and domains (Pietschnig & Voracek, 2015).

This increase in scores must be the result of environmental changes, as the genetic pool of a population would not be able to change over such a short time period. Although the particular environmental factors responsible for this development have not been mapped, it is likely that economic conditions, changes in nutrition and child rearing, higher levels of education, increased literacy and the influence of radio and television have had an impact (Ceci & Kanaya, 2010). At the same time, the increase in IQ is greater for non-verbal than for verbal intelligence, that is, tests or subtests believed to be relatively unaffected by cultural factors. The average IQ on the non-verbal Raven test – which is also considered a good measure of fluid intelligence – increased by 21 points over 30 years, with equal differences among 10-year-olds and 20-year-olds (Flynn, 1998). One possible explanation is that children growing up in the 1980s and later have had more exposure to graphic patterns through film, television and computer games than earlier generations (Greenfield, 1998). More recently, the **Flynn effect** seems to have declined somewhat, and is even in reverse in some countries (Flynn & Shayer, 2018; Sundet et al., 2004).

Owing to this "inflation" in test scores, children's cognitive abilities are assessed slightly differently, depending on when the test used was

DOI: 10.4324/9781003292500-40

last standardized (Fletcher et al., 2010). This also applies to children who score well below or above the mean. With each new standardization of the Wechsler tests, studies show a rapid increase in the proportion of children and adolescents classified as intellectually disabled (even though many specialists continue to use older versions of the tests). After that, the proportion gradually decreases over time until the appearance of a new standardization (Kanaya & Ceci, 2012). Similarly, the proportion of children classified as **gifted** increases with the length of time since the most recent standardization (Wai et al., 2012).

32

School Performance and Intelligence

By and large, there is a clear statistical relationship between IQ and academic performance at school. Access to education contributes positively to IQ, and interrupted and reduced schooling – which is often the case for children living in war areas and when the family is seeking refuge in another country – can lead to lower intellectual performance (Ceci, 1991; Nisbett et al., 2012). However, the effect of schooling interacts with general maturity: in spite of the fact that they had been equally long in school, the youngest children in the fourth grade and in the eighth grade scored a few percentiles lower than the oldest (Bedard & Dhuey, 2006). Mass education is considered one of the factors contributing to the Flynn effect (Baker et al., 2015). In Norway, a reform that increased obligatory schooling by 2 years increased the population mean among 19-year-olds by 3.7 IQ points (Brinch & Galloway, 2012).

Children with higher IQ scores typically do better in school than children with lower scores, but the relationship varies with the subject (Mayes et al., 2009; Roth et al., 2015). At the same time, a high IQ does not ensure academic success. Studies of children with an IQ above 130 show that social factors, motivation and self-regulation are also of importance. Some gifted children have specific learning disorders, and in many cases their positive skills as well as their learning disorders remain undetected (Lovett & Lewandowski, 2006; McCoach et al., 2001). Moreover, the best predictor of future grades is not IQ, but earlier school grades (Minton & Schneider, 1980).

DOI: 10.4324/9781003292500-41

33

Atypical Development

Intellectual Disability

Intellectual disability is a complex condition involving low intelligence (see Book 1, *Theoretical Perspectives and Methodology*, Chapter 32), and its developmental consequences are discussed in several of the topic books. These include low tolerance for novelty, complexity and uncertain situations, and difficulty understanding social and emotional cues (Whitman et al., 1997). The incidence of motor impairment, sensory impairment, epilepsy, autism spectrum disorder, attention deficit disorder and other disorders is often several times higher in children with intellectual disability than among children in general (Carr & O'Reilly, 2016a, b). Children with intellectual disability show a delayed development in most areas, and the differences from typically developing children increase with age (Hall et al., 2005). However, they only share a general difficulty with learning, but otherwise they are as different as other children. Regarding them as a homogeneous group would mask important differences in their possibilities and limitations and their needs for an adapted environment (Leonard & Wen, 2002).

There are five main causes of intellectual disability: lack of oxygen (hypoxia) or exposure to toxins during pregnancy, disturbances in brain development, genetic conditions, metabolic diseases, and neglect and psychosocial influences (Jimenez-Gomez & Standridge, 2014). Genetic factors are thought to have a major impact on severe intellectual disability. **Mutations** in individual genes, such as **phenylketonuria** (PKU) and **fragile X syndrome**, are of particular importance in moderate to profound intellectual disability. A single gene, however, can have many mutations, and the same gene can be involved in a number of conditions (Kleefstra et al., 2014). Mild intellectual disability seems more associated with variation in several genes and to

DOI: 10.4324/9781003292500-42

be part of the normal variation among the population. Siblings of children with severe intellectual disability have the same average IQ as the general population (around 100), indicating that they do not share the genetic disorder. Siblings of children with mild intellectual disability score about one standard deviation lower than the population mean, or roughly 85, which may reflect that they share relevant genes or environmental influences (Nichols, 1984).

The largest single group with a known cause for intellectual disability is represented by people with Down syndrome. With an incidence of one in 720 births, they make up about 6–8 percent of children with intellectual disability (Presson et al., 2013; Vissers et al., 2016). Other common **syndromes** involving various degrees of intellectual disability are **Rett syndrome**, Lesch–Nyhan syndrome, Williams syndrome, Cornelia de Lange syndrome, **Prader–Willi syndrome** and **Angelman syndrome** (see Book 2, *Genes, Fetal Development and Early Neurological Development*, Chapter 3). In about half the cases, the cause of the intellectual disability is unknown, but new syndromes are constantly being identified (Anazi et al., 2017; Udwin & Kuczynski, 2007; Vissers et al., 2016). There are, however, large individual differences among children with the same diagnosis, both with regard to their biological basis and their environment, and each child follows a unique developmental pathway.

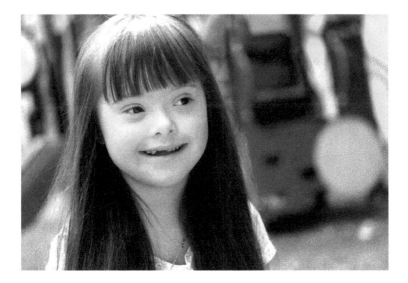

Down syndrome is a common cause of intellectual disability

For optimal development, children with intellectual disability depend more than other children on a specially adapted environment. Their developmental progress must be individually planned in far more detail than for other children. The child's individual education plan (IEP) can differ substantially from the school's usual curriculum, with greater emphasis on everyday skills and practical tasks. Children with intellectual disability often take an *outer directed* approach to problem solving. This means that they, more than other children, make use of the immediate situation and other external cues when solving problems, and to a lesser extent internal reflection or mental trial and error. They often lack the necessary concepts and mental strategies to reason beyond what they are able to perceive in the moment. They are unable to try out mental solutions and have to take a practical approach to problem solving (Bybee & Zigler, 1998). Children with intellectual disability may need a lot of help in developing the ability to play and interact with other children, as well as to explore their surroundings, learn to dress, eat and cope with the minor and major challenges of daily life. Special education at school also includes social skills and opportunities for interacting with other children.

For children with intellectual disability, the first 5 years of life are often a period of early intervention that typically includes direct intervention with the child and parent guidance (Baker et al., 2016). Early intervention is an important tool in leading children onto the best possible path of development (Guralnick, 2011, 2017; Ramey & Ramey, 1998b). It is partly based on the assumption of **sensitive periods**, that the brain is more plastic and that children learn more easily during their first few years of life (see Book 2, *Genes, Fetal Development and Early Neurological Development*, Chapter 16). Notwithstanding the possible presence of such periods, it is better to support a positive development early on, both in terms of development and resources, than having to attempt to change the child's developmental course at a later point.

A child with an intellectual disability requires time and effort and can take many of the family's resources, partly because of the child's problems with comprehension and self-regulation, and partly because the intellectual disability itself involves training, adaptation and care beyond the age required by other children (Blacher et al., 2007; Carr & O'Reilly, 2016b). At the same time, the family represents the most important resource and social network for children and adolescents with intellectual disability. Help and support for the family are therefore important in any work involving children with intellectual disability.

Albert Einstein

Giftedness and Talent

Although they represent a small group, especially gifted children may also need special support and adaptation for an optimal development: one in 1,000 is highly gifted, and one in 10,000 is exceptionally gifted

(Gagné, 2004). Their school may need to provide an individually tailored plan that incorporates opportunities for learning and social development that go beyond the school's ordinary curriculum and routines. The number of mildly gifted and moderately gifted children is considerably higher (1 in 10 and 1 in 100, respectively). They are often academically strong and may need some form of adaptation, but within the framework of the regular curriculum.

Traditional support for talented children has included starting earlier at school or skipping a grade (in some cases with a certain degree of curricular adaptation). As strong intellectual ability typically goes hand in hand with the ability to work independently, support may be directed at the children's own active learning. Encouraging exploration and curiosity is often a good way of exploiting the intellectual potential of gifted children (Porath, 2014). Tailored education for this group should therefore not simply consist of more work and more challenging tasks, but has to be rooted in an active engagement in the student's particular learning style and interests (VanTassel-Baska & Stambaugh, 2008).

For gifted children with specific learning disorders or behavioral disorders, there is a risk of failing to identify both their talent and their disorders, and hence for them to become underachievers in school. They need follow-up strategies that can promote their talent and reduce the impact of learning disorders, emotional problems and adjustment disorders (Buică-Belciu & Popovici, 2014; Gilman et al., 2013).

Summary of Part V

1   There is no widely accepted definition of intelligence, but intelligence involves the understanding of complex ideas, adaption to the environment, learning from experience, reasoning, overcoming and problem solving. Some believe intelligence is a *domain-general* ability, others that it consists of many *domain-specific* abilities, while others yet believe that it includes both a *g-factor* and several *s-factors*.

2   Sternberg's *triarchic theory of intelligence* consists of three parts: process, experience and adaptation. *Process* involves the mental processes that form the basis for intelligent action. The *experiential sub theory* deals with the application of processes in the outer world. The *contextual sub theory* is based on the notion that intelligent actions have a purpose, and that human beings use cognitive mechanisms to adapt to the world they live in.

3   Gardner's theory of *multiple intelligences* includes eight domain-specific modular *intelligences*. It is controversial, and there is disagreement on whether the different areas of competence can be called intelligence.

4   Intelligence tests build on the assumption that intelligence has a *normal distribution*. Tests are norm-referenced by testing a large, representative sample of children in the relevant age groups. IQ is a measure of how children perform on a test compared with their peers. Most intelligence tests consist of various types of tasks and provide a *cognitive profile* in addition to a full-scale IQ. The *age score* indicates the age at which children on average achieve a specific raw score. Experience, culture and language background affect the test results.

5   The most common reason for testing intelligence is to assess whether a child needs special education or support, based on the

DOI: 10.4324/9781003292500-43

assumption that tests are able to *predict future development*. Correlations between early test scores and later childhood IQ are low. Measures of information processing in the first year – but not later – have a higher average correlation with later IQ scores. After toddler age, IQ scores correlate relatively high with later IQs, although there is also significant variation. It is not the goal of tests to predict *too* well, as this would imply a predetermined view of intelligence. Interventions are based on the assumption that developmental problems and disorders can be remediated by training and adaptation.

6   Twin studies and other family studies show that genes are important to intellectual development, *and* that improvement to the environment results in higher IQ. The correlations between IQ scores increase with the amount of shared genetic material. Many genes have been associated with intelligence, but the effect of individual genes is very small. Children who are adopted into families with a higher socioeconomic background have higher IQs than children adopted into families with a lower socioeconomic background. Heredity estimates have been found to vary with socioeconomic background.

7   Many environmental factors impact children's intellectual development, including nutrition. *Orphanage studies* have shown that environmental factors can have a dramatic effect on children's intellectual development. Although lack of stimulation and social contact can lead to decreased cognitive functioning, the effects can be reversed. A low socioeconomic status is associated with risk factors that result in lower IQ. Most environments are stable, and the majority of children grow up in the same good or bad environment. Many countries have programs to support children who grow up in high-risk environments.

8   Based on the hypothesis of a *reaction range*, genes determine the amount of environmental impact on the development of a given area. The reaction range is also a *zone of modifiability*, with possibilities and constraints. The *Rosenthal effect* illustrates how assumptions about a child's intelligence can become a self-fulfilling prophecy.

9   The ability profiles of boys and girls show certain differences, most likely owing to differences in biology, culture and experience. The differences among boys and among girls are greater than the average difference between boys and girls as a group.

10   Many studies have found variation in average IQ scores among different ethnic groups. Some attribute differences to genes, others

to environmental factors. The difference between average IQ in the Black and the White populations is best explained by environmental factors.

11 The mean raw score on intelligence tests has increased in most countries over time, making it necessary to standardize tests at regular intervals. The *Flynn effect* is probably caused by changes in economic factors, nutrition, parenting, education, reading ability and the influences of media. In many countries, the effect is currently declining or even in reverse. The Flynn effect has an impact on the number of people categorized as intellectually disabled or especially gifted.

12 Performance on intelligence tests is positively influenced by education. Higher intelligence is associated with better academic achievement, but the achievement of gifted children is also dependent on social factors, motivation and self-regulation. Some gifted children have learning disorders.

13 *Intellectual disability* is a complex condition that affects all aspects of a child's functioning, and cognitive profiles vary as much as those of children with typical development. For optimal development, children with intellectual disability rely on a specially adapted environment. Child rearing requires more time and effort from parents, and parent guidance and support are important elements in any work involving children in this group.

14 Especially gifted children may require individually tailored programs beyond the school's ordinary curriculum. Other gifted children who do well in school may need some form of adaptation within the regular curriculum.

Core Issues

- The role of genes and environment in intelligence.
- The bases of ethnic differences in average IQ.
- The effect of public early intervention programs.

Suggestions for Further Reading

Dickens, W. T., & Flynn, J. R. (2006a). Black Americans reduce the racial IQ gap: Evidence from standardization samples. *Psychological Science, 17*, 913–920.

Drevon, D. D., Knight, R. M., & Bradley-Johnson, S. (2017). Nonverbal and language-reduced measures of cognitive ability: A review and evaluation. *Contemporary School Psychology, 21*, 255–266.

Guralnick, M. J. (2011). Why early intervention works: A systems perspective. *Infants and Young Children*, *24*, 6–28.

Jensen, A. R. (1985). The nature of the Black–White difference on various psychometric tests: Spearman's hypothesis. *Behavioral and Brain Sciences*, *8*, 193–219.

Ramey, C. T., & Ramey, S. L. (1998). Early intervention and early experience. *American Psychologist*, *53*, 109–120.

Sternberg, R. J. (2015). Multiple intelligences in the new age of thinking. In S. Goldstein, D. Princiotta, & J. A. Naglieri (Eds), *Handbook of intelligence* (pp. 229–241). New York, NY: Springer.

Part VI

Learning and Instruction

34

Learning and Adaptation

Learning may be defined as an experiential process which leads to relatively permanent changes in the knowledge, skills and behavior of an organism that are not caused by maturation, disease, fatigue or injury (Kolb, 1984). Learning is a central part of children's lives and adaptation (Siegler, 2000), and it is not always easy to distinguish learning and developmental processes (see Book 1, *Theoretical Perspectives and Methodology*, Chapter 5). The individual learns throughout the lifespan, but the acquisition of new knowledge and skills is especially important in childhood and adolescence. In new situations, adults can to a greater extent use the knowledge and skills they already have.

Children learn from their individual actions and exploration, but much of children's learning is social as other children and adults guide them toward what is important and relevant in their society (Tomasello, 2005). The transfer of knowledge across generations is basic to the evolution of human societies, and every society has ways of equipping children with knowledge, including children with atypical learning and development. Some have educational difficulties, and the most common learning disorders involve problems with reading, writing and math.

Among the developmental theories, logical and social constructivism have had a particular impact on education.

DOI: 10.4324/9781003292500-45

35

Types of Learning

Learning is an adaptive process and can take different forms, both formal in educational settings and informal in play and other everyday activities. Learning is related to cognitive development but also to emotional development and motivation. Early forms of learning are habituation, **conditioning** and imitation. As children grow older, reasoning and insight become more important in acquiring knowledge and skills (see Part III, this volume).

Habituation and Conditioning

Habituation and conditioning are basic, simple forms of learning and adaptation to the environment. Habituation can be demonstrated as early as the **embryonic stage** and is used in research on newborns (Leader, 2016). The particular types of stimulation to which infants habituate and dishabituate provide important insights into the characteristics of the physical and social surroundings they are aware of and capable of differentiating. In **classical conditioning**, children form associations between two stimuli that follow each other closely in time. **Operant conditioning** leads to learning when a child's action is followed by **reinforcement**, defined as an event that increases the likelihood of repeating the action. Good grades act as a reinforcement when they lead a child to spend more time on homework. An important characteristic of operant conditioning is that the reinforcing event need not take place every time the action is performed. Once an action has been learned, it often leads to more effective learning as long as it is reinforced at certain intervals (Skinner, 1969).

Imitation and Observational Learning

Imitation is the deliberate execution of an action performed by another person and is rooted in social learning (Tomasello, 2005). Observation

DOI: 10.4324/9781003292500-46

and then imitation of others reduce the need for time-consuming trial and error, lay the foundation for learning from others and their experiences and make it easier to establish social and emotional relationships. Of special interest from a developmental point of view are imitation in newborns and the emergence of immediate and deferred imitation as tools for learning new skills.

Imitation in Newborns

One of the major points of contention among developmental psychologists is the question of when children are able to "translate" actions they see others perform into movements they perform themselves (Oostenbroek et al., 2013). Meltzoff and Moore (1983) observed that 1–3-day-old infants spent more time mouth opening when the adult opened and closed the mouth and more time in tongue protrusion when the adult engaged in this activity. In another experiment, newborns were differentially influenced by adult tongue protrusion and head turning (Figure 35.1). Other studies have reported similar findings (Meltzoff & Moore, 1997; Nagy et al., 2013), including the observation that the finger movements of 2-day-old children were affected by the number of fingers shown to them (Nagy et al., 2014). Meltzoff and Moore explain their observations by suggesting that children have

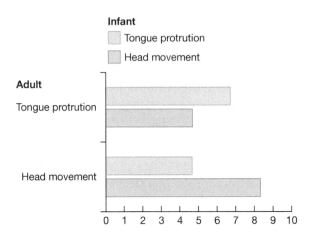

Figure 35.1 Tongue protrusion and head rotation in newborns.
Forty infants aged 1–3 days saw an adult either protruding the tongue or rotating the head. The figure shows that the infants more often stuck out their tongue when the adult performed a tongue-protrusion gesture and turned their head more often when the adult rotated his or her head (based on Meltzoff & Moore, 1989).

an innate ability to imitate other people's actions that they are able to master themselves.

Other studies have been unable to find a consistent correspondence between actions performed by the adult and the infant (Abravanel & DeYong, 1997; Anisfeld et al., 2001; Heimann et al., 1989; Ullstadius, 1998), and a number of theorists have questioned whether the infants in Meltzoff and Moore's studies actually imitated the adult's actions (Anisfeld, 2005; Jones, 2009; Oostenbroek et al., 2016). In a similar experiment, Jones (1996) found that 4-week-olds stuck out their tongue more often in response to tongue protrusion than to a mouth-opening gesture, consistent with the observations of Meltzoff and Moore (1983). Jones, however, also found that infants looked longer at a tongue-protruding face than at a mouth-opening face. Her interpretation is that tongue protrusion is more interesting for a newborn than mouth opening, and that tongue movements involve *oral exploration* (Jones, 2006). There is no doubt that the infants' tongue movements were elicited by the adult's actions, but they were not imitative – it was not the specific outward appearance of the adult's action that determined the child's behavior, but rather the interest aroused by seeing the tongue-protruding gesture. Furthermore, imitative behavior gradually diminishes: imitation of hand movements disappears at 2 months of age and returns once again at 7 months, while imitation of mouth movements disappears around 3 months and returns around 12 months. This suggests that the elicited actions of newborns and the later imitation of actions have different functions, and that early "imitation" needs a separate explanation (Elsner, 2005).

For newborns to be able to copy the actions of others, they must be born with a neurological structure that allows them to recognize and perform actions carried out by others without any previous experience. A number of researchers suggest that the mirror-neuron system (see Book 2, *Genes, Fetal Development and Early Neurological Development*, Chapter 15) is the neurological basis for imitation (Fabbri-Destro & Rizzolatti, 2008; Iacoboni, 2005; Stern, 2007). Such a system may possibly be of importance for the later development of imitation, but it can hardly explain imitation in newborns. One of the characteristics of mirror-neuron systems is that they are activated once the *goal* of a perceived action becomes clear, such as stretching out the hand to pick up an apple or pour water out of a glass (Jacob, 2009). The small action repertoire of newborns has no clear purpose, and infants only a few days of age have little knowledge about the intent of different actions.

Young children like to do the same as adults do

Moreover, **mirror neurons** have been found in a number of species that do not imitate (Oostenbroek et al., 2013; Suddendorf et al., 2013).

Another hypothesis is that the areas of the brain that control motor skills are generally activated when an individual observes the actions of others (Cattaneo & Rizzolatti, 2009). This implies the possibility of a rudimentary link between perception and action at birth that does not provide a basis for imitation in the narrow sense but has an activating function that increases the likelihood of the infant being attentive and acting in concert with other people. Conceivably, this could help ensure social attachment through mutual attention or represent a form of early "calibration" between external stimulation and individual action that later enables the child to acquire new skills by observing others.

Most researchers agree that newborns have a small repertoire of actions, and that children's actions can be triggered by those of adults. The point in question is how to explain the correspondences that have been found between the actions of newborns and adults. On the one hand, Meltzoff and Moore (1994) maintain that these actions are a form of imitation, performed with such effort as to suggest they have a purpose. Anisfeld (2005) and Jones (2009), on the other hand, suggest that watching the actions of adults activates part of infants' behavioral repertoire, although not in the way imitation is commonly defined. No matter which explanation may be right, actions elicited at this age do not seem to lead infants to learn new actions or where a particular action may be appropriate.

Imitation after the Age of 6 Months

By around 6 months, the behavioral repertoire of infants has grown, and they gradually begin to imitate new actions, although imitation in the first year of life generally remains sparse. Children and adults often interact by vocalizing, but it is usually the adult who imitates the child (Jones, 2009). One study investigated at what age more than 50 percent of children imitate some common actions (Jones, 2007). The mothers of 162 children aged 6–20 months performed different actions in front of their child. The age when half of the children performed the mother's action was 6 months for hitting the table when their mother did, 8 months for waving good-bye and vocalizing the sound *ah*, 10 months for clapping hands, 14 months for vocalizing the sound *eh-eh*, 16 months for performing sequential finger movements and putting one hand on their head, and 18 months for protruding their tongue when the mother protruded her tongue. However, the children rarely reiterated a specific action before the age of 1 year. Two-thirds of the 6-month-olds knocked on the table when their mother did, but did so just as often when their mother performed a different action. Only the mother's *ah* sound had a specific matching response before the age of 12 months, while the other actions matched between 12 and 18 months. It is worth noting that the children generally protruded their tongue quite often. Although 40 percent of the 6-month-olds protruded their tongue when their mother did, it was not until 18 months that they did so significantly more often when observing their mother's tongue protrusion than when she performed other actions. This supports the assumption that the imitation of actions after the age of 6 months has a different basis than the earliest tongue-protruding gestures (Elsner, 2005; Jones, 1996, 2007).

It is an important milestone in children's development when they begin to imitate actions they have not mastered earlier – imitation becomes a functional aspect of the learning process. This imitation is not random: children imitate actions more often when they have a clear goal, have an effect on something or trigger an action than when the action has no clear objective, such as just moving an object in a circle (Elsner, 2007). Children first imitate functional actions such as drinking from a cup or brushing their hair with a brush, and not until 2 years of age are they able to imitate non-functional actions such as using a toy car as a cup or a brush (Guillaume, 1926; Uzgiris, 1999). Children under 2½ years of age find it difficult to start using a new action to reach a goal without having seen the goal as well as the action that leads to it (Carpenter & Call, 2002). What children imitate also depends on their development and interests, and with age their imitation becomes progressively more selective (Harris & Want, 2005). Imitation is also reduced when the action is marked as undesired by an adult (Seehagen et al., 2017).

Deferred imitation means that children perform an action some-time after having observed it, and thus that the action must be remembered. Deferred imitation and memory are limited in the first year of life. With age, children need fewer demonstrations, recall more complex actions and their order and remember for longer (Elsner, 2007).

Learning does not only consist in acquiring new skills: children also use cues to learn *when* particular skills can be used. In many situations, imitating another person's action may be neither functional nor practical. A counter-imitation mechanism has therefore been suggested that inhibits "automatic" imitation, which is assumed to be part of the mirror-neuron system and self-regulation (see Book 6, *Emotions, Temperament, Personality, Moral, Prosocial and Antisocial Development*, Chapter 3) in general (Campbell & Cunnington, 2017).

The fact that a child uses an action or a strategy that has worked well for someone else does not always involve imitation in a straight-forward sense. The actions of adults also provide information about the properties of objects. When a child presses a button the way Daddy did, the action is not necessarily direct imitation but may be the result of having discovered new action possibilities afforded by the object (Yang et al., 2010). Deferred imitation can entail either direct copying of an action or the use of new knowledge in exploring the environment. Both are the result of **observational learning**.

Children do not imitate adults only: they start early to follow each other's example. A major **diary study** found that only children and children with siblings imitate with about the same frequency around the age of 1, but that only children almost exclusively imitate adults. Children with siblings imitate more spontaneously and more in the context of play, with fewer actions and routines based on instruction than only children. Thus, having a sibling affects what a child is imitating (Barr & Hayne, 2003). Two-year-olds often copy each other's actions, for example by taking the same toy another child has taken

(Nadel-Brulfert & Baudonniere, 1982). This suggests that imitation may be a tool for children to establish joint play and other activities. Around the age of 1 year, children learn one or two new skills per day by imitating others (Barr & Hayne, 2003). Much of children's play consists in copying the activities of adults, while adults adapt to children by imitating and expanding *their* actions. Imitation is especially important during the first years of life but continues as a learning strategy throughout life. The emergence of culture would be impossible to imagine without cooperation, imitation and observational learning and the fact that children imitate other people and are guided in modeling the actions of others (Rogoff, 2014; Tomasello, 2016).

Learning by Trial and Error, Insight and Heuristics

Children use a variety of strategies when they encounter "problems" they need to solve, depending on their development and experience (Schunk, 2012; Siegler, 2000). During early development, an important strategy is trial and error. The child is trying different solutions, without a clear plan, until one works, for example turning a triangle around or moving between holes when trying to put it into a box with differently shaped holes. This is typically a novice strategy. As younger children are new to many situations, they lack appropriate strategies to solve everyday problems. At first, they may use strategies that are not particularly adequate, but, over time, their trial-and-error exploration leads to better understanding and a larger action repertoire, as well as to more systematic and deliberate "guess and check" (Fessakis et al., 2013).

Four-year-old Mary is looking at a jigsaw puzzle. Suddenly she puts a piece exactly where it belongs. She has had an insight into how it fits. Insight is characterized by a sudden shift in skills. Sometimes it is the result of mental trial and error; other times it is the result of reasoning, combining different elements, arranging the situation in different ways and the like (Schunk, 2012). It is precisely this type of understanding Piaget and other researchers explore in their conversations with children about problem solving – their conscious reflection on the challenges they meet (see Chapter 3, this volume).

In heuristic problem solving, older children employ a set of general strategies, such as thinking of a similar problem, making a plan, drawing a conceptual map or working backward, that may help the child be systematic and reach a solution when encountering new problems. A child may start by identifying the problem, asking what she knows and needs

Young children learn about the physical world by trying out different solutions

to know to solve the problem and searching for strategies and solutions that were useful in the past. Heuristics functions best with new material in familiar situations in which the child may already have established useful strategies (Gigerenzer & Gaissmaier, 2011; Schunk, 2012).

36

Two Developmental Perspectives on Education

Children learn in a large variety of formal and informal situations. Informal learning is most common, but formal training and education in kindergarten and at school ensure that knowledge considered important by society is conveyed to the coming generation (Cole, 2005; Olson, 2003). Both logical and social constructivism have had a significant impact on education (deVries, 2000; Green & Gredler, 2002; Stoltz et al., 2015), each with its own perspective: Piaget views cognition as the basis for learning and education, while Vygotsky views learning and education as the basis for cognition (see Part I, this volume).

Logical Constructivism

According to Piaget (1969b, 1972), children's thinking is qualitatively different from adult thinking and limits what children are able to learn. Therefore, education can only be effective as long as it takes into account these differences. Educational objectives at school must be based on the child's level of development, for example by paying attention to the order in which basic concepts such as conservation of mass, weight, volume and causality are acquired (Elkind, 1976). Cognitive assessment of children who struggle or excel in school is an integral part of educational practice (see Book 1, *Theoretical Perspectives and Methodology*, Part III, and Part II, this volume).

According to Piaget, schools should promote children's thinking – factual knowledge is of secondary importance. The goal of education is to foster autonomous intellectual explorers rather than vessels of information to be reproduced, and schools should strive to encourage the best possible quality of thinking in children. This is in line with modern educational approaches, except that Piaget places relatively

DOI: 10.4324/9781003292500-47

little emphasis on children's interactions. In his view, learning mostly concerns individual exploration of the laws and rules of natural science. However, individual experience is not enough, and children must also learn to reconstruct knowledge selected by the school system (Martí, 1996).

The emphasis on children's abilities is also closely connected with Piaget's view of children as active participants in their own learning. In educational approaches based on Piaget's theory, the teacher is not an agent who fills passive children with the knowledge they lack. The teacher should adapt the situation and ask questions that promote children's independent learning based on their own prerequisites, but it is the individual child itself who creates intellectual growth (Furth & Wachs, 1975). Piaget has contributed to leading school education from blackboard and lecture to a more activity-oriented approach. Teachers should give students time to "work" rather than merely talking in front of the class all day. This does not represent a downgrading of the teacher's importance, but, to the contrary, places greater demands on teachers' knowledge about children's cognitive functioning. Although the teacher's function described above is less collaboration-oriented, it is not unlike the role of the teacher in Vygotsky's theory (see below).

Social Constructivism

In social constructivism, formal education is seen as an integral aspect of cognitive development, and educational work at all levels is a natural part of this (Karpov, 2014; Kozulin, 2002). "Instruction" is a central concept in Vygotsky's theory.

> Studying child thought apart from the influence of instruction, as Piaget did, excludes a very important source of change and bars the researcher from posing the question of the interaction of development and instruction peculiar to each age level. Our own approach focuses on this interaction.
>
> (Vygotsky, 1962, p. 117)

Like Piaget, Vygotsky (1935a, b) places emphasis on the independent and active child. Adults should not simply tell or show children what to do, but facilitate the child's own discovery of the problem as well as the solution together with the adult. In Vygotsky's theory, "independent" means that children themselves seek out knowledge, not that they find it on their own. They need the help of adults, and it is the adult's responsibility to guide the child to seek knowledge that is considered important by society. The learning process is a matter not merely of transferring information from teacher to student, but of guiding the student's construction of scientific concepts and theoretical understanding. In contrast with Piaget's theory, it is not the child's individual exploration that yields the best result, but the collaboration between the child and others. Children learn better when the adult takes part as a committed and active participant in the children's exploration (Kozulin, 2002).

Vygotsky argues that education must be based on the child's *zone of proximal development*, the area in which a child is able to master new tasks with help (see Chapter 6, this volume). The children in a school class are different both with respect to independent coping and the extent of their zone of proximal development in different fields of knowledge. The zone determines the types of tasks and activities that are meaningful for a child and the kind of instruction and guidance the child requires. Tasks children are able to manage independently lie below the zone and are therefore too simple. No matter how many such tasks a child solves, they will not lead to new knowledge. If a task lies above the zone of proximal development, the child will not be able to understand it, and watching somebody else solve the problem will not provide new knowledge. When a child or adolescent struggles or has atypical development, a thorough assessment will be necessary to ensure that the teaching is appropriate for their zone of proximal development in relevant areas. This zone thus acts as a bridge between the known and the unknown. Being within the child's proximal zone ensures that the instruction does not turn into tedious repetitions of familiar knowledge or frustrating encounters with the unfamiliar, but makes new insights achievable.

37

Cooperation among Children

Much of children's and adolescents' learning takes place in **vertical relationships** with teachers and other adults. It is an asymmetric relationship where the adult possesses the knowledge and skills, and the child or adolescent is the recipient. This is not to say that children are usually passive learners. They actively seek knowledge and help from more competent persons, both inside and outside of kindergarten and school. In a **horizontal relationship**, both parts are equal. Peer collaboration is based on a reciprocal relationship and can involve competition as well as cooperation.

Damon and Phelps (1989) distinguish between three types of collaboration between children. *Peer tutoring* means that older or more competent children help children who are novices. They assume the role of the teacher and create a vertical relationship. This can occur within the scope of a class, but often peer tutoring involves students from higher grades who act as "mentors" in cross-age tutoring. In **cooperative learning**, a group of children join forces to solve an assignment given by the teacher. The assignment is often divided into smaller tasks that are distributed among individual children. Every child works toward the same final goal, however, and the group members are a source of support and inspiration for each other. In *peer collaboration*, everyone is equal. The learning process consists of jointly exploring a topic, and the task is based on the group's interests rather than the teacher's authority. This also represents a more integrated and joint process in which preliminary ideas and proposals are discussed by all the group members. An important part of the process is that children gain a better understanding of their own as well as others' reasoning and have to adapt to different perspectives on the same topic.

DOI: 10.4324/9781003292500-48

Studies have shown that two or more children solve tasks of which they had no prior knowledge better in collaboration than separately (Battistich & Watson, 2003; Gillies, 2014; Johnson & Johnson, 2009). For example, Light and Glachan (1985) found that pairs of children aged 7–8 or 12–13 years needed on average about one-third fewer entries to solve Mastermind tasks than a group of children who solved the tasks individually. In fact, studies of adults have found that the "group intelligence" can be higher than the achievement of the highest scoring individual (Woolley et al., 2015). However, studies have also found that the effect of collaboration depends on the task and the interaction between the children. For example, in group mathematics, those who master mathematics best may dominate and hinder true collaboration. Children need help in learning to work together, as much of the group activity that goes on in classrooms may be distracting and have little educational value. In addition, peer collaboration in school also puts significant demands on the teacher (Gillies, 2014; Mercer, 2013).

The question is how and why collaboration makes learning more effective, why a collaborative solution can be better than the best individual solution. Howe (2010) suggests that a need to find a common solution elicits more in-depth discussions and hence better solutions. According to Doise (1978), collaborative learning is driven by "socio-cognitive conflicts" that arise because children have different perspectives and experiences. As children initially only have their own perspective (or perspectives, but nevertheless only their own), the individual child cannot achieve a similar level of problem solving. Another important factor is that the children themselves are active in the production of knowledge and therefore have a greater sense of ownership. A teacher would not be able to present different perspectives to the same extent. It should also be noted that, in this context, the word "conflict" should not be taken literally. It is not as if serious disagreement between children necessarily promotes learning. Children who accept each other's viewpoints without expressing disagreement learn more than children who quarrel. Howe (2009) emphasizes the importance of unresolved contradictions, analogous to the process of equilibration in Piaget's theory (see Chapter 3, this volume). Conflict entails a certain polarity between children's views that provides opportunity for agreement and disagreement in their dialogue, and that requires a mental reshuffling for conflicting views to be united (Kruger,

1993). Perspectives must be neither too different nor so similar as to leave no room for contradiction. Effective collaborative learning furthermore requires that children understand their role and have the opportunity to explore each other's views constructively (Gillies, 2003). In line with this, Mercer (2013) suggests that collaborative learning builds on mind understanding and the ability to share ideas and compare different perspectives.

38

Atypical Development: Learning Disorders

The school is society's main tool for providing shared knowledge and competence to all children, as well as ensuring the competence society needs. A learning disorder implies that the child has difficulty achieving some of the school's educational objectives beyond general cognitive resources and in spite of appropriate education. Low performance due to poor education is not considered a learning disorder. When a child has a learning disorder, teaching needs to be adapted to the child's problems, and severe disorders can necessitate an entirely different educational approach than other children benefit from. Moreover, a learning disorder can represent a significant emotional burden and require psychological support.

In line with a developmental understanding, multiple factors interact in the development of learning disorders (Kaufmann et al., 2013). A child may have early signs indicating **vulnerability** for a learning disorder, such as delayed language development or a high frequency of family members with dyslexia, and these may be a strong reason for preventive measures. However, correlations between early signs of vulnerability and later development are often small and moderate, and many vulnerable children show **resilience** and do not develop a learning disorder (Lee & Johnston-Wilder, 2015). A learning disorder does not present and cannot be diagnosed before the child has actually shown difficulties with school learning.

Reading and Writing Disorders

Disorders related to the comprehension and production of written language are common and a major problem in school (see Book 1, *Theoretical Perspectives and Methodology*, Chapter 32). There is considerable discussion about the definition of dyslexia, but core features are

DOI: 10.4324/9781003292500-49

problems with word decoding, poor reading fluency and spelling problems, and they can appear in children with high as well as low intelligence (Elliott & Grigorenko, 2014; Snowling, 2013). Written text is
the basic tool in most schoolwork, and problems with understanding
and composing written text may therefore have major influences on
motivation and academic achievement.

Research shows a clear relationship between language and reading
skills, and developmental language disorders entail a vulnerability for
developing reading and writing disorders (Grigorenko, 2007; Simkin & Conti-Ramsden, 2006). Children with dyslexia who learn an
alphabet-based language usually recognize the letters but have difficulty combining the sounds that correspond to the individual letters
into words (Peterson & Pennington, 2015). Chinese children can
have problems distinguishing written words with differences in stress
(tonemes) (Li & Ho, 2011). Dyslexia may be seen as a language disorder because the reading problems seem to be a developmental extension of the problems children have in language processing. Children
with phonological problems tend to have problems with word reading
and spelling; children with semantic problems have difficulties understanding text meaning (Bishop & Snowling, 2004; Nation et al., 2010).
However, children with dyslexia understand and use spoken language
much better than written. Reading must therefore imply additional
impaired processes, and reading is related to many non-verbal cognitive skills (Ricketts, 2011).

Reading problems are common in a variety of disorders. Among
children with severe motor impairments and unintelligible speech
(dysarthria), reading and writing disorders are the rule rather than the
exception (Smith, 2005). Many children with ADHD have problems
with reading and writing (McGrath et al., 2011). There are often several family members with dyslexia, indicating that it is hereditary, but
there are also influences from the environment (Bishop, 2015; Shaywitz & Shaywitz, 2013). Children with dyslexia, more often than other
children, have parents who left school early, do little reading and lack
the resources to follow up their child's disorders (Bonifacci et al., 2016).

Most often, reading disorders are noted when a child is unable to
read out loud, especially when it comes to new words and text with
more complex content. One exception is children with **hyperlexia**,
who have good mechanical reading abilities and read the text correctly aloud but do not comprehend what they are reading and cannot
answer even simple questions about the content (Grigorenko et al.,
2003). If they had heard someone else say the same sentences, they

would have been able to answer these questions without difficulty. They seem to be attentive to only a part of the reading process, the production of speech on the basis of letters. This emphasizes that the understanding of the meaning of a text involves more processes than just letter-sound decoding.

Some children are not hyperlexic but have *reading comprehension problems*. They appear to be able readers, and the people around them do not always notice their problems. After all, they are able to read out loud and understand what others say to them. As a result, they often do not receive the support they need for an adequate development of vocabulary and reading comprehension (Woolley, 2010). Reading comprehension problems can persist throughout adolescence and adulthood (Vaughn et al., 2014).

Prevention and Learning Support

Reading and writing are so fundamental to a child's future that early help is indicated for anyone with an increased risk of problems. For children with early language disorders or ADHD and other groups known to be at risk, early intervention is essential *before* the disorder appears, often already in kindergarten (Schulte-Körne, 2010). Shaywitz and colleagues (1998) found that 80 percent of children diagnosed with dyslexia in first grade did not meet the criteria for the disorder 4 years later. This underlines not only the importance of intervention and the fact that early difficulties do not necessarily predestine later problems, but also that care should be taken in giving this type of diagnosis during early school age. In later school age, learning disorders tend to stabilize. Most children diagnosed with dyslexia at 9 years of age remain poor readers 5 years later (Rutter et al., 1976).

Intervention and adaptation may be important throughout school life, but intervention seems to be more effective when implemented early rather than later in school age. A number of programs are available to help children with reading and writing disorders, and different methods seem to be effective in early and later interventions (Scammacca et al., 2015; Shaywitz et al., 2008; Schiff & Joshi, 2016). Some children derive only limited benefits from ordinary interventions (Shaywitz & Shaywitz, 2013). A large repertoire of strategies is essential, as a larger dose of what does not work serves little purpose. Audiobooks can be effective in countering the inevitable loss of knowledge brought about by poor reading skills; special assistive technology and text-to-speech computer programs can also be of help

(Saine et al., 2011; von Tetzchner et al., 1997). It is important, however, to distinguish between children who simply read slowly and children who struggle with the process of reading itself. Slow readers may need additional training to automate the reading process, preferably by using books that are exciting and easy to read and naturally speed up the child's reading pace. Children who struggle with the process of reading itself need support in learning the relationship between letters and speech sounds.

Research has found associations between reading disorders and emotional and behavioral problems. This demonstrates the impact such disorders can have on stress and **self-esteem** (Halonen et al., 2006; Mugnaini et al., 2009). Strategies for reducing or preventing severe reading and writing problems are thus crucial to a child's entire course of school as well as to prevent emotional and behavioral problems (Halonen et al., 2006).

Mathematics Disorders

Mathematics learning disorder, or *developmental dyscalculia*, implies math performance significantly below grade level, often operationally defined as two school grades below peers (see Book 1, *Theoretical Perspectives and Methodology*, Chapter 32). Therefore, the severity of problems often does not become noticeable until late in the second or third grade (Gifford & Rockliffe, 2012). Many children struggle with mathematics, and it is discussed whether children with a math disorder represent the extreme end of a continuum (or several continua) of mathematical ability or whether the arithmetic difficulties associated with dyscalculia are qualitatively different from more common mathematics difficulties. Some children are able to solve mathematical exercises but are slow performers and use far more time than their peers.

Dyscalculia was first described by Kosc (1974), and the fact that many children have difficulties with math may be one reason why these types of problems were only more recently acknowledged as a learning disorder (Butterworth, 2008). In addition, there are different types of mathematical problems, and there is still disagreement on how to diagnose dyscalculia and whether a uniform complex of math disorders actually exists (Emerson, 2015; Gillum, 2012). Studies show a relation between math performance and different cognitive skills, but there is no specific test profile capable of determining whether a child has a math disorder (Munro, 2003). Recent research has investigated the involvement of different brain areas and processes in mathematical thinking, which may give new insights into math learning and problems and, in the future, contribute to the design of special educational interventions (Bugden & Ansari, 2015; Gillum, 2012).

Mathematics also includes a linguistic aspect. Relational terms such as prepositions and words for quantity and size are part of early math language (Donlan, 2015). In addition, math requires a high degree of precision in both comprehension and expression. When children struggle with language, their ability to establish numeracy is also reduced (Landerl, 2015). Children with a minority language background, for example, can develop language skills that function well in daily life but are too rudimentary to acquire mathematical knowledge (Levels et al., 2008).

There is no consensus on the causes of mathematical disorders, but they can reflect individual differences in both numerical and non-numerical functions (Kaufmann et al., 2013). Working memory appears to be important for mathematics learning, and children with mathematics learning disorders have special difficulties with tasks involving working memory (Menon, 2016). However, this is also the case for children with autism spectrum disorder (Kercood et al., 2014) or ADHD (Martinussen et al., 2005). Butterworth (2008) suggests that a deficiency in an innate "number module" leads to a decrease in the ability to handle all types of mathematical operations. However, the assumption about a number module is inconsistent with brain studies (Bugden & Ansari, 2015) and the fact that many children with math disorders also have ADHD and problems with reading and writing. Math problems are found in many groups, with slight variations among children with different syndromes and disorders (Green & Gallagher, 2014; Reeve & Gray, 2015). Therefore, it is more likely that a number of different functions are involved in the development of mathematical skills and disorders (Fias et al., 2013; Henik et al., 2011). The heterogeneity of problems shows the complexity of mathematics, and comparison of different syndromes and disorders may shed light on the many factors influencing learning of mathematics (Bugden & Ansari, 2015; Kaufmann et al., 2013; Reeve & Gray, 2015).

Prevention and Learning Support

It seems possible to identify 5–6-year-olds who later show mathematical learning disabilities in the first and second grade (Stock et al., 2010). There are a large number of intervention programs for moderate problems as well as severe mathematical disorders (Dowker, 2017; Reeve &

Waldecker, 2017). The consequences of poor school–entry quantitative knowledge can be lifelong without appropriate intervention (Geary, 2015). One study found that first graders who were more than one standard deviation below average in the understanding of numerals had a four times higher probability of being functionally innumerate as adolescents than children with average numerical understanding in the first grade. The vulnerable children improved their math skills to a similar degree as their peers but did not gain on them, and the gap in mathematical competence remained (Geary et al., 2013). Although genes have been shown to influence the acquisition of mathematical skills, development is not determined by genes only but depends on education and other environmental factors. Studies on the prevention of mathematical disorders suggest that early detection of potential problems and remedial follow–up can reduce the incidence and consequences of disorders (Clarke et al., 2016; Gersten et al., 2015; Salminen et al., 2015). In primary school, there is no age effect, indicating that there is no "**critical period**": mathematics intervention can be effective at any age. However, the long–term effects may be small (Dowker, 2017). School instruction geared to demonstrate visual spatial relationships and strengthen executive reasoning skills can be of help (Cheng & Mix, 2014; Raghubar et al., 2010), as can language support (Gersten et al., 2009).

> It is worth acknowledging, while we are discussing the heterogeneous nature of children, that teachers, too, are a heterogeneous group.
>
> (Chinn, 2015, p. 7)

Some children receive special education in order to achieve the corresponding level of math skills as their peers, while others need lower educational targets (Holmes & Dowker, 2013). Number knowledge is important in many daily activities, and an appropriate goal for children with severe math disorders may be to provide them with the skills necessary to manage most practical situations and, possibly, compensatory strategies and assistive technology. Teaching can focus on a practical understanding of length, weight, time and money, for example. Also, the home environment can support the child's development, for example if parents focus children's attention on the numerical features of routine activities, such as counting children in a game or plates as they are put on the table (Hannula et al., 2010). Counseling can be of help in strengthening children's self-esteem and **self-efficacy** in tandem with more intensive and specially adapted math lessons (Green & Gallagher, 2014).

39

Learning Disorders and Mental Disorders

Many children and adolescents with learning disorders find school emotionally stressful and are vulnerable to developing internalizing and **externalizing disorders** (Alesi et al., 2014; Jenson et al., 2011). Learning disorders influence education and employment in adult life (Gerber, 2012). As adults, they also have a higher incidence of **internalizing disorders** (Klassen et al., 2013). Although some children are anxious about math, anxiety does not seem to be the main cause of their math disorder. At the same time, problems with math can lead to considerable emotional distress (Butterworth, 2008).

As many children with a learning **disability** are diagnosed late, they do not know what is wrong and may experience the first years of school as stressful. The situation can improve once they get better insight into their own difficulties in adolescence and realize that they are no less smart than their peers (Ingesson, 2007). Meanwhile, children's **self-image** is increasingly affected by their academic achievements. Whereas there is little connection between math disorders and self-image in second grade, there is a relatively strong connection in eighth grade (Linnanmäki, 2004). Many adolescents with dyslexia and mathematics learning disorders experience low self-esteem and a sense of despondency (Alexander-Passe, 2006; Graefen et al., 2015).

Some degree of emotional strain is probably unavoidable for children and adolescents with learning disorders, but the negative consequences of these disorders can be significantly reduced by early diagnosis and adequate educational and psychological support (Ingesson, 2007). When learning disorders are accompanied by social and emotional disorders, academic performance can be improved through parallel interventions aimed at these disorders (Alesi et al., 2014). Although learning disorders will not simply disappear with an improvement in the child's social and emotional life, better social and emotional functioning frees up resources that in turn allow the child to take better advantage of learning in school.

DOI: 10.4324/9781003292500-50

Summary of Part VI

1   *Learning* is commonly defined as a relatively permanent change in knowledge and skills that results from experience. *Instruction* includes both formal and informal strategies to provide children with knowledge and skills.

2   *Habituation* means that children react less after repeated presentations of a stimulus. **Dishabituation** occurs when the presentation of a new stimulus once again leads to an increase in reaction. Children regulate the stimulation from the environment.

3   *Classical conditioning* involves the association of two stimuli. In *operant conditioning*, learning occurs when a child's action is followed by *reinforcement*, an event that increases the likelihood of repeating the action.

4   *Imitation* is social learning, the deliberate replication of someone else's action. One point of discussion is *when* infants are able to "translate" other people's actions into movements they themselves perform. After the age of 6 months, infants learn many skills through *immediate* and *deferred imitation* and by observing and copying the actions of others. Imitation is particularly important during the first years, but remains a learning strategy throughout life. The development of cultural knowledge is based on cooperation, imitation and instruction.

5   Children are new to many situations and often have to use *trial and error* to find the strategy in their repertoire best suited to solving the problems they face. *Insight learning* is characterized by a sudden shift in skills as the result of mental trial and error, reasoning or by combining different elements.

6   A pedagogy based on *logical constructivism* assumes that children's development sets limits to what they are capable of learning. Learning in the narrow sense comes *after* development. *Social*

DOI: 10.4324/9781003292500-51

constructivism centers on children's active participation in the process while the adult lays the groundwork for the child to discover the problem and find a solution together with the adult. Training must remain within the child's *zone of proximal development* for different areas.

7   *Learning disorders* imply a difficulty meeting the school's educational objectives. Even milder forms of *reading and writing disorders* (dyslexia) can have major consequences for children's learning and development. Some children struggle most during childhood, but disorders can persist throughout adolescence and adulthood. Various strategies can mitigate and prevent reading and writing disorders, and different methods seem to be useful at earlier and later stages. Although many children struggle with math, some have such severe problems that they are diagnosed with *dyscalculia*. Early detection of potential disorders and remedial follow-up, with or without compensatory strategies and assistive technology, can reduce the incidence and consequences of these disorders.

8   Children and adolescents with learning disorders often have low self-esteem and are vulnerable to developing internalizing and externalizing disorders. When learning disorders are accompanied by social and emotional disorders, academic performance can be improved by parallel interventions.

9   *Vertical learning relationships* involve children together with adults or more competent children, while *horizontal learning relationships* are reciprocal. *Peer tutoring* means that more competent children teach children who need help. In *cooperative learning*, a group of children jointly solve an assignment given by the teacher. In *peer collaboration*, the learning process consists of jointly exploring an area of knowledge based on the group's interests rather than the teacher's authority. The fact that two or more children solve a task better together than on their own may be related to "socio-cognitive conflicts," where children have to integrate different perspectives and experiences.

Core Issues

- The basis and function of early imitation.
- The presence of domain-specific core functions in mathematical learning disorders.
- The relationship between cognition and learning.

Suggestions for Further Reading

Alexander-Passe, N. (2006). How dyslexic teenagers cope: An investigation of self-esteem, coping and depression. *Dyslexia, 12,* 256–275.

Jones, S. S. (2007). Imitation in infancy: The development of imitation. *Psychological Science, 18,* 593–599.

Kaufmann, L., Mazzocco, M. M., Dowker, A., von Aster, M., Goebel, S. M., Grabner, R. H., Henik, A., Jordan, N. C., Karmiloff-Smith, A., Kucia, K., et al. (2013). Dyscalculia from a developmental and differential perspective. *Frontiers in Psychology, 4,* 516.

Meltzoff, A. N., & Moore, M. K. (1983). Newborn infants imitate adult facial gestures. *Child Development, 54,* 702–709.

Mercer, N. (2013). The social brain, language, and goal-directed collective thinking: A social conception of cognition and its implications for understanding how we think, teach, and learn. *Educational Psychologist, 48,* 148–168.

Glossary

See subject index to find the terms in the text

A-not-B error   Children look for an object where they have previously found it (position A), rather than where they saw the object being hidden (position B).

Abstraction   A cognitive process that gives rise to a generalized category of something concrete, such as people, objects and events that are associated with less detailed features, aspects or similarities.

Accommodation   Alteration or formation of a new cognitive *schema* in order to better adapt the *cognitive structure* to external conditions; see *assimilation*.

Activity   A stable and complex system of goal-oriented activities or interactions that are related to each other by theme or situation and have taken place over a long period of time.

Activity theory   The elaboration and revision of Vygotsky's *theory* by neo-Vygotskians.

Activity-specific   Refers to skills and abilities that are unique to a particular activity; see *domain-general* and *domain-specific*.

Adaptation   Changes that increase the ability of a species or an individual to survive and cope with the environment.

Adaptive behavior   Behavior that enables an individual to survive and cope with the physical, social and cultural challenges of the environment.

Adolescence   The period between *childhood* and adulthood, age 12–18.

Age score   The average age at which children achieve a certain *raw score* on a *test*; sometimes called mental age in connection with *intelligence tests*.

Anatomically detailed dolls   Dolls with genitals used in connection with forensic interviews of younger children as well as older children with learning disabilities who may have been victims of sexual abuse.

Angelman syndrome   Genetic syndrome characterized by hyperactivity and severe learning disabilities; caused by a missing part of chromosome pair 15, inherited from the mother; the counterpart to *Prader-Willi syndrome.*

Assessment (in clinical work)   The mapping of an individual's strengths and weaknesses, competencies and problem areas.

Assimilation   The adaptation, integration or interpretation of external influences in relation to existing cognitive *schemas*; see *accommodation.*

Association   A link, such as between a stimulus and a reaction or action, or between ideas or thoughts.

Attachment   A *behavioral system* that includes various forms of *attachment behavior*; the system is activated when a child finds herself at a shorter or a longer distance from the person she is attached to, and experiences emotions such as pain, fear, stress, uncertainty or anxiety; the term is also used to describe emotional attachment to a caregiver; Attachment can be secure, insecure and disorganized; see *exploration.*

Attention deficit disorder; ADD   Characterized by impulsivity, low ability to concentrate on a task, and little sustained attention, may experience problems with emotional regulation, motor coordination, working memory, spatial perception and executive function.

Attention deficit hyperactivity disorder; ADHD   Attention deficit disorder with restlessness and a high level of activity.

Atypical development   Course of development that differs significantly from the development of the majority of a *population*; see *individual differences* and *typical development.*

Autism spectrum disorder   Neurodevelopmental disorder that appears in the first years of life; characterized by persistent deficits in social skills, communication and language, and by repetitive behavior and restricted interests.

Autobiographical memory   Memory of chronologically organized sequences of personally experienced events; see *long-term memory* and *working memory.*

Behavioral disorder   All forms of behavior that are socially unacceptable in one way or another, such as running away from home, screaming, cursing, messy eating manners, bed-wetting, ritual behavior, excessive dependency, poor *emotion regulation*, *aggression*, fighting and *bullying*.

Causality, understanding of   Understanding of the causal relationship or connection between actions and their consequences; the fundamental connection between things; see *physical causality*.

Childhood   Age 1–12 years.

Childhood amnesia   Describes the inability of older children and adults to remember experienced events that took place during the first 2–3 years of life.

Childhood dementia   Cognitive decline with onset in childhood.

Class inclusion   Refers to a class or category that is part of another class or category; essential feature of a hierarchical structure.

Classical conditioning   See *conditioning*.

Cognition   Thinking or understanding; includes some type of perception of the world, storage in the form of mental *representation*, different ways of managing or processing new and stored experiences, and action strategies.

Cognitive profile   The profile or pattern of performance in various cognitive areas.

Cognitive structure   Complex structure of mental representations and processes that forms the basis for thoughts, actions and the perception of the outside world; evolves and changes throughout development.

Collective monologue   Piaget's term for children's *egocentric speech* or *private speech*.

Communication   Intentional conveyance of thoughts, stories, desires, ideas, emotions, etc., to one or more persons.

Concept   Mental *representation* of a category of objects, events, persons, ideas, etc.; see *extension (of a concept)* and *intension (of a concept)*.

Concrete operational stage   According to Piaget, the third of four stages in cognitive development, approximately age 7–11; see *formal operational stage*, *preoperational stage* and *sensorimotor stage*.

Conditioning   The learning of a specific reaction in response to specific stimuli; includes classical and operant conditioning. In *classical conditioning*, a neutral stimulus is associated with an unlearned or *unconditioned stimulus* that elicits an unlearned or *unconditioned response*, eventually transforming the neutral stimulus into a conditioned stimulus that elicits a conditioned response similar to the unconditioned response. In *operant conditioning*, an action is followed by an event that increases or reduces the probability that the action will be repeated under similar circumstances; see *reinforcement*.

Connectionism   Theory within the information-processing tradition; based on a model of mental functioning by which external stimulation leads to various activating and inhibitory processes that may occur sequentially (following one another in time) or in parallel (simultaneously); knowledge is represented as a pattern of activation and inhibition, and new networks give rise to phenomena that differ qualitatively from the processes from which they emerged.

Conservation (in cognition)   A form of mental constancy; the ability to understand that the material or mass of an object does not change in mass, number, volume or weight unless something is taken away or added, even if external aspects of the object appear changed.

Constancy (in cognition)   The ability to understand that the attributes of objects and people remain the same, even if they seem to have changed, for example due to a different viewing angle and lighting conditions; see *object constancy* and *object permanence*.

Constraint (in development)   The organism's resistance to change and adaptation to new experiences; often used in connection with the nervous system.

Constructivism   Psychological theories based on the notion that an individual constructs his or her understanding of the outside world; see *logical constructivism* and *social constructivism*.

Continuity (in development)   Development in which later ways of functioning build directly on previous functions and can be predicted based on them; see *discontinuity*.

Cooperative learning; Collaborative learning   Two or more children solving problems together.

Core knowledge   In nativist theory, the innate abilities that form the basis for further perceptual, cognitive and linguistic development.

Correlation   Measure of the degree of covariation between two variables, ranging from −1.00 to +1.00; values close to 0.00 show a low degree of correlation; a positive correlation (+) means that a high score on one variable is associated with high score on the other; a negative correlation (−) indicates that a high score on one variable is associated with a low score on the other.

Correspondence (cognitive)   In Piaget's New Theory, the perception of structural similarity that provides a basis for comparing people, objects, events, actions, etc.; see *morphism*.

Critical period   Limited time period in which an individual is especially susceptible to specific forms of positive or negative

stimulation and experience; if the stimulation or experience fails
to take place during this period, a similar stimulation or experience later in life will neither benefit nor harm the individual to
any appreciable extent; see *sensitive period.*

Critical psychology   Theoretical tradition influenced by radical
social constructivism and women's studies, as well as postmodern
socology and psychoanalytic interpretation; challenges the idea
that regular developmental features have a biological basis.

Crystallized intelligence   Ability to solve problems that require
cultural and personal knowledge acquired through experience,
such as vocabulary or factual information; see *fluid intelligence.*

Cultural tool   According to Vygotsky, a skill that has developed
through generations in a culture, and that is passed on to children,
such as language, the numerical system or calendar time.

Culture   The particular activities, tools, attitudes, beliefs, values,
norms, etc., that characterize a group or a community.

Deductive reasoning   The process of ascertaining whether
a statement is true or false based on a given premise; drawing
conclusions about a specific case based on general principles; see
hypothetical-deductive reasoning and *inductive reasoning.*

Defense mechanism   In *psychodynamic theory,* unconscious mental strategies for dealing with inner psychological conflicts and
reducing anxiety that follows the drives and impulses of the *id* and
threatens control by the *ego.*

Deferred imitation; Delayed imitation   Deliberate repetition
of another person's action at some later point in time; see *immediate imitation.*

Development   Changes over time in the structure and functioning
of human beings and animals as a result of interaction between
biological and environmental factors.

Developmental disorder   Disorder that is congenital or appears
in *infancy* or *childhood* without the presence of external injuries or
similar.

Developmental pathway   One of several possible courses of
development within the same area or domain.

Developmental phase   Time period central to a particular developmental process.

Developmental quotient (DQ)   *Standard score* in developmental
tests; corresponds to the *intelligence quotient (IQ)* in intelligence tests.

Dialectical reasoning   The process of basing decisions and conclusions on dialectical reflection or argumentation.

Diary Study (in research on children)   Research method based on parents' written record of their child's actions or utterances.

Disability   The difference between an individual's abilities and the demands of the environment.

Discontinuity (in development)   Development in which new functions are associated with qualitative differences rather than merely a quantitative growth in previously established functions, and where the effect of past development can be altered by subsequent experiences; see *continuity*.

Dishabituation   Increased response to a new stimulus or aspect of a stimulus following a reduction in response intensity due to repeated presentation of a stimulus; see *habituation*.

Domain   A delimited sphere of knowledge; an area in which something is active or manifests itself.

Domain-genera   Abilities and skills that include most domains of knowledge; see *domain-specific*.

Domain-specific   Abilities and skills within a specific domain of knowledge; see *domain-general*.

Down syndrome; Trisomy 21   Syndrome that causes varying degrees of *intellectual disability*; caused by an error in cell division that results in a partial or complete extra copy of chromosome 21.

Dynamic assessment   The mapping of children's cognitive abilities by recording how much progress they make in the solution of a certain type of task after having received specific help and training for a given period.

Dyslexia   Severe reading and writing disorder, despite adequate sensory and intellectual abilities and appropriate training; see *learning disorder*.

Egocentric; egocentrism   Tendency to interpret events from one's own perspective; partial or complete inability to distinguish between one's own and other people's perspective.

Embryonic period   Weeks 2–8 of prenatal development.

Emotion   A state caused by an event important to the person and characterized by the presence of feelings; involves physiological reactions, conscious inner experience, directed action and outward expression.

Empathy   Feel with someone; emotional reaction similar to the emotion another person is perceived to experience; see *sympathy*.

Encoding   Conversion of external stimulation to mental *representations*.

Equilibration   According to Piaget, a process that leads children to search for solutions to cognitive contradictions and to integrate established cognitive *schemas* and new experiences.

Executive functions   Cognitive functions that monitor and regulate attention and plan and supervise the execution of voluntary actions, including the inhibition to act on inappropriate impulses.

Experiment   Method to test a hypothesis on specific causal relationships or connections. One or several conditions are systematically altered, and the effect is recorded. As many conditions as possible are kept constant in order not to affect the outcome, increasing the probability that the results are solely related to the conditions being studied.

Exploration   According to Bowlby, a behavioral system whose function is to provide information about the environment and enable the individual to better adapt to it; activated by unfamiliar and/or complex objects; deactivated once the objects have been examined and become familiar to the individual; see *attachment*.

Expressive language   The language that the child produces.

Extension (of a concept)   All actual and possible exemplars encompassed by a concept; see *intension (of a concept)*.

Externalizing disorder   Negative emotions directed at others; often expressed in the form of antisocial and aggressive behavior.

First-order belief attribution; First-order theory of mind   The ability to understand what another person is thinking; see *second-order belief attribution*.

Fluid intelligence   Basic skills such as memory and spatial perception whose development is relatively independent of specific cultural experiences; see *crystallized intelligence*.

Flynn effect   Increase in skills and knowledge that over time leads to changes in the norms of IQ tests.

Formal operational stage   According to Piaget, the fourth and final stage in cognitive development, starting around the age of 11; see *concrete operational stage*, *preoperational stage* and *sensorimotor stage*.

Formal operational thinking   According to Piaget, the highest form of cognitive functioning, where thinking is completely free of specific objects and experiences.

Fragile X syndrome   Hereditary condition that mainly affects boys; caused by damage to the X chromosome. Characterized by the development of an elongated head, a large forehead, a high palate and a prominent chin following *puberty*. Often, but not always, entails *learning disabilities* of widely varying degree, from mild to severe, and occasionally *autism*.

Functional equivalence   Refers to the fact that characteristics, behavior patterns or stimulation fulfill the same function in different individuals (for example in different cultures), or in the same individual at different age levels.

Gender difference; Sex difference   Characteristic, ability or behavior pattern that differs between the two sexes.

Generalize   To perceive and react in the same way to events that are similar in some respects.

Genotype   The genetic makeup of an individual.

Gesture   Distinct movement primarily used as a means of communication and interpreted consistently within a social system.

Gifted; giftedness (intelligence)   Scores in the high end of the IQ distribution, above 130.

Group play   Play in which several children interact; see *symbolic play*.

Habituation   Gradual reduction in the intensity of a reaction or response following repeated stimulation; allows an individual to ignore familiar objects and direct attention at new ones.

Head Start   American preschool program during the 1960s and 1970s with the aim of providing support for children from low-income and socially disadvantaged families.

Heritability estimate   Calculation of heritability based on the difference between the correlations of fraternal and identical twins.

Hierarchical structure (of concepts)   Organization of objects or concepts into categories and subcategories that are part of larger categories.

Horizontal relationship   Relationship in which both parties share an equal amount of knowledge and social power; see *vertical relationship*.

Horizontal structure (in language)   Utterances consisting of several words that all lie within the same intonation contour.

Hospitalization syndrome   Bad health and delayed development in children due to being raised in poor institutional environments.

Hyperactivity   Unusually high activity level that is difficult for an individual to control.

Hyperlexia   Mechanical reading ability without understanding.

Hypothetical-deductive reasoning   Method of solving problems or seeking knowledge that proceeds from a general assumption about the relationship between different factors and develops hypotheses that can be tested systematically; see *deductive reasoning* and *inductive reasoning*.

Identity   An individual's sense of who he or she is, as well as of affiliation with larger and smaller social groups and communities.

Imitation   The deliberate execution of an action to create a correspondence between what oneself does and what someone else does; see *delayed imitation* and *modeling.*

Immediate imitation   Deliberate repetition of another person's action immediately after it has been performed; see *deferred imitation.*

Incidence   The appearance of new occurrences of a trait, disease or similar in a particular *population* during a particular time span, often expressed as the number of incidences per 1,000 individuals per year.

Individual differences   Variation in skills and characteristics between the individuals in a *population*; see *atypical development* and *typical development.*

Induced memory   Memory of an experienced event that is "planted" in a person without the latter actually having experienced the event.

Inductive reasoning   The establishment of a general rule based on specific experience; see *deductive reasoning* and *hypothetical-deductive reasoning.*

Infancy   The first year of life.

Information processing (theory)   Psychological theories based on the assumption that all mental phenomena can be described and explained by models in which the flow of information is processed by one or more systems.

Integration (in development)   Coordination; progress toward greater organization and a more complex structure.

Intellectual disability; Learning disability; Mental retardation   Significant problems learning and adjusting that affect most areas of functioning; graded mild (IQ 70–50), moderate (IQ 49–35), severe (IQ 34–20) and profound (IQ below 20); in clinical contexts, a significant reduction in social adjustment is an additional criterion.

Intelligence quotient (IQ)   Numerical representation of an individual's *intelligence* in relation to peers. Formerly, IQ was based on the relationship between mental age and chronological age, calculated by dividing the *age score* on an IQ test by the individual's chronological age; today, IQ tests are based on a *standard score* with a mean of 100 and a *standard deviation* of 15 or 16, depending on the *test* being used.

Intension (of a concept)   The content, all of the attributes embraced by a *concept*; see *extension.*

Intentionality   Goal-oriented determination; includes a notion of the goal of an action, and emotions and plans related to achieving the goal.

Internalization   Process whereby external processes are reconstructed to become internal processes, such as when children independently adopt problem-solving strategies they have previously used in interaction with others, or adopt the attitudes, characteristics and standards of others as their own.

Internalizing disorder   Negative emotions directed at oneself, anxiety, depression; often involving a negative self-image, shyness and seclusion; see *externalizing disorder*.

Interpretative mind   Describes the fact that two people can perceive the same information differently; see *mind understanding*.

Joint attention   Two or more individuals share a common focus of attention, while at the same time being aware that the same focus of attention is shared by the other person(s).

Landmark   Distinctive spatial feature used to orient oneself in one's surroundings, such as the color of the walls or the placement of windows, doors and objects.

Language function   The purpose of speech; the objective one wants to achieve by conveying something to another person using language.

Learning   Relatively permanent change in understanding and behavior as the result of experience; see *development* and *maturation*.

Learning disorder   Significant problems developing skills in a specific area of knowledge, such as language impairment, reading/writing disorders (*dyslexia*) and difficulties with math (dyscalculia); often referred to as specific learning disorder as opposed to general learning disability; see *intellectual disability*.

Logical constructivism   Psychological tradition that includes Piaget's theory and the theories of others that build on it; its main principle is that children actively construct their own understanding of the outside world, and that *perception* and *cognition* are affected by logical and conceptually driven processes; see *constructivism* and *social constructivism*.

Logical reasoning   Reasoning whose deductions are limited by the rules of logic.

Long-term memory   Part of the memory system that stores memories over time and contains most of an individual's knowledge; see *autobiographical memory* and *working memory*.

Longitudinal study   Research method that involves the observation of the same individuals at various age levels.

Maturation   Developmental change caused by genetically determined regulating mechanisms that are relatively independent of
the individual's specific experiences; see *development* and *learning*.

Memory span   The amount of information an individual is able to
keep in *working memory*, such as the number of digits a child can
recall after seeing or hearing them once.

Mental age   See *age score*.

Mental disorder   Behavioral or psychological pattern that occurs
in an individual and leads to clinically significant distress or
impairment in one or more important areas of functioning.

Mental model   Subjective mind model of how the world functions
and how things are connected.

Mentalizing   The interpretation of one's own and others' behavior
as an expression of mental states, desires, feelings, perceptions, etc.;
according to Fonagy, a process that includes all thoughts about
relationships, human interactions and psychological processes in
humans.

Meta-knowledge   Knowledge about knowledge, for example met-
alinguistic insight into language itself.

Metaphor   A type of *analogy*; meaning expressed illustratively or
figuratively.

Mind understanding   Understanding that other people have
internal states, such as knowledge, feelings and plans, that may be
different from one's own and may affect their actions; see *social
cognition* and *theory of mind*.

Mind-oriented   Relating to other people as cognitive individuals.

Minority language   Language spoken by a minority of a society's
population.

Mirror neuron   Nerve cell that is activated both when an individual observes an action and when he or she performs the action.

Modeling   Type of observational learning, whereby an individual
learns by observing and imitating other people's behavior and its
consequences; see *imitation*.

Module (in cognition)   Isolated brain system that deals with a
particular type of stimulation and knowledge.

Moral reasoning   Reasoning about real or hypothetical moral
dilemmas.

Morphism   In Piaget's new theory, *correspondence* beyond identical
resemblance.

Multiple intelligences   According to Gardner, different forms of
intelligence among human beings.

Mutation   Sudden change in a gene.

Nativism   Theoretical assumption that development proceeds according to a plan that in some way is represented genetically, and that experience has little or no effect on the developmental outcome; see *maturation*.

New theory   See *The new theory*.

Norm (in a test)   A standard or normative score for a certain age level, based on the results from a large number of individuals.

Norm-referenced test   *Test* that is *standardized* based on a representative group and scaled in such a way that the score reflects an individual's performance relative to the performance of the standardized group.

Normal distribution   Statistically defined distribution around a mean; also called Gaussian curve.

Novelty preference   Tendency to be more attentive to new rather than familiar stimulation; appears in infants after the age of 3 months.

Object (in psychodynamic theory)   Mental representation of a person or an object that is the goal of a drive, or through which a drive can achieve its goal.

Object constancy   Understanding that an object remains the same despite changes in how it appears in different light, perspective or distance.

Object permanence   Understanding that an object continues to exist even though it cannot be perceived by the senses.

Observational learning   Learning by observing the behavior of others and the consequences of their behavior.

Operant conditioning   See *conditioning*.

Operation (cognitive)   According to Piaget, the mental *representation* of actions that follow logical rules.

Parenting style   General description of how parents raise their children.

Perception   Knowledge gained through the senses; discernment, selection and processing of sensory input.

Personal narrative   See *autobiographical memory*.

Phenylketonuria (PKU)   Hereditary disorder in the production of the enzyme phenylalanine hydroxylase, leading to elevated levels of phenylalanine in the blood; causes severe mental and physical impairment if left untreated by a dietary regimen.

Physical causality, understanding of   Understand ing of how physical objects behave and interact with one another; see *causality*.

Population (in statistics)   The sum total of individuals, objects, events and the like included in a study. Also used to describe a group of individuals with a common measurable attribute, such as children in a certain school grade or young people in cities.

Prader-Willi syndrome   Genetic syndrome characterized by short stature, *hypotonia*, an insatiable appetite and often mild learning disabilities; caused by a missing or unexpressed part of chromosome pair 15, inherited from the father; the counterpart to *Angelman syndrome*.

Pragmatic reasoning   Reasoning based on *schemas* abstracted from one's own past experiences in similar situations.

Pragmatics (in language)   Functions of language in everyday use.

Preference method   Method of measuring the proportion of time a child is attentive to each of two different stimuli, such as a simple checkerboard and a more complex visual pattern, or the mother's voice and the voice of a stranger; children are said to show a preference for the stimulus they are attentive to for more than half the time.

Pre-linguistic   Refers to children's skills and abilities before they begin to speak, for example pre-linguistic *communication*.

Preoperational stage   According to Piaget, the second of four stages in cognitive development, approx. age 4–7; see *concrete operational stage*, *formal operational stage* and *sensorimotor stage*.

Preschool age   Age 3–6 years.

Pretend play   Form of *symbolic play* that involves make-believe actions.

Private speech   Speech that does not convey enough information to allow the listener to understand what is being communicated.

Protection (in development)   Conditions that reduce the negative effects of *vulnerability* and *risk*.

Prototype   Typical exemplar of a concept.

Prototype category   *Conceptual category* derived from a prototypical exemplar.

Punishment   In behavioral psychology, any event that reduces the probability of repeating an action under similar circumstances; see *reinforcement*.

Qualitative change   Change in the nature or quality of a phenomenon.

Raw score (in testing)   The total number of points scored on a test; see *standard score*.

Reaction range   The degree to which a developmental process can be influenced at a particular point during development.

Recall   Recollection of an experience without perceptual support; see *recognition*.

Recognition The process of experiencing something in the moment that has been experienced before, such as when children consciously or non-consciously show that they have seen a particular image before; see *recall*.

Refreshment (of memory) Repeated presentation of an object or event previously experienced by an individual.

Reinforcement (in conditioning) In *classical conditioning*: presentation of an *unconditioned stimulus* and a *neutral stimulus* that becomes a *conditioned stimulus*, such that the *conditioned response* is triggered more consistently. In *operant conditioning*: events that follow the execution of an action and increase the likelihood of repeating the action under similar circumstances.

Representation (mental) An individual's mental storage of understanding and knowledge about the world.

Representative sample A group of individuals with the same distribution of relevant characteristics as the *population* represented by the sample, so that the results of the sample can be assumed to be valid for the entire population.

Resilience Attributes that lead to a positive development under difficult childhood conditions, such as children who are biologically or socially at *risk* of aberrant or delayed development; see *vulnerability*.

Rett syndrome Genetic syndrome that almost exclusively affects girls; characterized by severe *intellectual disability* and motor and language impairment; development is often normal for the first 6–18 months of life, with a consequent decline in functioning. Believed to be mainly caused by a defective control gene (MeCP2) on the X chromosome that fails to switch off other X chromosome genes at the right time.

Risk Increased likelihood of a negative developmental outcome; may be linked to biological and environmental factors.

Role Expectations of certain action patterns and behaviors associated with an individual by virtue of their function or position in society, for example as a girl, teenager or boy scout.

Role-play Form of *pretend play* in which the participants make-believe they are another person, an animal or a human-like figure.

Scaffold, scaffolding In *social constructivism*, the external regulation, help and support provided by adults or more experienced peers to children, adapted to their level and allowing them to transcend their independent coping skills and develop new skills and knowledge; see *zone of proximal development*.

Schema Mental *representation* that emerges when actions are generalized by means of repetition and transformed through mental processing, thus shaping the individual's perception of the environment; see *cognitive structure*.

School age Age 6–12.

Script (cognition) Generalized mental *representation* of a sequence of events that recur within the context of a specific situation; provides among other things the basis for an individual's expectations of how to behave in different situations, such as at school or at a restaurant.

Second-order belief attribution; Second-order theory of mind The belief of one person's thoughts about another person's thoughts, what A thinks B is thinking; see *mind understanding* and *theory of mind*.

Self Personal awareness, perception or evaluation of oneself.

Self-efficacy The experience of acting and having control over one's own life; belief in one's own ability to deal with different situations and events.

Self-evaluation; Self-esteem The assessment of one's own characteristics in relation to an inner standard that includes how and who one wishes to be; can also refer to questionnaires, surveys and the like about a person's characteristics.

Self-image Positive or negative perception of oneself and one's own characteristics.

Self-regulation The ability to monitor and adapt one's own thoughts, feelings, reactions and actions in order to cope with the requirements, challenges and opportunities of the environment and be able to achieve one's goals; also referred to as self-control.

Sensitive period Limited period of time when an individual is particularly susceptible to specific forms of positive or negative stimulation and experience; if the stimulation or experience does not take place during the given time period, the individual will still be able to take advantage of, or be impaired by, similar types of stimulation or experience later in life, but to a lesser extent; see *critical period*.

Sensitivity (of a caregiver) Ability to understand a child's condition, respond quickly and adequately to the child's *signals* and behavior, and provide challenges the child is able to master.

Sensorimotor stage According to Piaget, the first of four stages in cognitive development, lasting until the age of 2; see *concrete operational stage*, *formal operational stage* and *preoperational stage*.

Sign language   Visual-manual language, primarily using movements of the arms, hands and fingers, supported by body movements, mouth movements and facial gestures.

Social cognition   Cognitive processes that form the basis for understanding one's own and other people's intentions, motives, emotions, thoughts and social relations.

Social construction   Anything rooted in or created by means of social interaction.

Social constructivism   Psychological theories based on the notion that children construct their understanding of the outside world through interaction and cooperation with other people, and that people in different cultures (including the subcultures of a society) can perceive one and the same phenomenon in different ways; see *logical constructivism*.

Socioeconomic status (SES)   Assessment of an individual's economic and social status in society; for children, usually based on information about the parents' education and occupation.

Stability (in development)   Describes the constancy of an individual's position in relation to peers with respect to a particular characteristic; the fact that individual differences in the execution of a skill are constant from one developmental stage to another.

Stage (in development)   Delimited period of time in which thoughts, feelings and behavior are organized in a way that is qualitatively different from the preceding or following periods.

Stage theory   Theory based on the assumption that development proceeds in distinct and qualitatively different *stages*.

Standard deviation   Measure of the spread of *quantitative* data; indicates the average degree of deviation in the score or numerical value of a variable from the total average; see *normal distribution*.

Standard score (in testing)   Score based on *standard deviation*; indicates the relative ranking of an individual's performance on a test compared with the statistical average and the distribution of scores in the standardization sample; see *raw score*.

Standard theory   See *The standard theory*.

Standardization (of tests)   Systematic survey of *test* items among a *representative sample* of the *population* targeted by the test; aims to estimate the distribution of scores among a given population.

Stanford-Binet Intelligence Scales   IQ test for ages 2–23; the 5th revised English-language edition (SB5) was released in 2003.

Stanine scale   STAndard NINE is a method of scaling test scores based on a division of the *normal distribution curve* into nine steps, with a mean of five and a standard deviation of two.

Symbol   Something that represents something other than itself, such as a sign, a word, an image or the like.

Symbolic play   Play in which children take on the role of a person or an animal, and connect objects with a function unlike the one they usually have, performing a make-believe activity; see *group play*.

Sympathy   Understanding why another person experiences the emotions that they express.

Syndrome   Set of attributes and behavioral characteristics that regularly occur together.

Temperament   A biologically determined pattern of emotional reactivity and regulation unique to an individual; includes the degree of *emotionality*, *irritability* and *activity level*, and reactions to and ability to cope with emotional situations, new impressions and changes.

Test   Measurement instrument; a collection of questions or tasks that provide a basis for assessing an individual's performance relative to peers or a specific set of criteria; see *norm-referenced test*.

The new theory   A common term for Piaget's final revision of his theory of cognitive development, which makes allowances for some of the criticism directed at *the standard theory*, in particular issues concerning Piaget's assumptions on *domain-general* development.

The standard theory   A common term for Piaget's theory of cognitive development as it appeared in its basic form in the 1950s and 1960s; see *the new theory*.

Theory of mind   The understanding that human beings are thinking and sentient beings who act according to how they perceive a given situation; see *social cognition* and *mind understanding*.

Transactional model   Developmental model based on mutual interaction between an individual and the environment over time: the environment changes the individual, the individual changes the environment, which in turn changes the individual, and so on.

Transitive relation   Relation that makes it possible to infer the relation between A and C based on the relations A–B and B–C, for example that A must be greater than C when A is greater than B and B is greater than C.

Triarchic model of intelligence   According to Sternberg, a model of intelligence with three integrated sub-theories: 1) *cognition* and the processes that form the basis for intelligent action, 2) experiences of relationships between the inner and the outer world, and 3) use of cognitive mechanisms to adapt to the world one lives in on a practical everyday basis.

Turner syndrome   *Chromosomal abnormality* caused by the presence of only a single X chromosome (X0) in females; characterized by a slightly low weight at birth, heart failure, distinctive facial features, short and chubby fingers, short stature, inability to reproduce and *learning disabilities*.

Twin Study   Study comparing identical and fraternal twins who have grown up together and separately in order to shed light on the importance of genes and the environment in the development of different traits.

Typical development   Course of development that characterizes the majority of a *population*; see *atypical development* and *individual differences*.

Unconscious   Not within the sphere of conscious attention; in *psychoanalytic theory*, an inaccessible part of consciousness where repressed, often anxiety-eliciting memories and desires are stored.

Under-stimulation   Deprivation, lack of or a reduction in stimulation considered important for normal development.

Vertical relationship   Relationship in which one part has more knowledge and social power than the other, such as parent–child; see *horizontal relationship*.

Visual perspective   Ability to understand what others are able or unable to see.

Vocabulary spurt   A rapid increase in productive vocabulary that typically characterizes children's language from the end of the second year of life; often defined as the first month in which a child's vocabulary increases by 15 words or more, often coinciding with the child's earliest two-word utterances.

Vulnerability   An individual's susceptibility to be adversely affected by particular conditions or circumstances in the environment; see *resilience* and *risk*.

Williams syndrome   Genetic syndrome characterized by heart defects, distinctive facial features, a short stature, developmental delays in the fetal stage and later, problems thriving during *infancy*, mild or moderate *learning disabilities*, good language abilities compared with other skills, and trusting behavior toward other people.

Working memory   Part of the memory system related to what an individual does while trying to remember something for a short period of time or dealing with a problem. Characterized by limited storage and processing capacity, and a rapid reduction in content if not repeated; see *autobiographical memory* and *long-term memory*.

Zone of modifiability   The reaction range which represents the child's developmental constraints, the upper and lower level of possible development.

Zone of proximal development   Children's mastery of skills in collaboration with more competent individuals within a specific area of knowledge or expertise, as opposed to self-mastery; see *scaffold*.

Zygote   Cell resulting from the fusion of an egg and a sperm cell.

Bibliography

Abravanel, E., & DeYong, N. G. (1997). Exploring the roles of peer and adult video models for infant imitation. *Journal of Genetic Psychology*, *158*, 133–150.

Acredolo, C. (1997). Understanding Piaget's new theory requires assimilation and accommodation. *Human Development*, *40*, 235–237.

Agnew, S. E., & Powell, M. B. (2004). The effect of intellectual disability on children's recall of an event across different question types. *Law and Human Behavior*, *28*, 273–294.

Alderson-Day, B., & Fernyhough, C. (2015). Inner speech: Development, cognitive functions, phenomenology, and neurobiology. *Psychological Bulletin*, *141*, 931–965.

Alea, N., & Wang, Q. (2015). Going global: The functions of autobiographical memory in cultural context. *Memory*, *23*, 1–10.

Alesi, M., Rappo, G., & Pepi, A. (2014). Depression, anxiety at school and self-esteem in children with learning disabilities. *Journal of Psychological Abnormalities in Children*, *3*, 125.

Alexander, J. M., & Schwanenflugel, P. J. (1994). Strategy regulation: The role of intelligence, metacognitive attributions, and knowledge base. *Developmental Psychology*, *30*, 709–723.

Alexander-Passe, N. (2006). How dyslexic teenagers cope: An investigation of self-esteem, coping and depression. *Dyslexia*, *12*, 256–275.

Allen, J. G. (2003). Mentalizing. *Bulletin of the Menninger Clinic*, *67*, 91–112.

Almeida, L. S., Prieto, M. D., Ferreira, A. I., Bermejo, M. R., Ferrando, M., & Ferrándiz, C. (2010). Intelligence assessment: Gardner multiple intelligence theory as an altenative. *Learning and Individual Differences*, *20*, 225–230.

Anazi, S., Maddirevula, S., Faqeih, E., Alsedairy, H., Alzahrani, F., Shamseldin, H. E., Patel, N., Hashem, M., Ibrahim, N., Abdulwahab, F., etal. (2017). Clinical genomics expands the morbid genome of intellectual disability and offers a high diagnostic yield. *Molecular Psychiatry*, *22*, 615–624.

Andersen, P. N., Hovik, K. T., Skogli, E. W., Egeland, J., & Øie, M. (2013). Symptoms of ADHD in children with high-functioning autism are related to impaired verbal working memory and verbal delayed recall. *PloS One*, *8* (5), e64842.

Andrés-Roqueta, C., Adrian, J. E., Clemente, R. A., & Katsos, N. (2013). Which are the best predictors of theory of mind delay in children with specific language impairment? *International Journal of Language and Communication Disorders, 48*, 726–737.

Anisfeld, M. (2005). No compelling evidence to dispute Piaget's timetable of the development of representational imitation in infancy. In S. Hurley & N. Chater (Eds), *Perspectives on imitation: From neuroscience to social science, Volume 2: Imitation, human development, and culture* (pp. 107–131). Cambridge, MA: MIT Press.

Anisfeld, M., Turkewitz, G., Rose, S. A., Rosenberg, F. R., Sheiber, F. J., Couturier-Fagan, D. A., Ger, J. S., & Sommer, I. (2001). No compelling evidence that newborns imitate oral gestures. *Infancy, 2*, 111–122.

Antshel, K. M., & Olszewski, A. K. (2014). Cognitive behavioral therapy for adolescents with ADHD. *Child and Adolescent Psychiatric Clinics, 23*, 825–842.

Apperly, I. A. (2008). Beyond simulation–theory and theory–theory: Why social cognitive neuroscience should use its own concepts to study "Theory of Mind". *Cognition, 107*, 266–283.

Apperly, I. A. (2011). *Mindreaders: The cognitive basis of "theory of mind"*. New York, NY: Psychology Press.

Arden, R., & Plomin, P. (2006). Sex differences in variance of intelligence across childhood. *Personality and Individual Differences, 41*, 39–48.

Arsenault, D. J., & Foster, S. L. (2012). Attentional processes in children's overt and relational aggression. *Merrill-Palmer Quarterly, 58*, 409–436.

Astington, J. W., & Gopnik, A. (1988). Knowing you have changed your mind: Children's understanding of representational change. In J. W. Astington, P. L. Harris & D. R. Olsen (Eds), *Developing theories of mind* (pp. 193–206). Cambridge: Cambridge University Press.

Avis, J., & Harris, P. L. (1991). Belief desire reasoning among Baka children: Evidence for a universal conception of mind. *Child Development, 62*, 460–467.

Ayoub, C., O'Connor, E., Rappolt-Schlictmann, G., Vallotton, C., Raikes, H., & Chazan-Cohen, R. (2009). Cognitive skill performance among young children living in poverty: Risk, change, and the promotive effects of Early Head Start. *Early Childhood Research Quarterly, 24*, 289–305.

Baillargeon, R. (1987). Young infants' reasoning about the physical and spatial properties of a hidden object. *Cognitive Development, 2*, 179–200.

Baillargeon, R. (1994). How do infants learn about the physical world? *Current Directions in Psychological Science, 3*, 133–140.

Baillargeon, R. (2004). Infants' physical world. *Current Directions in Psychological Science, 13*, 89–94.

Baillargeon, R. (2008). Innate ideas revisited: For a principle of persistence in infants' physical reasoning. *Perspectives on Psychological Science, 3*, 2–13.

Baillargeon, R., Kotovsky, L., & Needham, A. (1995). The acquisition of physical knowledge in infancy. In D. Sperber, D. Premack & A. J. Premack (Eds), *Causal cognition* (pp. 79–116). Oxford: Oxford University Press.

Baillargeon, R., Scott, R. M., & Bian, L. (2016). Psychological reasoning in infancy. *Annual Review of Psychology, 67*, 159–186.

Baillargeon, R., Scott, R. M., & He, Z. (2010). False-belief understanding in infants. *Trends in Cognitive Sciences, 14*, 110–118.

Baillargeon, R., Li, J., Ng, W., & Yuan, S. (2009). An account of infants' physical reasoning. In A. Woodward & A. Needham (Eds), *Learning and the infant mind* (pp. 66–116). New York, NY: Oxford University Press.

Baillargeon, R., He, Z., Setoh, P., Scott, R. M., Sloane, S., & Yang, D. Y. J. (2013). False-belief understanding and why it matters. In M. Banaji & S. Gelman (Eds), *Navigating the social world: What infants, children, and other species can teach us* (pp. 88–95). New York, NY: Oxford University Press.

Baker, B. L., Marquis, W. A., & Abbott Feinfield, K. (2016). Early intervention and parent education. In A. Carr, S. Linehan, G. O'Reilly, P. N. Walsh & J. McEnvoy (Eds), *The handbook of intellectual disability and clinical psychology practice, Second edition* (pp. 311–338). Abingdon, UK: Routledge.

Baker, D. P., Eslinger, P. J., Benavides, M., Peters, E., Dieckmann, N. F., & Leon, J. (2015). The cognitive impact of the education revolution: A possible cause of the Flynn effect on population IQ. *Intelligence, 49*, 144–158.

Baron, I. S. (2004). *Neuropsychological evaluation of the child.* New York, NY: Oxford University Press.

Baron-Cohen, S. (1995). *Mindblindness: An essay on autism and theory of mind.* Boston, MA: MIT press.

Baron-Cohen, S., Leslie, A. M., & Frith, U. (1985). Does the autistic child have a "theory of mind"? *Cognition, 21*, 37–46.

Baron-Cohen, S., Leslie, A. M., & Frith, U. (1986). Mechanical, behavioural and intentional understanding of picture stories in autistic children. *British Journal of Developmental Psychology, 4*, 113–125.

Barr, R., & Hayne, H. (2003). It's not what you know, it's who you know: Older siblings facilitate imitation during infancy. *International Journal of Early Years Education, 11*, 7–21.

Barrasso-Catanzaro, C., & Eslinger, P. J. (2016). Neurobiological bases of executive function and social-emotional development: Typical and atypical brain changes. *Family Relations, 65*, 108–119.

Barrouillet, P. (2015). Theories of cognitive development: From Piaget to today. *Developmental Review, 38*, 1–12.

Barrouillet, P., & Poirier, L. (1997). Comparing and transforming: An application of Piaget's morphisms theory to the development of class inclusion and arithmetic problem solving. *Human Development, 40*, 216–234.

Battistich, V., & Watson, M. (2003). Fostering social development in preschool and the early elementary grades through cooperative classroom activities. In R. M. Gillies & A. F. Ashman (Eds), *Cooperative learning: The social and intellectual outcomes of learning in groups* (pp. 19–35). London: Routledge.

Bauer, P. J. (1997). Development of memory in early childhood. In N. Cowan (Ed.), *The development of memory in childhood* (pp. 83–111). Hove, UK: Psychology Press.

Bauer, P. J. (2006) Event memory. In D. Kuhn & R. Siegler (Eds), *Handbook of child psychology: Cognition, perception, and language, Sixth edition* (pp. 373–425). London: Wiley.

Bauer, P. J. (2013). Memory. In P. D. Zelazo (Ed.), *Oxford handbook of developmental psychology, Volume 1: Mind and body* (pp. 505–541). New York, NY: Oxford University Press.

Bauer, P. J. (2014). The development of forgetting: Childhood amnesia. In P. Bauer & R. Fivush (Eds), *The Wiley handbook on the development of children's memory, Volume I–II* (pp. 513–544). London: Wiley.

Bauer, P. J. (2015). Development of episodic and autobiographical memory: The importance of remembering forgetting. *Developmental Review, 38*, 146–166.

Bauer, P. J., & Fivush, R. (1992). Constructing event representations: Building on a foundation of variation and enabling relations. *Cognitive Development, 7*, 381–401.

Bauer, P. J., & Larkina, M. (2014). The onset of childhood amnesia in childhood: A prospective investigation of the course and determinants of forgetting of early-life events. *Memory, 22*, 907–924.

Bauer, P. J., & Werkera, S. S. (1995). One- to two-year-olds' recall of events: The more expressed, the more impressed. *Journal of Experimental Child Psychology, 59*, 475–496.

Bauer, P. J., & Werkera, S. S. (1997). Saying is revealing: Verbal expression of event memory in the transition from infancy to early childhood. In P. W. van den Broek, P. J. Bauer & T. Bourg (Eds), *Developmental spans in event comprehension and representation: Bridging fictional and actual events* (pp. 139–168). Hillsdale, NJ: Erlbaum.

Bauer, P. J., Hertsgaard, L. A., & Wewerka, S. S. (1995). Effects of experience and reminding on long term recall in infancy: Remembering not to forget. *Journal of Experimental Child Psychology, 59*, 260–298.

Bauer, P. J., Doydum, A. O., Pathman, T., Larkina, M., Güler, O. E., & Burch, M. (2012). It's all about location, location, location: Children's memory for the "where" of personally experienced events. *Journal of Experimental Child Psychology, 113*, 510–522.

Bayley, N. (2006). *Bayley Scales of Infant and Toddler Development, Third edition.* San Antonio, Texas: Harcourt Assessment.

Beckett, C., Maughan, B., Rutter, M., Castle, J., Colvert, E., Groothues, C., Hawkins, A., Kreppner, J., O'Connor, T. G., Stevens, S., & Sonuga-Barke, E. J. (2007). Scholastic attainment following severe early institutional deprivation: A study of children adopted from Romania. *Journal of Abnormal Child Psychology, 35*, 1063–1073.

Bedard, K., & Dhuey, E. (2006). The persistence of early childhood maturity: International evidence of long-run age effects. *The Quarterly Journal of Economics, 121*, 1437–1472.

Bedell, G., Coster, W., Law, M., Liljenquist, K., Kao, Y. C., Teplicky, R., Anaby, D., & Khetani, M. A. (2013). Community participation, supports, and barriers of school-age children with and without disabilities. *Archives of Physical Medicine and Rehabilitation, 94*, 315–323.

Beilin, H. (1992). Piaget's new theory. In H. Beilin & P. B. Pufall (Eds), *Piaget's theory: Prospects and possibilities* (pp. 1–17). Hillsdale, NJ: Erlbaum.

Belli, R. F. (Ed.) (2012). *True and false recovered memories: Toward a reconciliation of the debate*. New York, NY: Springer.

Belmonte, M. K. (2009). What's the story behind "theory of mind" and autism? *Journal of Consciousness Studies, 16*, 118–139.

Berg, C. A., & Sternberg, R. J. (1985). Response to novelty: Continuity versus discontinuity in the developmental course of intelligence. *Advances in Child Development and Behavior, 19*, 2–47.

Best, J. R., Miller, P. H., & Jones, L. L. (2009). Executive functions after age 5: Changes and correlates. *Developmental Review, 29*, 180–200.

Bidell, T. R., & Fischer, K. W. (1992). Beyond the stage debate: Action, structure, and variability in Piagetian theory and research. In R. J. Sternberg & C. A. Berg (Eds), *Intellectual development* (pp. 100–140). Cambridge: Cambridge University Press.

Binet, A. (1975). *Modern ideas about children*. Menlo Park, CA: Suzanne Heisler.

Bishop, D. V. M. (2005). *Test for Reception of Grammar, TROG*. London: Psychological Corporation.

Bishop, D. V. M. (2015, May). The interface between genetics and psychology: Lessons from developmental dyslexia. *Proceedings of the Royal Society B, 282 (1806)*, 20143139.

Bishop, D. V. M., & Snowling, M. J. (2004). Developmental dyslexia and specific language impairment: Same or different? *Psychological Bulletin, 130*, 858–886.

Bishop, E. G., Cherny, S. S., Corley, R., Plomin, R., DeFries, J. C., & Hewitt, J. K. (2003). Development genetic analysis of general cognitive ability from 1 to 12 years in a sample of adoptees, biological siblings, and twins. *Intelligence, 31*, 31–49.

Bjorklund, D. F. (1995). *Children's thinking: Developmental functions and individual differences, Second edition*. Pacific Grove, CA: Brooks.

Bjorklund, D. F., & Harnishfeger, K. K. (1987). Developmental differences in mental effort requirements for the use of an organizational strategy in free recall. *Journal of Experimental Child Psychology, 44*, 109–125.

Bjorklund, D. F., Dukes, C., & Brown, R. D. (2009). The development of memory strategies. In M. L. Courage & N. Cowan, (Eds). *The development of memory in infancy and childhood* (pp. 146–175). Hove, UK: Psychology Press.

Blacher, J., Feinfield, K. A., & Kraemer, B. R. (2007). Supporting families who have children with disabilities. In A. Carr, G. O'Reilly, P. N. Walsh & J. McEvoy (Eds), *The handbook of intellectual disability and clinical psychology practice* (pp. 303–335). New York, NY: Routledge.

Blair, C. (2016). Executive function and early childhood education. *Current Opinion in Behavioral Sciences, 10*, 102–107.

Bleie, T. (2003). Evolution, brains and the predicament of sex in human cognition. *Sexualities, Evolution and Gender, 5*, 149–189.

Blumberg, F. (2008). *Freaks of nature: What anomalies tell us about development and evolution*. Oxford: Oxford University Press.

Boland, A. M., Haden, C. A., & Ornstein, P. A. (2003). Boosting children's memory by training mothers in the use of an elaborative conversational style as an event unfolds. *Journal of Cognition and Development, 4*, 39–65.

Bonifacci, P., Storti, M., Tobia, V., & Suardi, A. (2016). Specific learning disorders: A look inside children's and parents' psychological well-being and relationships. *Journal of Learning Disabilities, 49,* 532–545.

Bono, K. E., & Bizri, R. (2014) The role of language and private speech in pre-schoolers' self-regulation. *Early Child Development and Care, 184,* 658–670.

Brambring, L., & Asbrock, D. (2010). Validity of false belief tasks in blind children. *Journal of Autism and Developmental Disorders, 40,* 1471–1484.

Brant, A. M., Munakata, Y., Boomsma, D. I., DeFries, J. C., Haworth, C. M., Keller, M. C., Martin, N. G., McGue, M., Petrill, S. A., Plomin, R., et al (2013). The nature and nurture of high IQ: An extended sensitive period for intellectual development. *Psychological Science, 24,* 1487–1495

Briley, D. A., & Tucker-Drob, E. M. (2013). Explaining the increasing heritability of cognitive ability across development: A meta-analysis of longitudinal twin and adoption studies. *Psychological Science, 24,* 1704–1713.

Brinch, C. N., & Galloway, T. A. (2012). Schooling in adolescence raises IQ scores. *Proceedings of the National Academy of Sciences, 109,* 425–430.

Brown, A. L. (1989). Analogical learning and transfer: What develops? In S. Vosniadou & A. Ortony (Eds), *Similarity and analogical reasoning* (pp. 369–412). Cambridge: Cambridge University Press.

Brown, J. R., & Dunn, J. (1991). You can cry, Mum: The social and developmental implications of talk about internal states. *British Journal of Developmental Psychology, 9,* 237–256.

Bruck, M., Ceci, S. J., & Principe, G. F. (2006). The child and the law. In W. Damon, R. M. Lerner, K. A. Renninger & I. E. Sigel (Eds), *Handbook of child psychology, Sixth edition, Volume 4: Child psychology in practice* (pp. 776–816). New York, NY: Wiley.

Bruck, M., Ceci, S. J., Francoeur, E., & Renick, A. (1995b). Anatomically detailed dolls do not facilitate preschoolers' reports of a pediatric examination involving genital touching. *Journal of Experimental Psychology: Applied, 1,* 95–109.

Bugden, S., & Ansari, D. (2015). How can cognitive developmental neuroscience constrain our understanding of developmental dyscalculia? In S. Chinn (Ed.), *International handbook of dyscalculia and mathematical learning difficulties* (pp. 18–43). London: Routledge.

Buică-Belciu, C., & Popovici, D.-V. (2014). Being twice exceptional: Gifted students with learning disabilities. *Procedia-Social and Behavioral Sciences, 127,* 519–523.

Bulloch, M. J., & Opfer, J. E. (2009). What makes relational reasoning smart? Revisiting the relational shift in cognitive development. *Developmental Science, 12,* 114–122.

Burack, J. A., Russo, N., Kovshoff, H., Palma Fernandes, T., Ringo, J., Landry, O., & Iarocci, G. (2016). How I attend – not how well do I attend: Rethinking developmental frameworks of attention and cognition in autism spectrum disorder and typical development. *Journal of Cognition and Development, 17,* 553–567.

Burman, J. T. (2013). Updating the Baldwin effect: The biological levels behind Piaget's new theory. *New Ideas in Psychology, 31,* 363–373.

Bushnell, E. W., McKenzie, B. E., Lawrence, D. A., & Connell, S. (1995). The spatial coding strategies of 1-year-old infants in a locomotor search task. *Child Development, 66,* 937–958.

Buttelmann, D., Carpenter, M., & Tomasello, M. (2009). Eighteen-month-old infants show false belief understanding in an active helping paradigm. *Cognition, 112,* 337–342.

Buttelmann, D., Over, H., Carpenter, M., & Tomasello, M. (2014). Eighteen-month-olds understand false beliefs in an unexpected-contents task. *Journal of Experimental Child Psychology, 119,* 120–126.

Butterfill, S. A. (2007). What are modules and what is their role in development? *Mind and Language, 22 (4),* 450–473.

Butterworth, B. (2008). Developmental dyscalculia. In J. Reed & J. Warner-Rogers (Eds), *Child Neuropsychology* (pp. 274–357). Oxford: Blackwell.

Bybee, J., & Zigler, E. (1998). Outerdirectedness employed in individuals with and without mental retardation: A review. In R. M. Hodap, J. A. Burack, & E. Zigler (Eds), *Handbook of mental retardation and development* (pp. 434–461). Cambridge: Cambridge University Press.

Callaghan, T., Rochat, P., Liilard, A., Claux, M., Odden, H., Itakura, S., Tapanya, S., & Singh, S. (2005). Synchrony in the onset of mental state reasoning: Evidence from five cultures. *Psychological Science, 16,* 378–384.

Calvin, C. M., Fernandes, C., Smith, P., Visscher, P. M., & Deary, I. J. (2010). Sex, intelligence and educational achievement in a national cohort of over 175,000 11-year-old schoolchildren in England. *Intelligence, 38,* 424–432.

Campbell, F. A., & Ramey, C. T. (1994). Effects of early intervention on intellectual and academic achievement: A follow up study of children from low income families. *Child Development, 65,* 684–698.

Campbell, F. A., Ramey, C. T., Pungello, E., Sparling, J., & Miller-Johnson, S. (2002). Early childhood education: Young adult outcomes from the Abecedarian Project. *Applied Developmental Science, 6,* 42–57.

Campbell, M. E., & Cunnington, R. (2017). More than an imitation game: Top-down modulation of the human mirror system. *Neuroscience and Biobehavioral Reviews, 75,* 195–202.

Campbell, S. B., Halperin, J. M., & Sonuga-Barke, E. S. J. (2014). A developmental perspective on attention deficit/hyperactivity disorder (ADHD). In M. Lewis & K. Rudolp (Eds), *Handbook of developmental psychopathology* (pp. 427–448). New York, NY: Springer.

Campos, J. J., Anderson, D. I., Barbu-Roth, M. A., Hubbard, E. M., Hertenstein, M. J., & Witherington, D. (2000). Travel broadens the mind. *Infancy, 1,* 149–219.

Campos, J. J., Witherington, D., Anderson, D. I., Frankel, C. I., Uchiyama, I., & Barbu-Roth, M. (2008). Rediscovering development in infancy. *Child Development, 79,* 1625–1632.

Capron, C., & Duyme, M. (1989). Assessment of effects of socio-economic status on IQ in a full cross-fostering study. *Nature, 340,* 552–554.

Caraballo, R. H., Cejas, N., Chamorro, N., Kaltenmeier, M. C., Fortini, S., & Soprano, A. M. (2014). Landau–Kleffner syndrome: A study of 29 patients. *Seizure, 23,* 98–104.

Carey, S. (1985). *Conceptual change in childhood*. London: MIT Press.

Carey, S. (1992). Becoming a face expert. *Philosophical Transactions of the Royal Society of London. B: Biological Science, 335*, 95–103.

Carey, S., Zaitchik, D., & Bascandziev, I. (2015). Theories of development: In dialog with Jean Piaget. *Developmental Review, 38*, 36–54.

Carlson, S. M., Zelazo, P. D., & Faja, S. (2013). Executive function. In P. Zelazo (Ed.), *The Oxford handbook of developmental psychology, Volume 1* (pp. 706–743). Oxford: Oxford University Press.

Caron, A. J. (2009). Comprehension of the representational mind in infancy. *Developmental Review, 29*, 69–95.

Carpendale, J. I. M., & Chandler, M. J. (1996). On the distinction between false belief understanding and subscribing to an interpretive theory of mind. *Child Development, 67*, 1686–1706.

Carpendale, J. I. M., & Lewis, C. (2004). Constructing an understanding of mind: The development of children's social understanding within social interaction. *Behavioral and Brain Sciences, 27*, 79–151.

Carpendale, J. I. M., & Lewis, C. (2015). The development of social understanding. In R. M. Lerner, L. S. Liben & U. Mueller (Eds), *Handbook of child psychology and developmental science, Seventh edition, Volume 2: Cognitive processes* (pp. 381–424). Hoboken, NJ: Wiley.

Carpendale, J. I. M., Lewis, C., Susswein, N., & Lunn, J. (2009). Talking and thinking: The role of speech in social understanding. In A. Winsler, C. Fernyhough & I. Montero (Eds), *Private speech, executive functioning, and the development of verbal self-regulation* (pp. 83–94). Cambridge: Cambridge University Press.

Carpenter, M., & Call, J. (2002). The chemistry of social learning. *Developmental Science, 5*, 23–25.

Carr, A., & O'Reilly, G. (2016a). Diagnosis, classification and epidemiology. In A. Carr, G. O'Reilly, P. N. Walsh & J. McEvoy (Eds), *The handbook of intellectual disability and clinical psychology practice* (pp. 3–44). Hove, UK: Routledge.

Carr, A., & O'Reilly, G. (2016b). Lifespan development and the family lifecycle. In A. Carr, G. O'Reilly, P. N. Walsh & J. McEvoy (Eds), *The handbook of intellectual disability and clinical psychology practice* (pp. 45–74). Hove, UK: Routledge.

Carruthers, P. (2006). *The architecture of the mind: Massive modularity and the flexibility of thought*. Oxford: Oxford University Press.

Carruthers, P. (2008). Précis of the architecture of the mind: Massive modularity and the flexibility of thought. *Mind and Language, 23*, 257–262.

Case, R. (1985). *Intellectual development: Birth to adulthood*. London: Academic Press.

Case, R. (1998). The development of conceptual structures. In W. Damon & N. Eisenberg (Eds), *Handbook of child psychology, Fifth edition, Volume 3. Cognition, perception, and language* (pp. 311–388). New York, NY: Wiley.

Cattaneo, L., & Rizzolatti, G. (2009). The mirror neuron system. *Archives of Neurology, 66*, 557–560.

Cattell, R. B. (1963). Theory of fluid and crystallized intelligence: A critical experiment. *Journal of Educational Psychology, 54*, 1–22.

Ceci, S. J. (1991). How much does schooling influence general intelligence and its cognitive components? A reassessment of the evidence. *Developmental Psychology*, *27*, 703–722.

Ceci, S. J., & Kanaya, T. (2010). "Apples and oranges are both round": Furthering the discussion on the Flynn effect. *Journal of Psychoeducational Assessment*, *28*, 441–447.

Ceci, S. J., Kulkofsky, S., Klemfuss, Z., Sweeney, C. D., & Bruck, M. (2007). Unwarranted assumptions about children's testimonial accuracy. *Annual Review of Clinical Psychology*, *3*, 311–328.

Chabris, C. F., Hebert, B. M., Benjamin, D. J., Beauchamp, J., Cesarini, D., Van der Loos, M., Johannesson, M., Magnusson, P. K., Lichtenstein, P., Atwood, C. S., etal. (2012). Most reported genetic associations with general intelligence are probably false positives. *Psychological Science*, *23*, 1314–1323.

Charman, T. (2000). Theory of mind and the early diagnosis of autism. In S. Baron-Cohen, H. Tager-Flusberg & D. J. Cohen (Eds), *Understanding other minds, Second edition* (pp. 422–441). Oxford: Oxford University Press.

Chen, J.-Q., & Gardner, H. (1997). Alternate assessment from a multiple intelligences theoretical perspective. In D. P. Flanagan, J. L. Genshaft & P. L. Harrison (Eds), *Contemporary intellectual assessment* (pp. 105–212). London: Guilford Press.

Chen, Z., & Klahr, D. (2008). Remote transfer of scientific reasoning and problem-solving strategies in children. In R. V. Kail (Ed.), *Advances in child development and behavior, Volume 36* (pp. 419–470). Amsterdam: Elsevier.

Cheng, P. W., & Holyoak, K. J. (1985). Pragmatic reasoning schema. *Cognitive Psychology*, *17*, 391–416.

Cheng, Y.-L., & Mix, K. S. (2014). Spatial training improves children's mathematics ability. *Journal of Cognition and Development*, *15*, 2–11.

Chi, M. T. H., & Koeske, R. D. (1983). Network representation of a child's dinosaur knowledge. *Developmental Psychology*, *19*, 29–39.

Chinn, S. (2015). The Routledge international handbook of dyscalculia and mathematical learning difficulties: An overview. In S. Chinn (Ed.), *The Routledge international handbook of dyscalculia and mathematical learning difficulties* (pp. 1–17). New York, NY: Routledge.

Chomsky, N. (2000). *New horizons in the study of language and mind*. Cambridge: Cambridge University Press.

Christianson, S. Å., Azad, A., Leander, L., & Selenius, H. (2013). Children as witnesses to homicidal violence: What they remember and report. *Psychiatry, Psychology and Law*, *20*, 366–383.

Clark, A. (2008). Pressing the flesh: A tension in the study of the embodied, embedded mind? *Philosophy and Phenomenological Research*, *76*, 37–59.

Clark, E. V. (1973). What's in a word? On the child's acquisition of semantics in his first language. In T. E. Moore (Ed.), *Cognitive development and the acquisition of language* (pp. 65–110). New York, NY: Academic Press.

Clarke, B., Doabler, C. T., Smolkowski, K., Baker, S. K., Fien, H., & Strand Cary, M. (2016). Examining the efficacy of a Tier 2 kindergarten mathematics intervention. *Journal of Learning Disabilities*, *49*, 152–165.

Cohen, L. B., & Cashon, C. H. (2006). Infant cognition. In W. Damon & R. M. Lerner (Eds), *Handbook of child psychology, Sixth edition, Volume 1: Theoretical models of human development* (pp. 793–828). New York, NY: Wiley.

Cohen, L. B., Chaput, H. H., & Cashon, C. H. (2002). A constructivist model of infant cognition. *Cognitive Development, 17*, 1323–1343.

Cole, M. (2005). Cross-cultural and historical perspectives on developmental consequences of education. *Human Development, 48*, 195–216.

Cole, M. (2006). Internationalization in psychology: We need it now more than ever. *American Psychologist, 61*, 904–917.

Colombo, J. (2001). Infants' detection of contingency: A cognitive-neuroscience perspective. *Bulletin of the Menninger Clinic, 65*, 321–334.

Conn, C. (2014). Investigating the social engagement of children with autism in mainstream schools for the purpose of identifying learning targets. *Journal of Research in Special Educational Needs, 14*, 153–159.

Conway, A. R., & Kovacs, K. (2015). New and emerging models of human intelligence. *Wiley Interdisciplinary Reviews: Cognitive Science, 6*, 419–426.

Cordón, I. M., Pipe, M. E., Sayfan, L., Melinder, A., & Goodman, G. S. (2004). Memory for traumatic experiences in early childhood. *Developmental Review, 24*, 101–132.

Corrigan, R., & Denton, P. (1996). Causal understanding as a developmental primitive. *Developmental Review, 16*, 162–202.

Cortese, S., Ferrin, M., Brandeis, D., Buitelaar, J., Daley, D., Dittmann, R. W., Holtmann, M., Santosh, P., Stevenson, J., Stringaris, A., etal. (2015). Cognitive training for attention-deficit/hyperactivity disorder: Meta-analysis of clinical and neuropsychological outcomes from randomized controlled trials. *Journal of the American Academy of Child and Adolescent Psychiatry, 54*, 164–174.

Cortina, M., & Liotti, G. (2010). Attachment is about safety and protection, intersubjectivity is about sharing and social understanding. *Psychoanalytic Psychology, 27*, 410–441.

Coull, G. J., Leekam, S. R., & Bennett, M. (2006). Simplifying second-order belief attribution: What facilitates children's performance on measures of conceptual understanding? *Social Development, 15*, 260–275.

Cowan, N. (2014). Short-term and working memory in childhood. In P. J. Bauer & R. Fivush (Eds), *The Wiley handbook on the development of children's memory, Volume 2* (pp. 202–229). Chichester, UK: Wiley.

Crippa, A., Marzocchi, G. M., Piroddi, C., Besana, D., Giribone, S., Vio, C., Maschietto, D., Fornaro, E., Repossi, S., & Sora, M. L. (2015). An integrated model of executive functioning is helpful for understanding ADHD and associated disorders. *Journal of Attention Disorders, 19*, 455–467.

Cronch, L. E., Viljoen J. L., & Hansen, D. J. (2006). Forensic interviewing in child sexual abuse cases: Current techniques and future directions. *Aggression and Violent Behavior, 11*, 195–207.

Cuevas, K., Rajan, V., Morasch, K. C., & Bell, M. A. (2015). Episodic memory and future thinking during early childhood: Linking the past and future. *Developmental Psychobiology, 57*, 552–565.

Cutting, A. L., & Dunn, J. (2002). The cost of understanding other people: Social cognition predicts young children's sensitivity to criticism. *Journal of Child Psychology and Psychiatry and Allied Disciplines, 43*, 849–860.

D'Souza, D., & Karmiloff-Smith, A. (2011). When modularization fails to occur: A developmental perspective. *Cognitive Neuropsychology, 28*, 276–287.

Dahlgren, S. O., Dahlgren Sandberg, A., & Larsson, M. (2010). Theory of mind in children with severe speech and physical impairments. *Research in Developmental Disabilities, 31*, 617–624.

Daley, T. C., Whaley, S. E., Sigman, M. D., Espinosa, M.P., & Neumann, C. (2003). IQ on the rise: The Flynn effect in rural Kenyan children. *Psychological Science, 14*, 215–219.

Damon, W. (1984). Peer education: The untapped potential. *Journal of Applied Developmental Psychology, 5*, 331–343.

Damon, W., & Phelps, E. (1989). Strategic uses of peer learning in children's education. In T. J. Berndt & G.-W. Ladd (Eds), *Peer relationships in child development* (pp. 135–157). New York, NY: Wiley.

Danforth, J. S., Connor, D. F., & Doerfler, L. A. (2016). The development of comorbid conduct problems in children with ADHD: An example of an integrative developmental psychopathology perspective. *Journal of Attention Disorders, 20*, 214–229.

Dapul, H., & Laraque, D. (2014). Lead poisoning in children. *Advances in Pediatrics, 61*, 313–333.

de Rosnay, M., Pons, F., Harris, P. L., & Morrell, J. (2004). A lag between understanding false belief and emotion attribution in young children: Relationships with linguistic ability and mothers' mental-state language. *British Journal of Developmental Psychology, 22*, 197–218.

Deary, I. J., Pattie, A., & Starr, J. M. (2013). The stability of intelligence from age 11 to age 90 years: The Lothian birth cohort of 1921. *Psychological Science, 24*, 2361–2368.

Delgado, B., Gómez, J. C., & Sarriá, E. (2009). Private pointing and private speech: Developing parallelisms. In A. Winsler, C. Fernyhough & I. Montero (Eds), *Private speech, executive functioning, and the development of verbal self-regulation* (pp. 162–163). New York, NY: Cambridge University Press.

Delgado, B., Gómez, J. C., & Sarriá, E. (2011). Pointing gestures as a cognitive tool in young children: Experimental evidence. *Journal of Experimental Child Psychology, 110*, 299–312.

DeLoache, J. S., & Marzolf, D. P. (1995). The use of dolls to interview young children: Issues of symbolic representation. *Journal of Experimental Child Psychology, 60*, 155–173.

DeLoache, J. S., Miller, K. F., & Pierroutsakos, S. L. (1998). Reasoning and problem solving. In W. Damon, D. Kuhn & R. S. Siegler (Eds), *Handbook of child psychology, Fifth edition, Volume 2: Cognition, perception, and language* (pp. 801–850). New York, NY: Wiley.

DeMarie, D., & López, L. M. (2014). Memory in schools. In P. J. Bauer & R. Fivush (Eds), *The Wiley handbook on the development of children's memory, Volume 2* (pp. 836–864). Chichester, UK: Wiley.

Demetriou, A., Christou, C., Spanoudis, G., & Platsidou, M. (2002). The development of mental processing: Efficiency, working memory, and thinking. *Monographs of the Society of Research in Child Development, 67*, 268.

Dempster, F. N. (1981). Memory span: Sources of individual and developmental differences. *Psychological Bulletin, 89*, 63–100.

Desforges, C. (1998). Learning and teaching: Current views and perspectives. In D. Shorrocks-Taylor (Ed.), *Directions in educational psychology* (pp. 5–18). London: Whurr.

deVries, R. (2000). Vygotsky, Piaget, and education: A reciprocal assimilation of theories and educational practices. *New Ideas in Psychology, 18*, 187–213.

Diamond, A. (2013). Executive functions. *Annual Review of Psychology, 64*, 135–168.

Diamond, A., & Lee, K. (2011). Interventions shown to aid executive function development in children 4 to 12 years old. *Science, 333* (*6045*), 959–964.

Diamond, A., & Ling, D. S. (2016). Conclusions about interventions, programs, and approaches for improving executive functions that appear justified and those that, despite much hype, do not. *Developmental Cognitive Neuroscience, 18*, 34–48.

Dickens, W. T., & Flynn, J. R. (2006a). Black Americans reduce the racial IQ gap: Evidence from standardization samples. *Psychological Science, 17*, 913–920.

Dickens, W. T., & Flynn, J. R. (2006b). Common ground and differences. *Psychological Science, 17*, 923–924.

Ding, X. P., Wellman, H. M., Wang, Y., Fu, G., & Lee, K. (2015). Theory-of-mind training causes honest young children to lie. *Psychological Science, 26*, 1812–1821.

Doggett, A. M. (2004). ADHD and drug therapy: Is it still a valid treatment? *Journal of Child Health Care, 8*, 69–81.

Doherty, M. J. (2009). *Theory of mind: How children understand others' thoughts and feelings*. Hove, UK: Psychology Press.

Doise, W. (1978). *Groups and individuals: Explanantions in social psychology*. Cambridge: Cambridge University Press.

Donaldson, M. (1978). *Children's minds*. London: Fontana.

Donlan, C. (2015). Linguistic factors in the development of basic calculation. In S. Chinn (Ed.), *The Routledge international handbook of dyscalculia and mathematical learning difficulties* (pp. 346–356). Abingdon, UK: Routledge.

Dowker, A. (2017). Interventions for primary school children with difficulties in mathematics. *Advances in Child Development and Behavior, 53*, 255–287.

Dramé, C., & Ferguson, C. J. (2019). Measurements of intelligence in sub-Saharan Africa: Perspectives gathered from research in Mali. *Current Psychology, 38*, 110–115.

Duncan, R., & Tarulli, D. (2009). On the persistence of private speech: Empirical and theoretical considerations. In A. Winsler, C. Fernyhough & I. Montero (Eds), *Private speech, executive functioning, and the development of verbal self-regulation* (pp. 176–187). New York, NY: Cambridge University Press.

Dunn, J., Brown, J. R., & Beardsall, J. (1991). Family talk about feeling states and children's later understanding of others' emotions. *Developmental Psychology, 27*, 448–455.

Dunn, J., & Cutting, A. L. (1999). Understanding others, and individual differences in friendship interactions in young children. *Social Development, 8*, 201–219.

Dunn, L., & Dunn, D. (2007). *Peabody Picture Vocabulary Test, Fourth edition* (PPVT-IV). Bloomington, MN: Pearson.

Dye, M. W., & Hauser, P. C. (2014). Sustained attention, selective attention and cognitive control in deaf and hearing children. *Hearing Research, 309,* 94–102.

Eimas, P. D., & Quinn, P. C. (1994). Studies on the formation of perceptually based basic-level categories in young infants. *Child Development, 65,* 903–917.

Eisen, M. L., Goodman, G. S., Qin, J. J., & Davis, S. L. (2002). Memory and suggestibility in maltreated children: Age, stress arousal, dissociation, and psychopathology. *Journal of Experimental Child Psychology, 83,* 167–212.

Elkind, D. (1976). *Child development and education.* Oxford: Oxford University Press.

Ellefson, M. R., Ng, F. F. Y., Wang, Q., & Hughes, C. (2017). Efficiency of executive function: A two-generation cross-cultural comparison of samples from Hong Kong and the United Kingdom. *Psychological Science, 28,* 555–566.

Elliott, J. G., & Grigorenko, E. L. (2014). *The dyslexia debate.* Cambridge: Cambridge University Press.

Elman, J. L. (2005). Connections models of development: Where next? *Trends in Cognitive Science, 9,* 111–117.

Elman, J. L., Bates, E. A., Johnson, M. H., Karmiloff-Smith, A., Parisi, D., & Plunkett, K. (1996). *Rethinking innateness. A connectionist perspective on development.* London: MIT Press.

Elsner, B. (2005). Novelty and complexity: Two problems in animal (and human) imitation. In S. L. Hurley & N. Chater (Eds), *Perspectives on imitation: From neuroscience to social science, Volume 1* (pp. 287–290). Cambridge, MA: MIT Press.

Elsner, B. (2007). Infants' imitation of goal-directed actions: The role of movements and action effects. *Acta Psychologica, 124,* 44–59.

Emerson, J. (2015). The enigma of dyscalculia. In S. Chinn (Ed.), *International handbook of dyscalculia and mathematical learning difficulties* (pp. 217–227). Abingdon, UK: Routledge.

Ensor, R., Devine, R. T., Marks, A., & Hughes, C. (2014). Mothers' cognitive references to 2-year-olds predict Theory of Mind at ages 6 and 10. *Child Development, 85,* 1222–1235.

Ewing, D., Zeigler-Hill, V., & Vonk, J. (2016). Spitefulness and deficits in the social–perceptual and social–cognitive components of Theory of Mind. *Personality and Individual Differences, 91,* 7–13.

Ezkurdia, I., Juan, D., Rodriguez, J. M., Frankish, A., Diekhans, M., Harrow, J., Vazquez, J., Valencia, A., & Tress, M. L. (2014). Multiple evidence strands suggest that there may be as few as 19 000 human protein-coding genes. *Human Molecular Genetics, 23,* 5866–5878.

Fabbri-Destro, M., & Rizzolatti, G. (2008). Mirror neurons and mirror systems in monkeys and humans. *Physiology, 23,* 171–179.

Fagan, J. F., & Detterman, D. K. (1992). The Fagan Test of Infant Intelligence: A technical summary. *Journal of Applied Developmental Psychology, 13,* 173–193.

Fagan, J. F., & Holland, C. R. (2007). Racial equality in intelligence: Predictions from a theory of intelligence as processing. *Intelligence, 35* (4), 319–334.

Fagan, J. F., Holland, C. R., & Wheeler, K. (2007). The prediction from infancy of adult IQ and achievement. *Intelligence, 35,* 22–231.

Fan, J. (2013) Attentional network deficits in autism spectrum disorders. In J. D. Buxbaum & P. R. Hof (Eds), *The neuroscience of autism spectrum disorders* (pp. 281–288). Oxford: Elsevier.

Feinfield, K. A., Lee, P. P., Flavell, E. R., Green, F. L., & Flavell, J. H. (1999). Young children's understanding of intention. *Cognitive Development, 14,* 463–486.

Feldman, D. H. (2004). Piaget's stages: The unfinished symphony of cognitive development. *New Ideas in Psychology, 22,* 175–231.

Ferrara, K., & Landau, B. (2015). Geometric and featural systems, separable and combined: Evidence from reorientation in people with Williams syndrome. *Cognition, 144,* 123–133.

Fessakis, G., Gouli, E., & Mavroudi, E. (2013). Problem solving by 5–6 years old kindergarten children in a computer programming environment: A case study. *Computers and Education, 63,* 87–97.

Fias, W., Menon, V., & Szucs, D. (2013). Multiple components of developmental dyscalculia. *Trends in Neuroscience and Education, 2,* 43–47.

Fink, E., Begeer, S., Peterson, C. C., Slaughter, V., & Rosnay, M. (2015). Friendlessness and theory of mind: A prospective longitudinal study. *British Journal of Developmental Psychology, 33,* 1–17.

Fivush, R. (1997). Event memory in early childhood. In N. Cowan (Ed.), *The development of memory in childhood* (pp. 139–161). Hove, UK: Psychology Press.

Fivush, R. (2009). Coconstructing memories and meaning over time. In J. A. Quas & R. Fivush (Eds), *Emotion and memory in development* (pp. 343–354). Oxford: Oxford University Press.

Fivush, R. (2011). The development of autobiographical memory. *Annual Review of Psychology, 62,* 559–582.

Fivush, R., Haden, C. A., & Reese, E. (2006). Elaborating on elaborations: The role of maternal reminiscing style on children's cognitive and socioemotional development. *Child Development, 77,* 1568–1588.

Fivush, R., & Hamond, N. R. (1989). Time and again: Effects of repetition and retention interval on 2-year-olds' event recall. *Journal of Experimental Child Psychology, 47,* 259–273.

Fivush, R., & Hamond, N. R. (1990). Autobiographical memory across the preschool years: Toward reconceptualizing childhood amnesia. In R. Fivush & J. A. Hudson (Eds), *Emory symposia in cognition, Volume 3. Knowing and remembering in young children* (pp. 223–248). New York, NY: Cambridge University Press.

Fivush, R., Kue bli, J., & Clubb, P. A. (1992). The structure of events and event representations: A developmental analysis. *Child Development, 63,* 188–201.

Fivush, R., & Nelson, K. (2004). Culture and language in the emergence of autobiographical memory. *Psychological Science, 15,* 573–577.

Flavell, J. H. (1971). Stage related properties of cognitive development. *Cognitive Psychology, 2,* 421–453.

Flavell, J. H. (1992). Perspectives on perspective taking. In H. Beilin & P. B. Pufall (Eds), *Piaget's theory: Prospects and possibilities* (pp. 107–139). Hillsdale, NJ: Erlbaum.

Flavell, J. H. (2004). Development of knowledge about vision. In D. T. Levin (Ed.), *Thinking and seeing: Visual metacognition in adults and children* (pp. 13–36). Cambridge, MA: MIT Press.

Flavell, J. H., Beach, D. R., & Chinsky, J. M. (1966). Spontaneous verbal rehearsal in a memory task as a function of age. *Child Development, 37*, 283–299.

Flavell, J. H., Botkin, P. T., Fry, C. L., Wright, J. V., & Jarvis, P. E. (1968). *The development of role-taking and communication skills in children.* New York, NY: John Wiley.

Fletcher, J. M., Stuebing, K. K., & Hughes, L. C. (2010). IQ scores should be corrected for the Flynn effect in high-stakes decisions. *Journal of Psychoeducational Assessment, 28*, 469–473.

Fletcher-Watson, S., Collis, J. M., Findlay, J. M., & Leekam, S. R. (2009). The development of change blindness: Children's attentional priorities whilst viewing naturalistic scenes. *Developmental Science, 12*, 438–445.

Fletcher-Watson, S., McConnell, F., Manola, E., & McConachie, H. (2014). Interventions based on the Theory of Mind cognitive model for autism spectrum disorder (ASD). *The Cochrane Library.*

Flynn, E., Pine, K. J., & Lewis, C. (2007). Using the microgenetic method to investigate cognitive development: An introduction. *Infant and Child Development, 15*, 1–6.

Flynn, J. R. (1998). IQ gains over time: Toward finding the causes. In U. Neisser (Ed.), *The rising curve* (pp. 25–66). Washington, DC: American Psychological Association.

Flynn, J. R., & Shayer, M. (2018). IQ decline and Piaget: Does the rot start at the top? *Intelligence, 66*, 112–121.

Fodor, J. (1983). *Modularity of mind: An essay on faculty psychology.* Cambridge, MA: MIT Press.

Fodor, J. (1985). Précis of "Modularity of mind". *Behavioral and Brain Sciences, 8*, 1–42.

Fonagy, P., Gergely, G., & Jurist, E. L. (Eds) (2004). *Affect regulation, mentalization and the development of the self.* London: Karnac books.

Fonagy, P., Gergely, G., Jurist, E., & Target. (2002). *Affect regulation, mentalization and the development of the self.* New York, NY: Other Press.

Franklin, T. (2017). Best practices in multicultural assessment of cognition. In R. S. McCallum (Ed.), *Handbook of nonverbal assessment, Second edition* (pp. 39–46). Cham, Switzerland: Springer.

Freeman, N. H., & Lacohée, H. (1995). Making explicit 3-year-olds' implicit competence with their own false beliefs. *Cognition, 56*, 31–60.

Freud, S. (1905). *Three essays on the theory of sexuality.* London: Allen and Unwin.

Frick, P. J., Ray, J. V., Thornton, L. C., & Kahn, R. E. (2014). Annual research review: A developmental psychopathology approach to understanding callous-unemotional traits in children and adolescents with serious conduct problems. *Journal of Child Psychology and Psychiatry, 55*, 532–548.

Friedman, W. J. (2005). Developmental and cognitive perspectives on humans' sense of the times of past and future events. *Learning and Motivation, 36,* 145–158.

Friedman, W. J. (2014). The development of memory for the times of past events. In P. J. Bauer & R. Fivush (Eds), *The Wiley-Blackwell handbook on the development of children's memory* (pp. 394–407). Chichester, UK: Wiley-Blackwell.

Friedman, W. J., Gardner, A. G., & Zubin, N. R. E. (1995). Children's comparisons of the recency of two events from the past year. *Child Development, 66,* 970–983.

Friedman, W. J., Cederborg, A.-C., Hultman, E., Änghagen, O., & Magnusson, K. F. (2010). Children's memory for the duration of a paediatric consultation. *Applied Cognitive Psychology, 24,* 545–556.

Friedman, W. J., Reese, E., & Dai, X. (2011). Children's memory for the times of events from the past years. *Applied Cognitive Psychology, 25,* 156–165.

Furth, H. G., & Wachs, H. (1975). *Thinking goes to school: Piaget's theory in practice.* Oxford: Oxford University Press.

Gagné, F. (2004) Transforming gifts into talents: The DMGT as a developmental theory. *High Ability Studies, 15,* 119–147.

Gardner, H. (1983). *Frames of mind: The theory of multiple intelligence.* New York, NY: Basic Books.

Gardner, H. (1993). *Multiple intelligences: The theory in practice.* New York, NY: Basic Books.

Gardner, H. (2006). *Multiple intelligences: New horizons.* New York, NY: Basic Books.

Gathercole, S. E., Pickering, S. J., Ambridge, B., & Wearing, H. (2004). The structure of working memory from 4 to 15 years of age. *Developmental Psychology, 40,* 177–190.

Gauvain, M., & Perez, S. (2015). Cognitive development and culture. In R. M. Lerner, L. S. Liben & U. Müller (Eds), *Handbook of child psychology and developmental science, Seventh edition, Volume 2: Cognitive processes* (pp. 854–896) Hoboken, NJ: Wiley.

Geary, D. C. (2015). The classification and cognitive characteristics of mathematical disabilities in children. In R. C. Kadosh & A. Dowker (Eds), *Oxford handbook of numerical cognition* (pp. 767–786). Oxford: Oxford University Press.

Geary, D. C., Hoard, M. K., Nugent, L., & Bailey, H. D. (2013). Adolescents' functional numeracy is predicted by their school entry number system knowledge. *Plos One, 8* (1), e54651.

Gelman, R., & Williams, E. M. (1998). Enabling constraints for cognitive development and learning: Domain specificity and epigenesis. In W. Damon, D. Kuhn & R. S. Siegler (Eds), *Handbook of child psychology, Volume 2: Cognition, perception and language* (pp. 575–630). New York, NY: Wiley.

Gerber, P. J. (2012). The impact of learning disabilities on adulthood: A review of the evidenced-based literature for research and practice in adult education. *Journal of Learning Disabilities, 45,* 31–46.

Gersten, R., Chard, D. J., Jayanthi, M., Baker, S. K., Morphy, P., & Flojo, J. (2009). Mathematics instruction for students with learning disabilities: A meta-analysis of instructional components. *Review of Educational Research, 79,* 1202–1242.

Gersten, R., Rolfhus, E., Clarke, B., Decker, L. E., Wilkins, C., & Dimino, J. (2015). Intervention for first graders with limited number knowledge: Large-scale replication of a randomized controlled trial. *American Educational Research Journal*, *52*, 516–546.

Gibson, E. J., & Schmuckler, M. A. (1989). Going somewhere: An ecological and experimental approach to development of mobility. *Ecological Psychology*, *1*, 3–25.

Gifford, S., & Rockliffe, F. (2012). Mathematics difficulties: Does one approach fit all? *Research in Mathematics Education*, *14*, 1–15.

Gigerenzer, G., & Gaissmaier, W. (2011). Heuristic decision making. *Annual Review of Psychology*, *62*, 451–482.

Gillies, R. M. (2003). The behaviors, interactions, and perceptions of junior high school students during smallgroup learning. *Journal of Educational Psychology*, *95*, 137 –147.

Gillies, R. M. (2014). Cooperative learning: Developments in research. *International Journal of Educational Psychology*, *3*, 125–140.

Gillum, J. (2012). Dyscalculia: Issues for practice in educational psychology. *Educational Psychology in Practice*, *28*, 287–297.

Gilman, B. J., Lovecky, D. V., Kearney, K., Peters, D. B., Wasserman, J. D., Silverman, L. K., Postma, M. G., Robinson, N. M., Amend, E. R., Ryder-Schoeck, M., etal. (2013). Critical issues in the identification of gifted students with co-existing disabilities: The twice-exceptional. *Sage Open*, *3*, 2158244013505855.

Girotto, V., Light, P., & Colbourn, C. (1988). Pragmatic schemas and conditional reasoning in children. *The Quarterly Journal of Experimental Psychology*, *40*, 469–482.

Glenberg, A. M. (2010). Embodiment as a unifying perspective for psychology. *Wiley Interdisciplinary Reviews: Cognitive Science*, *1*, 586–596.

Goldstein, S. (2015). The evolution of intelligence. In S. Goldstein, D. Princiotta & J. A. Naglieri (Eds), *Handbook of intelligence* (pp. 3–7). New York, NY: Springer.

Goldstein, S., &. Naglieri, J. A. (Eds) (2014). *Handbook of executive functioning*. New York, NY: Springer.

Gómez, J. C. (2005). Species comparative studies and cognitive development. *Trends in Cognitive Science*, *9*, 118–125.

Goodman, G. S., & Reed, R. S. (1986). Age differences in eyewitness testimony. *Law and Human Behavior*, *10*, 317–322.

Goodman, G. S., Bottoms, B., Schwartz-Kenney, B., & Rudy, L. (1991). Children's memory for a stressful event: Improving children's reports. *Journal of Narrative and Life History*, *1*, 69–99.

Goodman, G. S., Rudy, L., Bottoms, B., & Aman, C. (1990). Children's concerns and memory: Issues of ecological validity in the study of children's eyewitness testimony. In R. Fivush & J. Hudson (Eds), *Knowing and remembering in young children* (pp. 249–284). Cambridge: Cambridge University Press.

Gopnik, A., & Astington, J. W. (1988). Children's understanding of representational change and its relation to the understanding of false belief and the appearance–reality distinction. *Child Development*, *59*, 26–37.

Gopnik, A., & Bonawitz, E. (2015). Bayesian models of child development. *Wiley Interdisciplinary Reviews: Cognitive Science*, *6*, 75–86.

Gopnik, A., & Meltzoff, A. N. (1997). *Words, thoughts and theories*. London: MIT Press.

Gordon, R. M. (1986). Folk psychology as simulation. *Mind and Language, 1*, 158–171.

Goswami, U. (1992). *Analogical reasoning in children*. Hillsdale, NJ: Lawrence Erlbaum.

Gottesman, I. I. (1963). Genetic aspects of intelligent behavior. In N. R. Ellis (Ed.), *Handbook of mental deficiency: Psychological theory and research* (pp. 253–296). New York, NY: McGraw-Hill.

Gouze, K. R. (1987). Attention and social problem solving as correlates of aggression in preschool males. *Journal of Abnormal Child Psychology, 15*, 181–197.

Graefen, J., Kohn, J., Wyschkon, A., & Esser, G. (2015). Internalizing problems in children and adolescents with math disability. *Zeitschrift für Psychologie, 22*, 93–101.

Grant, C. M., Riggs, K. J., & Boucher, J. (2004). Counterfactual and mental state reasoning in children with autism. *Journal of Autism and Developmental Disorders, 34*, 177–188.

Green, A. E., Kenworthy, L., Mosner, M. G., Gallagher, N. M., Fearon, E. W., Balhana, C. D., & Yerys, B. E. (2014). Abstract analogical reasoning in high-functioning children with autism spectrum disorders. *Autism Research, 7*, 677–686.

Green, K. B., & Gallagher, P. A. (2014). Mathematics for young children: A review of the literature with implications for children with disabilities. *Bas,kent University Journal of Education, 1*, 81–92.

Green, S., Pring, L., & Swettenham, J. (2004). An investigation of first-order false belief understanding of children with congenital profound visual impairment. *British Journal of Developmental Psychology, 22*, 1–17.

Green, S. K., & Gredler, M. E. (2002). A review and analysis of constructivism for school-based practice. *School Psychology Review, 31*, 53–70.

Greenfield, P. M. (1998). The cultural evolution of IQ. In U. Neisser (Ed.), *The rising curve* (pp. 81–123). Washington, DC: American Psychological Association.

Greenspan, S. I., & Woods, G. W. (2014). Intellectual disability as a disorder of reasoning and judgement: The gradual move away from intelligence quotient-ceilings. *Current Opinion in Psychiatry, 27*, 110–116.

Griffiths, P. (1986). Early vocabulary. In P. Fletcher & M. Garman (Eds), *Language acquisition, Second edition* (pp. 279–306). Cambridge: Cambridge University Press.

Grigorenko, E. L. (2007). Rethinking disorders of spoken and written language: Generating workable hypotheses. *Journal of Developmental and Behavioral Pediatrics, 28*, 478–486.

Grigorenko, E. L., Klin, A., & Volkmar, F. (2003). Annotation: Hyperlexia: Disability or superability? *Journal of Child Psychology and Psychiatry, 44*, 1079–1091.

Guilford, J. P. (1988). Some changes in the structure of intellect model. *Educational and Psychological Measurement, 48*, 1–4.

Guillaume, P. (1926). *Imitation in children*. Chicago: University of Chicago Press.

Guralnick, M. J. (2011). Why early intervention works: A systems perspective. *Infants and Young Children, 24*, 6–28.

Guralnick, M. J. (2017). Early intervention for children with intellectual disabilities: An update. *Journal of Applied Research in Intellectual Disabilities*, *30*, 211–229.

Hala, S., & Carpendale, J. I. M. (1997). All in the mind: Children's understanding of mental life. In S. Hala (Ed.), *The development of social cognition* (pp. 189–329). Hove, UK: Psychology Press.

Halford, G. S. (1989). Reflections on 25 years of Piagetian cognitive psychology. *Human Development*, *32*, 325–357.

Halford, G. S. (1992). Analogical reasoning and conceptual complexity in cognitive development. *Human Development*, *35*, 193–217.

Halford, G. S., & Andrews, G. (2004). The development of deductive reasoning: How important is complexity? *Thinking and Reasoning*, *10*, 123–145.

Halford, G. S., & Andrews, G. (2006). Reasoning and problem solving. In D. Kuhn & R. Siegler (Eds), *Handbook of child psychology, Volume 2. Cognitive, language and perceptual development* (pp. 557–608). Hoboken, NJ: Wiley.

Halford, G. S., & Andrews, G. (2011). Information processing models of cognitive development. In U. Goswami (Ed.), *The Wiley-Blackwell handbook of childhood cognitive development* (pp. 697–722). Oxford: Blackwell.

Hall, I., Strydom, A., Richards, M., Hardy, R., Bernal, J., & Wadsworth, M. (2005). Social outcomes in adulthood of children with intellectual impairment: Evidence from a birth cohort. *Journal of Intellectual Disability Research*, *49*, 171–182.

Halonen, A., Aunola, K., Ahonen, T., & Nurmi, J. E. (2006). The role of learning to read in the development of problem behaviour: A cross-lagged longitudinal study. *British Journal of Educational Psychology*, *76*, 517–534.

Halpern, D. F., Benbow, C. P., Geary, D. C., Gur, R., Hyde, J. S., & Gernsbacher, M. A. (2007). The science of sex differences in science and mathematics. *Psychological Science in the Public Interest*, *8*, 1–51.

Hamilton, A. F. de C. (2009). Research review: Goals, intentions and mental states: Challenges for theories of autism. *Journal of Child Psychology and Psychiatry*, *50*, 881–892.

Hannula, M. M., Lepola, J., & Lehtinen, E. (2010). Spontaneous focusing on numerosity as a domain-specific predictor of arithmetical skills. *Journal of Experimental Child Psychology*, *107*, 394–406.

Hanscombe, K. B., Trzaskowski, M., Haworth, C. M., Davis, O. S., Dale, P. S., & Plomin, R. (2012). Socioeconomic status (SES) and children's intelligence (IQ): In a UK-representative sample SES moderates the environmental, not genetic, effect on IQ. *PLoS One*, *7* (*2*), e30320.

Happé, F. G. E. (1994). *Autism: An introduction to psychological theory*. London: University College London Press.

Happé, F. G. E., & Conway, J. R. (2016). Recent progress in understanding skills and impairments in social cognition. *Current Opinion in Pediatrics*, *28*, 736–742.

Happé, F. G. E., & Ronald, A. (2008). The "fractionable autism triad": A review of evidence from behavioural, genetic, cognitive and neural research. *Neuropsychology Review*, *18*, 287–304.

Harner, L. (1975). Yesterday and tomorrow: Development of early understanding of the terms. *Developmental Psychology*, *11*, 864–865.

Harris, J. C., & Greenspan, S. (2016). Definition and nature of intellectual disability. In N. N. Singh (Ed.), *Handbook of evidence-based practices in intellectual and developmental disabilities* (pp. 11–39). Cham, Switzerland: Springer.

Harris, P. L. (1992). From simulation to folk psychology: The case for development. *Mind and Language, 7*, 120–144.

Harris, P. L., & Núñez, M. (1996). Understanding of permission rules by preschool children. *Child Development, 67*, 1572–1591.

Harris, P. L., & Want, S. (2005). On learning what not to do: The emergence of selective imitation in tool use by young children. In S. Hurley & N. Chater, (Eds) *Perspectives on imitation: From neuroscience to social science, Volume 2* (pp. 149–162). Cambridge, MA: MIT Press.

Hartshorn, K. (2003). Reinstatement maintains a memory in human infants for 1½ years. *Developmental Psychobiology, 42*, 269–282.

Hay, D. F. (2014). Social cognition: Commentary: Do theory of mind deficits lead to psychopathology or is it the other way around? *Journal of Personality Disorders, 28*, 96–100.

Hayes, B. K., Heit, E., & Swendsen, H. (2010). Inductive reasoning. *Wiley Interdisciplinary Reviews: Cognitive Science, 1*, 278–292.

Hayne, H. (1990). The effect of multiple reminders on long term retention in human infants. *Developmental Psychobiology, 23*, 453–477.

Hayne, H., & Jack, F. (2011). Childhood amnesia. *Wiley Interdisciplinary Reviews: Cognitive Science, 2*, 136–145.

Hayne, H., MacDonald, S., & Barr, R. (1997). Developmental changes in the specificity of memory over the second year of life. *Infant Behavior and Development, 20*, 237–249.

Heimann, M., Nelson, K. E., & Schaller, J. (1989). Neonatal imitation of tongue protrusion and mouth opening: Methodological aspects and evidence of early individual differences. *Scandinavian Journal of Psychology, 30*, 90–101.

Hemmer, I., Hemmer, M., Neidhardt, E., Obermaier, G., Uphues, R., & Wrenger, K. (2015). The influence of children's prior knowledge and previous experience on their spatial orientation skills in an urban environment. *Education 3–13, 43*, 184–196.

Henik, A., Rubinsten, O., & Ashkenazi, S. (2011). The "where" and "what" of developmental dyscalculia. *Clinical Neuropsychologist, 25*, 989–1008.

Henry L. A., & Gudjonsson, G. H. (2003). Eyewitness memory, suggestibility and repeated recall sessions in children with mild and moderate intellectual disabilities. *Law and Human Behavior, 27*, 481–505.

Herrnstein, R. J., & Murray, C. (1994). *The bell curve: The reshaping of American life by differences in intelligence*. New York, NY: Free Press.

Heyman, G. D., Phillips, A. T., & Gelman, S. A. (2003). Children's reasoning about physics within and across ontological kinds. *Cognition, 89*, 43–61.

Hibel, J., Farkas, G., & Morgan, P. L. (2010). Who is placed into special education? *Sociology of Education, 83*, 312–332.

Hinshaw, S. P., & Scheffler, R. M. (2014). *The ADHD explosion: Myths, medication, money, and today's push for performance*. Oxford: Oxford University Press

Holmes, C. J., Kim-Spoon, J., & Deater-Deckard, K. (2016). Linking executive function and peer problems from early childhood through middle adolescence. *Journal of Abnormal Child Psychology, 44*, 31–42.

Holmes, J., & Gathercole, S. E. (2014). Taking working memory training from the laboratory into schools. *Educational Psychology, 34*, 440–450.

Holmes, W., & Dowker, A. (2013). Catch up numeracy: A targeted intervention for children who are low-attaining in mathematics. *Research in Mathematics Education, 15*, 249–265.

Holyoak, K. J. (2005). Analogy. In K. J. Holyoak & R. G. Robinson (Eds), *The Cambridge handbook of thinking and reasoning* (pp. 315–340). Cambridge: Cambridge University Press.

Hoogenhout, M., & Malcolm-Smith, S. (2014). Theory of mind in autism spectrum disorder: Does DSM classification predict development? *Research in Autism Spectrum Disorders, 8*, 597–607.

Hoogenhout, M., & Malcolm-Smith, S. (2017). Theory of mind predicts severity level in autism. *Autism, 21*, 242–252.

Hovik, K. T., Saunes, B. K., Aarlien, A. K., & Egeland, J. (2013). RCT of working memory training in ADHD: Long-term near-transfer effects. *PLoS One, 8*, e80561.

Howe, C. (2009). Collaborative group work in middle childhood. *Human Development, 52*, 215–239.

Howe, C. (2010). *Peer groups and children's development.* Oxford: Wiley-Blackwell

Howe, M. L. (2015). Memory development. In R. M. Lerner, L. S. Liben & U. Müller (Eds), *Handbook of child psychology and developmental science, Seventh edition, Volume 2: Cognitive processes* (pp. 203–249). Hoboken, NJ: Wiley.

Hudson, J. A. (1993). Reminiscing with mothers and others: Autobiographical memory in young two-year-olds. *Journal of Narrative and Life History, 3*, 1–32.

Hudson, J. A., & Mayhew, E. M. Y. (2009). The development of memory for recurring events. In M. L. Courage & N. Cowan (Eds), *The development of memory in infancy and childhood, Second edition* (pp. 69–91). Hove, UK: Psychology Press.

Hudson, J. A., & Sheffield, E. (1995). *Extending young children's event memory: Effects of reminder on 16–24-month-olds long-term recall.* Paper presented at American Psychological Society, New York, USA.

Hughes, C., & Devine, R. T. (2015). Individual differences in theory of mind from preschool to adolescence: Achievements and directions. *Child Development Perspectives, 9*, 149–153.

Hughes, C., & Dunn, J. (1998). Understanding mind and emotion: Longitudinal associations with mental-state talk between young friends. *Developmental Psychology, 34*, 1026–1034.

Hughes, C., Devine, R. T., & Wang, Z. (2018). Does parental mind-mindedness account for cross-cultural differences in preschoolers' Theory of Mind? *Child Development, 89*, 1296-1310.

Hundeide, K. (1977). *Piaget i kritisk lys (Critical light on Piaget).* Oslo, Norway: Cappelen.

Huston, A. C., & Bentley, A. C. (2010). Human development in societal context. *Annual Review of Psychology*, *61*, 411–437.

Hyde, J. S., Fennema, E., & Lamon, S. J. (1990). Gender differences in mathematics performance: A meta-analysis. *Psychological Bulletin*, *107*, 139–155.

Iacoboni, M. (2005). Neural mechanisms of imitation. *Current Opinion in Neurobiology*, *15*, 632–637.

Ingesson, S. G. (2007). Growing up with dyslexia: Interviews with teenagers and young adults. *School Psychology International*, *28*, 574–591.

Inhelder, B., & Piaget, J. (1964). *The early growth of logic in the child: Classification and seriation*. London: Routledge and Kegan Paul.

Ionescu, T. (2012). Exploring the nature of cognitive flexibility. *New Ideas in Psychology*, *30*, 190–200.

Isbell, E., Fukuda, K., Neville, H. J., & Vogel, E. K. (2015). Visual working memory continues to develop through adolescence. *Frontiers in Psychology*, *6*, 696.

Jacob, P. (2009). The tuning-fork model of human social cognition: A critique. *Consciousness and Cognition*, *18*, 229–243.

Jensen, A. R. (1985). The nature of the Black–White difference on various psychometric tests: Spearman's hypothesis. *Behavioral and Brain Sciences*, *8*, 193–219.

Jenson, W. R., Harward, S., & Bowen, J. M. (2011). Externalizing disorders in children and adolescents: Behavioral excess and behavioral deficits. In M. A. Bray & T. J. Kehle (Eds), *The Oxford handbook of school psychology* (pp. 379–410). New York, NY: Oxford University Press.

Jimenez-Gomez, A., & Standridge, S. (2014). A refined approach to evaluating global developmental delay for the international medical community. *Pediatric Neurology*, *51*, 198–206.

Johnson, D. W., & Johnson, R. T. (2009). An educational psychology success story: Social interdependence theory and cooperative learning. *Educational Researcher*, *38*, 365–379.

Johnson, S. P., & Hannon, E. E. (2015). Perceptual development. In L. S. Liben, U. Müller & R. M. Lerner (Eds), *Handbook of child psychology and developmental science, Seventh edition, Volume 2: Cognitive processes* (pp. 63–112). Hoboken, NJ: Wiley.

Johnson, W., Carothers, A., & Deary, I. J. (2008). Sex differences in variability in general intelligence: A new look at the old question. *Perspectives on Psychological Science*, *3*, 518–531.

Johnson, W., Carothers, A., & Deary, I. J. (2009). A role for the X chromosome in sex differences in variability in general intelligence? *Perspectives on Psychological Science*, *4*, 598–611.

Johnson-Laird, P. N. (1999). Deductive reasoning. *Annual Review of Psychology*, *50*, 109–135.

Jones, C. M., Braithwaite, V. A., & Healy, S. D. (2003). The evolution of sex differences in spatial ability. *Behavioral Neuroscience*, *117*, 403–411.

Jones, E. A., Carr, E. G., & Feeley, K. M. (2006). Multiple effects of joint attention intervention for children with autism. *Behavior Modification*, *30*, 782–834.

Jones, S. S. (1996). Imitation or exploration? Young infants' matching of adults' oral gestures. *Child Development, 67,* 1952–1969.

Jones, S. S. (2007). Imitation in infancy: The development of imitation. *Psychological Science, 18,* 593–599.

Jones, S. S. (2009). The development of imitation in infancy. *Philosophical Transactions of the Royal Society, B Biological Sciences, 364,* 2325–2335.

Joshi, R. M., Padakannaya, P., & Nishanimath, S. (2010), Dyslexia and hyperlexia in bilinguals. *Dyslexia, 16,* 99–118.

Kagan, J. (2008a). In defense of qualitative changes in development. *Child Development, 79,* 1606–1624.

Kahneman, D. (2011). *Thinking, fast and slow.* New York, NY: Farrar, Straus and Giroux.

Kail, R. V. (2004). Cognitive development includes global and domain-specific processes. *Merrill-Palmer Quarterly, 50,* 445–455.

Kail, R. V., & Bisanz, J. (1992). The information-processing perspective on cognitive development in childhood and adolescence. In R. J. Sternberg & C. A. Berg (Eds), *Intellectual development* (pp. 229–260). Cambridge: Cambridge University Press.

Kail, R. V., & Miller, C. A. (2006) Developmental change in processing speed: Domain specificity and stability during childhood and adolescence. *Journal of Cognition and Development, 7,* 119–137.

Kan, K. -J., Wicherts, J. M., Dolan, C. V., & van der Maas, H. L. J. (2013). On the nature and nurture of intelligence and specific cognitive abilities: The more heritable, the more culture dependent. *Psychological Science, 24,* 2420–2428.

Kanaya, T., & Ceci, S. J. (2012). The impact of the Flynn Effect on LD diagnoses in special education. *Journal of Learning Disabilities, 45,* 319–326.

Karmiloff-Smith, A. (2007). Atypical epigenesis. *Developmental Science, 10,* 84–88.

Karmiloff-Smith, A. (2009). Nativism versus neuroconstructivism: Rethinking the study of developmental disorders. *Developmental Psychology, 45,* 56–63.

Karmiloff-Smith, A. (2015). An alternative to domain-general or domain-specific frameworks for theorizing about human evolution and ontogenesis. *AIMS neuroscience, 2,* 91–104.

Karns, C. M., Isbell, E., Giuliano, R. J., & Neville, H. J. (2015). Auditory attention in childhood and adolescence: An event-related potential study of spatial selective attention to one of two simultaneous stories. *Developmental Cognitive Neuroscience, 13,* 53–67.

Karpov, Y. V. (2005). *The neo-Vygotskian approach to child development.* Cambridge: Cambridge University Press.

Karpov, Y. V. (2014). *Vygotsky for educators.* Cambridge: Cambridge University Press.

Kaufmann, L., Mazzocco, M. M., Dowker, A., von Aster, M., Goebel, S. M., Grabner, R. H., Henik, A., Jordan, N. C., Karmiloff-Smith, A., Kucia, K., etal. (2013) Dys calculia from a developmental and differential perspective. *Frontiers in Psychology, 4,* 516.

Kavšek, M. (2004). Predicting later IQ from infant visual habituation and dishabituation: A meta-analysis. *Journal of Applied Development Psychology, 25,* 369–393.

Keehn, B., Müller, R. A., & Townsend, J. (2013). Atypical attentional networks and the emergence of autism. *Neuroscience and Biobehavioral Reviews, 37*, 164–183.

Kercood, S., Grskovic, J. A., Banda, D., & Begeske, J. (2014). Working memory and autism: A review of literature. *Research in Autism Spectrum Disorders, 8*, 1316–1332.

Kidd, C., Palmeri, H., & Aslin, R. N. (2013). Rational snacking: Young children's decision-making on the marshmallow task is moderated by beliefs about environmental reliability. *Cognition, 126*, 109–114.

Kimhi, Y. (2014). Theory of mind abilities and deficits in autism spectrum disorders. *Topics in Language Disorders, 34*, 329–343.

Kimura, D. (1999). *Sex and cognition*. Cambridge, MA: MIT Press.

Kimura, D. (2004). Human sex differences in cognition, fact, not predicament. *Sexualities, Evolution and Gender, 6*, 45–53.

King, D. L., Haagsma, M. C., Delfabbro, P. H., Gradisar, M. S., & Griffiths, M. D. (2013). Toward a consensus definition of pathological video-gaming: A systematic review of psychometric assessment tools. *Clinical Psychology Review, 33*, 331–342

Kirk, H., Gray, K., Ellis, K., Taffe, J., & Cornish, K. (2017). Impact of attention training on academic achievement, executive functioning, and behavior: A randomized controlled trial. *American Journal on Intellectual and Developmental Disabilities, 122*, 97–117.

Klassen, R. M., Tze, V. M., & Hannok, W. (2013). Internal izing problems of adults with learning disabilities: A meta-analysis. *Journal of Learning Disabilities, 46*, 317–327.

Kleefstra, T., Schencka, A., Kramera, J. M., & van Bokhove, H. (2014). The genetics of cognitive epigenetics. *Neuropharmacology, 80*, 83–94.

Klingberg, T., Forssberg, H., & Westerberg, H. (2002). Training of working memory in children with ADHD. *Journal of Clinical and Experimental Neuropsychology, 24*, 781–791.

Kolb, D. A. (1984). *Experiential learning: Experience as the source of learning and development*. Englewood Cliffs, NJ: Prentice-Hall.

Kokin, J., Younger, A., Gosselin, P., & Vaillancourt, T. (2016). Biased facial expression interpretation in shy children. *Infant and Child Development, 25*, 3–23.

Kosc, L. (1974). Developmental dyscalculia. *Journal of Learning Disabilities, 7*, 164–177.

Kozulin, A. (2002). Sociocultural theory and the mediated learning experience. *School Psychology International, 23*, 7–35.

Kruger, A. C. (1993). Peer collaboration: Conflict, cooperation, or both? *Social Development, 2*, 165–182.

Kuhn, D. (2013). Reasoning. In P. D. Zelazo (Ed.), *The Oxford handbook of developmental psychology, Volume 1: Body and mind* (pp. 744–764). Oxford: Oxford University Press.

Kuhn D., & Franklin, S. (2008). The second decade: What develops (and how). In. W. Damon & R. M. Lerner (Eds), *Child psychology and adolescent psychology: An advanced course* (pp. 517–550). New York, NY: Wiley.

Kuo, Z.Y. (1967). *The dynamics of behavior development: An epigenetic view*. New York, NY: Random House.

Kyllonen, P., & Kell, H. (2017). What is fluid intelligence? Can it be improved? In M. Rosen, K.Y. Hansen & U. Wolff (Eds), *Cognitive abilities and educational outcomes* (pp. 15–38). Cham, Switzerland: Springer.

LaBlonde, C. E., & Chandler, M. J. (1995). False belief understanding goes to school: On the social-emotional consequences of coming early or late to a first theory of mind. *Cognition and Emotion, 9,* 167–185.

Lagattuta, K. H., Kramer, H. J., Kennedy, K., Hjortsvang, K., Goldfarb, D., & Tashjian, S. (2015). Beyond Sally's missing marble: Further development in children's understanding of mind and emotion in middle childhood. *Advances in Child Development and Behavior, 48,* 185–217.

Lakoff, G. (1987). *Women, fire and dangerous things*. Chicago, IL: University of Chicago Press.

Lamb, M. E., La Rooy, D. J., Malloy, L. C., & Katz, C. (Eds) (2011). *Children's testimony: A handbook of psychological research and forensic practice, Second edition*. Chichester, UK: Wiley.

Landau, B., & Ferrara, K. (2013). Space and language in Williams syndrome: Insights from typical development. *Wiley Interdisciplinary Reviews: Cognitive Science, 4,* 693–706.

Landerl, K. (2015). How specific is the specific disorder of arithmetic skills? In S. Chinn (Ed.), *The Routledge international handbook of dyscalculia and mathematical learning difficulties* (pp. 115–124). New York, NY: Routledge.

Lawton, C. A. (2010). Gender, spatial abilities, and wayfinding. In J. Chrisler & D. McCreary (Eds), *Handbook of gender research in psychology* (pp. 317–341). New York, NY: Springer.

Lazar, I., & Darlington, R. (1982). Lasting effects of early education. *Monographs of the Society for Research in Child Development, 47,* 2–3.

Leader, L. R. (2016). The potential value of habituation in the fetus. In N. Reissland & B. S. Kisilevsky (Eds), *Fetal development* (pp. 189–209). Cham, Switzerland: Springer.

Learmonth, A. E., Newcombe, N. S., Sheridan, N., & Jones, M. (2008). Why size counts: Children's spatial reorientation in large and small enclosures. *Developmental Science, 11,* 414–426.

Lecce, S., Caputi, M., Pagnin, A., & Banerjee, R. (2017). Theory of mind and school achievement: The mediating role of social competence. *Cognitive Development, 44,* 85–97.

Lecce, S., & Hughes, C. (2010). The Italian job? Comparing theory of mind performance in British and Italian children. *British Journal of Developmental Psychology, 28,* 747–766.

Lee, C., & Johnston-Wilder, S. (2015). Mathematical resilience. In S. Chinn (Ed.), *The Routledge international handbook of dyscalculia and mathematical learning difficulties* (pp. 337–345). New York, NY: Routledge.

Lee, K. (2013). Little liars: Development of verbal deception in children. *Child Development Perspectives, 7,* 91–96.

Leevers, H. J., & Harris, P. L. (2000). Counterfactual syllogistic reasoning in normal 4-year-olds, children with learning disabilities, and children with autism. *Journal of Experimental Child Psychology*, *76*, 64–87.

Leonard, H., & Wen, X. (2002). The epidemiology of mental retardation: Challenges and opportunities in the new millennium. *Developmental Disabilities Research Reviews*, *8*, 117–134.

Leslie, A. M. (2005). Developmental parallels in understanding minds and bodies. *Trends in Cognitive Sciences*, *9*, 459–462.

Leslie, A. M., Friedman, O., & German, T. (2004). Core mechanisms in "theory of mind". *Trends in Cognitive Sciences*, *8*, 528–533.

Levels, M., Dronkers, J., & Kraaykamp, G. (2008). Immigrant children's educational achievement in western countries: Origin, destination, and community effects on mathematical performance. *American Sociological Review*, *73*, 835–853.

Levin, I. (1977). The development of time concepts in young children: Reasoning about duration. *Child Development*, *48*, 435–444.

Levin, I. (1989). Principles underlying time measurement: The development of children's constraints on counting time. In I. Levin & D. Zakay (Eds), *Time and human cognition: A life-span perspective* (pp. 145–183). Amsterdam, NL: Elsevier.

Lewis, C., Freeman, N. H., Hagestadt, C., & Douglas, H. (1994). Narrative access and production in preschoolers' false belief reasoning. *Cognitive Development*, *9*, 397–424.

Lewis, M., Stanger, C., & Sullivan M. W. (1989). Deception in three-year-olds. *Developmental Psychology*, *25*, 439–443.

Lewontin, R. (1970). Race and intelligence. *Bulletin of the Atomic Scientists*, *26*, 2–8.

Li, W. S., & Ho, C. S. H. (2011). Lexical tone awareness among Chinese children with developmental dyslexia. *Journal of Child Language*, *38*, 793–808.

Light, P., & Glachan, M. (1985). Facilitation of individual problem solving through peer interaction. *Educational Psychology*, *5*, 217–225.

Light, P. H., Girotto, V., & Legrenzi, P. (1990). Children's reasoning on conditional promises and permissions. *Cognitive Development*, *5*, 369–383.

Lillard, A. S. (1993). Pretend play skills and the child's theory of mind. *Child Development*, *64*, 348–371.

Lillard, A. S. (2001). Pretend play as Twin Earth. *Developmental Review*, *21*, 1–33.

Lingwood, J., Blades, M., Farran, E. K., Courbois, Y., & Matthews, D. (2015). The development of wayfinding abilities in children: Learning routes with and without landmarks. *Journal of Environmental Psychology*, *41*, 74–80.

Linnanmäki, K. (2004). Självuppfattning och utveckling av matematikprestationer. *Nordisk Tidskrift för Spesialpedagogikk*, *81*, 210–220.

Loftus, E. F. (1993). The reality of repressed memories. *American Psychologist*, *48*, 518–537.

Loftus, E. F., & Davis, D. (2006). Recovered memories. *Annual Review of Clinical Psychology*, *2*, 469–498.

Lourenço, O. M. (2016). Developmental stages, Piagetian stages in particular: A critical review. *New Ideas in Psychology*, *40*, 123–137.

Lovett, B. J., & Lewandowski, L. J. (2006). Gifted students with learning disabilities: Who are they? *Journal of Learning Disabilities, 39*, 515–527.

Low, J., & Perner, J. (2012). Implicit and explicit theory of mind: State of the art. *British Journal of Developmental Psychology, 30*, 1–13.

Lucariello, J. (1998). Together wherever we go: The ethnographic child and the developmentalist. *Child Development, 69*, 355–358.

Lucariello, J., & Nelson, K. (1985). Slot-filler categories as memory organizers for young children. *Developmental Psychology, 21*, 272–282.

Lucariello, J., & Nelson, K. (1987). Remembering and planning talk between mothers and children. *Discourse Processes, 10*, 219–235.

Luciana, M., Conklin, H. M., Hooper, C. J., & Yarger, R. S. (2005). The development of nonverbal working memory and executive control processes in adolescents. *Child Development, 76*, 697–712.

Lukowski, A. F., Phung, J. N., & Milojevich, H. M. (2015). Language facilitates event memory in early childhood: Child comprehension, adult-provided linguistic support and delayed recall at 16 months. *Memory, 23*, 848–863.

Luna, B., Garver, K. E., Urban, T. A., Lazar, N. A., & Sweeney, J. A. (2004). Maturation of cognitive processes from late childhood to adulthood. *Child Development, 75*, 1357–1372.

Lupyan, G. (2016). The centrality of language in human cognition. *Language Learning, 66*, 516–553.

Luria, A. R. (1961). *The role of speech in the regulation of normal and abnormal behavior*. Oxford: Pergamon Press.

Luria, A. R. (1976). *Cognitive development: Its cultural and social foundations*. London: Harvard University Press.

MacLeod, C., & Clarke, P. J. (2015). The attentional bias modification approach to anxiety intervention. *Clinical Psychological Science, 3*, 58–78.

Macnamara, J. (1982). *Words for things*. Cambridge, MA: MIT Press.

Mandler, J. M. (2004). *The foundations of mind: Origins of conceptual thought*. Oxford: Oxford University Press.

Mandler, J. M. (2008). On the birth and growth of concepts. *Philosophical Psychology, 21*, 207–230.

Mandler, J. M. (2010). The spatial foundations of the conceptual system. *Language and Cognition, 2*, 21–44.

Mandler, J. M. (2012). On the spatial foundations of the conceptual system and its enrichment. *Cognitive Science, 36*, 421–451.

Mandler, J. M., Bauer, P. J., & McDonough, L. (1991). Separating the sheep from the goats: Differing global categories. *Cognitive Psychology, 23*, 263–298.

Mandler, J. M., & McDonough, L. (1996). Drinking and driving don't mix: Inductive generalization in infancy. *Cognition, 59*, 307–335.

Manfra, L., Davis, K. D., Ducenne, L., & Winsler, A. (2014). Preschoolers' motor and verbal self-control strategies during a resistance-to-temptation task. *The Journal of Genetic Psychology, 175*, 332–345.

Mareschal, D., Johnson, M. H., Sirois, S., Spratling, M., Thomas, M., & Westermann, G. (2007a). *Neuroconstructivism, Volume I. How the brain constructs cognition*. Oxford: Oxford University Press.

Mareschal, D., Sirois, S., Westermann, G., & Johnson, M. H. (2007b). *Neurocon-structivism, Volume II. Per spectives and prospects.* Oxford: Oxford University Press.

Marini, Z., & Case, R. (1994). The development of abstract reasoning about the physical and social world. *Child Development, 65,* 147–159.

Markovits, H., Schleifer, M., & Fortier, L. (1989). Development of elementary deductive reasoning in young children. *Developmental Psychology, 25,* 787–793.

Martí, E. (1996). Piaget and school education: A socio-cultural challenge. *Prospects, 26,* 141–158.

Martin, S. (2014). *Play in children with motor disabilities.* Doctoral Dissertation, University of Kentucky, USA.

Martinussen, R., Hayden, J., Hogg-Johnson, S., & Tannock, R. (2005). A meta-analysis of working memory impairments in children with attention-deficit/hyperactivity disorder. *Journal of the American Academy of Child and Adolescent Psychiatry, 44,* 377–384.

Masangkay, Z. S., McCluskey, K. A., McIntyre, C. W., Sims-Knight, J., Vaughn, B. E., & Flavell, T. H. (1974). The early development of inferences about the visual percepts of others. *Child Development, 45,* 357–366.

Matsuda, F. (2001). Development of concepts of interrelationship among duration, distance, and speed. *International Journal of Behavioral Development, 25,* 466–480.

Mayer, A., & Träuble, B. E. (2013). Synchrony in the onset of mental state understanding across cultures? A study among children in Samoa. *International Journal of Behavioral Development, 37,* 21–28.

Mayes, S. D., Calhoun, S. L., Bixler, E. O., & Zimmerman, D. N. (2009). IQ and neuropsychological predictors of academic achievement. *Learning and Individual Differences, 19,* 238–241.

McAlister, A., & Peterson, C. C. (2007). A longitudinal study of child siblings and theory of mind development. *Cognitive Development, 22,* 258–270.

McAllister, R., & Gray, C. (2007). Low vision: Mobility and independence training for the early years child. *Early Child Development and Care, 177,* 839–852.

McCall, R. B. (1989). Commentary. *Human Development, 32,* 177–186.

McCall, R. B. (1994). What process mediates predictions of childhood IQ from infant habituation and recognition memory? Speculations on the roles of inhibition and rate of information processing. *Intelligence, 18,* 107–125.

McCall, R. B., Applebaum, M. I., & Hogarty, P. S. (1973). Developmental changes in mental performance. *Monographs of the Society for Research in Child Development, 38,* 3.

McCall, R. B., & Carriger, M. S. (1993). A meta-analysis of infant habituation and recognition memory performance as predictors of later IQ. *Child Development, 64,* 57–79.

McCoach, D. B., Kehle, T., Bray, M. A., & Siegle, D. (2001). Best practices in the identification of gifted students with learning disabilities. *Psychology in the Schools, 38,* 403–411.

McCormack, T. (2015). The development of temporal cognition. In R. M. Lerner, L. S. Liben & U. Mueller (Eds), *Handbook of child psychology and developmental science, Seventh edition, Volume 2: Cognitive Processes* (pp. 624–670). Hoboken, NJ: Wiley-Blackwell.

McCormack, T., & Hanley, M. (2011). Children's reasoning about the temporal order of past and future events. *Cognitive Development, 26,* 299–314.

McCrory, E., Henry, L. A., & Happé, F. (2007). Eye-witness memory and suggestibility in children with Asperger syndrome. *Journal of Child Psychology and Psychiatry, 48,* 482–489.

McGarrigle, J., Grieve, R., & Hughes, M. (1978). Interpreting inclusions: A contribution to the study of the child's cognitive and linguistic development. *Journal of the Experimental Child Psychology, 28,* 528–550.

McGonigle-Chalmers, M., Slater, H., & Smith, A. (2014). Rethinking private speech in preschoolers: The effects of social presence. *Developmental Psychology, 50,* 829–836.

McGrath, L. M., Pennington, B. F., Shanahan, M. A., Santerre-Lemmon, L. E., Barnard, H. D., Willcutt, E. G., DeFries, J. C., & Olson, R. K. (2011). A multiple deficit model of reading disability and attention-deficit/hyper-activity disorder: Searching for shared cognitive deficits. *Journal of Child Psychology and Psychiatry, 52,* 47–557.

McLaughlin, K. A., & Lambert, H. K. (2017). Child trauma exposure and psychopathology: Mechanisms of risk and resilience. *Current Opinion in Psychology, 14,* 29–34.

McNally, R. J. (2012). Searching for repressed memory. In R. F. Belli (Ed.), *Nebraska Symposium on Motivation: True and false recovered memories. Toward a reconciliation of the debate,* Volume *58* (pp. 121–147). New York, NY: Springer.

McWilliams, K., Narr, R., Goodman, G. S., Ruiz, S., & Mendoza, M. (2013). Children's memory for their mother's murder: Accuracy, suggestibility, and resistance to suggestion. *Memory, 21,* 591–598.

Meins, E., & Fernyhough, C. (1999). Linguistic acquisitional style and mentalising development: The role of maternal mind-mindedness. *Cognitive Development, 14,* 363–380.

Meins, E., Fernyhough, C., Wainwright, R., Clark-Carter, D., Das Gupta, M., Fradley, E., & Tuckey, M. (2003). Pathways to understanding mind: Construct validity and predictive validity of maternal mind-mindedness. *Child Development, 74,* 1194–1211.

Melby-Lervåg, M., Redick, T. S., & Hulme, C. (2016). Working memory training does not improve performance on measures of intelligence or other measures of "far transfer": Evidence from a meta-analytic review. *Perspectives on Psychological Science, 11,* 512–534.

Melinder, A., Alexander, K., Cho, Y. I., Goodman, G. S., Thoresen, C., Lonnum, K., & Magnussen, S. (2010). Children's eyewitness memory: A comparison of two interviewing strategies as realized by forensic professionals. *Journal of Experimental Child Psychology, 105,* 156–177.

Meltzoff, A. N., & Moore, M. K. (1983). Newborn infants imitate adult facial gestures. *Child Development, 54,* 702–709.

Meltzoff, A. N., & Moore, M. K. (1989). Imitation in newborn infants: Exploring the range of gestures imitated and the underlying mechanisms. *Developmental Psychology, 25,* 954–962.

Meltzoff, A. N., & Moore, M. K. (1994). Imitation, memory, and the representations of persons. *Infant Behavior and Developmental, 17*, 83–99.

Meltzoff, A. N., & Moore, M. K. (1997). Explaining facial imitation: A theoretical model. *Early Development and Parenting, 6*, 179–192.

Memon, A., Cronin, O., Eaves, R., & Bull, R. (1993). The cognitive interview and child witnesses. *Issues in Criminological and Legal Psychology, 20*, 3–9.

Memon, A., Meissner, C. A., & Fraser, J. (2010). The cognitive interview: A meta-analytic review and study space analysis of the past 25 years. *Psychology, Public Policy, and Law, 16*, 340–372.

Menon, V. (2016). Working memory in children's math learning and its disruption in dyscalculia. *Current Opinion in Behavioral Sciences, 10*, 125–132.

Mercer, N. (2013). The social brain, language, and goal-directed collective thinking: A social conception of cognition and its implications for understanding how we think, teach, and learn. *Educational Psychologist, 48*, 148–168.

Mervis, C. B., & Rosch, E. (1981). Categorization of natural objects. *Annual Review of Psychology, 32*, 89–115.

Miller, C. A. (2001). False belief understanding in children with specific language impairment. *Journal of Communication Disorders, 34*, 73–86.

Miller, M. R., Müller, U., Giesbrecht, G. F., Carpendale, J. I., & Kerns, K. A. (2013). The contribution of executive function and social understanding to preschoolers' letter and math skills. *Cognitive Development, 28*, 331–349.

Miller, S. A. (2009). Children's understanding of second-order mental states. *Psychological Bulletin, 135*, 749–773.

Milligan, K., Astington, J. W., & Dack, L. A. (2007). Language and theory of mind: Meta-analysis of the relation between language ability and false-belief understanding. *Child Development, 78*, 622–646.

Mink, D., Henning, A., & Aschersleben, G. (2014). Infant shy temperament predicts preschoolers theory of mind. *Infant Behavior and Development, 37*, 66–75.

Minton, H. L., & Schneider, F. W. (1980). *Differential psychology*. Monterey, CA: Brooks/Cole.

Mischel, W., Shoda, Y., & Rodriguez, M. I. (1989). Delay of gratification in children. *Science, 244 (4907)*, 933–938.

Mistry, J., Rogoff, B., & Herman, H. (2001). What is the meaning of meaningful purpose in children's remembering? Istomina Revisited. *Mind, Culture, and Activity, 8*, 28–41.

Moffitt, T. E., Caspi, A., Harkness, A. R., & Silva, P. A. (1993). The natural history of change in intellectual performance: Who changes? How much? Is it meaningful? *Journal of Child Psychology and Psychiatry, 34*, 455–506.

Moll, H., & Tomasello, M. (2004). 12- and 18-month-old infants follow gaze to spaces behind barriers. *Developmental Science, 7*, F1–F9.

Montgomery, J. W., Polunenko, A., & Marinellie, S. A. (2009). Role of working memory in children's understanding spoken narrative: A preliminary investigation. *Applied Psycholinguistics, 30*, 485–509.

Morelli, G., Rogoff, B., & Angelillo, C. (2003). Cultural variation in young children's access to work or involvement in specialised child-focused activities. *International Journal of Behavioral Development, 27*, 264–274.

Morra, S., & Borella, E. (2015). Working memory training: From metaphors to models. *Frontiers in Psychology, 6*, 1097.

Morra, S., Gobbo, C., Marini, Z., & Sheese, R. (2008). *Cognitive development: Neo-Piagetian perspectives*. New York, NY: Lawrence Erlbaum.

Moser, M. B., & Moser, E. I. (2016). Where am I? Where am I going? Scientists are figuring out how the brain navigates. *Scientific American, 614*, 26–33.

Mugnaini, D., Lassi, S., La Malfa, G., & Albertini, G. (2009). Internalizing correlates of dyslexia. *World Journal of Pediatrics, 5*, 255–264.

Mullen, E. M. (1995). *Mullen Scales of Early Learning*. Circle Pines: American Guidance Service.

Munakata, Y. (2006). Information processing approaches to development. In W. Damon, R. M. Lerner, D. Kuhn & R. S. Siegler (Eds), *Handbook of child psychology, Sixth edition, Volume 2: Cognition, perception, and language* (pp. 426–463). New York, NY: Wiley.

Munro, J. (2003). Dyscalculia: A unifying concept in understanding mathematics learning disabilities. *Australian Journal of Learning Difficulties, 8*, 25–32.

Nadel-Brulfert, J., & Baudonniere, P. M. (1982). The social function of reciprocal imitation in 2-year-old peers. *International Journal of Behavioral Development, 5*, 95–109.

Naglieri, J. A. (2015). Hundred years of intelligence testing: Moving from traditional IQ to second-generation intelligence tests. In S. Goldstein, D. Princiotta & J. A. Naglieri (Eds), *Handbook of intelligence: Evolutionary theory, historical perspective and current concepts* (pp. 295–316). New York, NY: Springer.

Nagy, E., Pal, A., & Orvos, H. (2014). Learning to imitate individual finger movements by the human neonate. *Developmental Science, 17*, 841–857.

Nagy, E., Pilling, K., Orvos, H., & Molnar, P. (2013). Imitation of tongue protrusion in human neonates: Specificity of the response in a large sample. *Developmental Psychology, 49*, 1628–1638.

Nation, K., Cocksey, J., Taylor, J. S., & Bishop, D. V. (2010). A longitudinal investigation of early reading and language skills in children with poor reading comprehension. *Journal of Child Psychology and Psychiatry, 51*, 1031–1039.

Needleman, H. (2004). Lead poisoning. *Annual Review of Medicine, 55*, 209–222.

Negen, J., & Nardini, M. (2015). Four-year-olds use a mixture of spatial reference frames. *PloS One, 10*, e0131984.

Neisser U. (2004). Memory development: New questions and old. *Developmental Review, 24*, 154–158.

Neisser, U., Boodoo, G., Bouchard, T. J., Boykin, A. W., Brody, N., Ceci, S. J., Halpern, D. F., Loehlin, J. C., Perloff, R., Sternberg, R. J., & Urbina, S. (1996). Intelligence: Knowns and unknowns. *American Psychologist, 51*, 77–101.

Nelson, C. A., Thomas, K. M., & de Haan, M. (2006b). Neural bases of cognitive development. In W. Damon, R. M. Lerner, D. Kuhn, R. & S. Siegler (Eds),

Handbook of child psychology, Sixth edition, Volume 2: Cognition perception, and language (pp. 3–57). Hoboken, NJ: Wiley.

Nelson, D. K., O'Neill, K., & Asher, Y. M. (2008). A mutually facilitative relationship between learning names and learning concepts in preschool children: The case of artifacts. *The Journal of Cognition and Development, 9,* 171–193.

Nelson, K. (1988). Constraints on word learning? *Cognitive Development, 3,* 221–246.

Nelson, K. (1996). *Language in cognitive development.* Cambridge: Cambridge University Press.

Nelson, K. (2007a). *Young minds in social worlds: Experience, meaning and memory.* Cambridge, MA: Harvard University Press.

Nelson, K. (2007b). Development of extended memory. *Journal of Physiology, 101,* 223–229.

Nelson, K. (2011). "Concept" is a useful concept in developmental research. *Journal of Theoretical and Philosophical Psychology, 31,* 96–101.

Nelson, K. (2014). Pathways from infancy to the community of shared minds/ El camino desde la primera infancia a la comunidad de mentes compartidas. *Infancia y Aprendizaje, 37,* 1–24.

Nelson, K. (2015). Making sense with private speech. *Cognitive Development, 36,* 171–179.

Nelson, K., & Fivush, R. (2004). The emergence of auto-biographical memory: A social cultural developmental theory. *Psychological Review, 11,* 486–511.

Nelson, K., & Gruendel, J. M. (1981). Generalized event representations: Basic building blocks of cognitive development. In M. E. Lamb & A. L. Brown (Eds), *Advances in developmental psychology,* Volume 1 (pp. 131–158). Hillsdale, NJ: Erlbaum.

Newcombe, N. S. (2002). The nativist-empiricist controversy in the context of recent research on spatial and quantitative development. *Psychological Science, 13,* 395–401.

Newcombe, N. S. (2013). Cognitive development: Changing views of cognitive change. *Wiley Interdisciplinary Reviews: Cognitive Science, 4,* 479–491.

Newcombe, N. S., & Huttenlocher, J. (1992). Children's early ability to solve perspective-taking problems. *Developmental Psychology, 28,* 635–643.

Newcombe, N. S., Huttenlocher, J., Drummey, A. B., & Wiley, J. G. (1998). The development of spatial location coding: Place learning and dead reckoning in the second and third years. *Cognitive Development, 13,* 185–200.

Newcombe, N. S., Uttal, D. H., & Sauter, M. (2013). Spatial development. In P. Zelazo (Ed.), *Oxford handbook of developmental psychology,* Volume 1 (pp. 564–590). New York, NY: Oxford University Press.

Newman, G. E., Choi, H., Wynn, K., & Scholl, B. J. (2008). The origins of causal perception: Evidence from postdictive processing in infancy. *Cognitive Psychology, 57,* 262–291.

Nguyen, S. P., & Murphy, G. L. (2003). An apple is more than just a fruit: Cross-classification in children's concepts. *Child Development, 74,* 1783–1806.

Nichols, P. L. (1984). Familial mental retardation. *Behavior Genetics, 14,* 161–170.

Nilsson, K. K., & de López, K. J. (2016). Theory of mind in children with specific language impairment: A systematic review and meta-analysis. *Child Development, 87,* 143–153.

Nisbett, R. E. (2005). Heredity, environment, and race differences in IQ: A commentary on Rushton and Jensen. *Psychology, Public Policy, and Law, 11,* 302–310.

Nisbett, R. E., Aronson, J., Blair, C., Dickens, W., Flynn, J., Halpern, D. F., & Turkheimer, E. (2012). Intelligence: New findings and theoretical developments. *American Psychologist, 67,* 130–159.

Nisbett, R. E., & Norenzayan, A. (2002). Culture and cognition. In H. Pashler & D. L. Medin (Eds), *Stevens' handbook of experimental psychology, Third edition* (pp. 561–597). New York, NY: Wiley.

Noel, K. K., & Westby, C. (2014). Applying theory of mind concepts when designing interventions targeting social cognition among youth offenders. *Topics in Language Disorders, 34,* 344–361.

Nunes, T., & Bryant, P. (2015). The development of quantitative reasoning. In R. M. Lerner, L. S. Liben & U. Müller (Eds), *Handbook of child psychology and developmental science, Seventh edition, Volume 2: Cognitive processes* (pp. 715–764). Hoboken, NJ: Wiley.

Nunes, T., Schlieman, A. D., & Carraher, D. W. (1993). *Street mathematics and school mathematics.* Cambridge: Cambridge University Press.

O'Connor, T. G., & Hirsch, N. (1999). Intra-individual differences and relationship-specificity of mentalising in early adolescence. *Social Development, 8,* 256–274.

Oakes, L. M. (1994). Development of infants' use of continuity cues in their perception of causality. *Developmental Psychology, 30,* 869–879.

Oakes, L. M., & Luck, S. J. (2014). Short-term memory in infancy. In P. J. Bauer & R. Fivush (Eds), *The Wiley handbook on the development of children's memory* (pp. 157–180). New York, NY: Wiley.

Oakland, T. (2004). Use of educational and psychological tests internationally. *Applied Psychology, 53,* 157–172.

Olson, D. R. (2003). *Psychological theory and educational reform: How school remakes mind and society.* New York, NY: Cambridge University Press.

Olson, I. R., & Newcombe, N. S. (2014). Binding together the elements of episodes: Relational memory and the developmental trajectory of the hippocampus. In P. J. Bauer & R. Fivush (Eds), *Handbook on the development of children's memory* (pp. 285–308). New York, NY: Wiley.

Onishi, K. H., & Baillargeon, R. (2005). Do 15-month-old infants understand false beliefs? *Science, 308,* 255–258.

Oostenbroek, J., Slaughter, V., Nielsen, M., & Suddendorf, T. (2013). Why the confusion around neonatal imitation? A review. *Journal of Reproductive and Infant Psychology, 31,* 328–341.

Oostenbroek, J., Suddendorf, T., Nielsen, M., Redshaw, J., Kennedy-Costantini, S., Davis, J., Clark, S., & Slaughter, V. (2016). Comprehensive longitudinal study challenges the existence of neonatal imitation in humans. *Current Biology, 26,* 1334–1338.

Orbach, Y., & Lamb, M. E. (2007). Young children's references to temporal attributes of allegedly experienced events in the course of forensic interviews. *Child Development, 78,* 1100–1120.

Osborne, J. (2010). Arguing to learn in science: The role of collaborative, critical discourse. *Science, 328* (*5977*), 463–466.

Overton, W. F., Ward, S. L., Noveck, I. A., Black, J., & O'Brien, D. P. (1987). Form and content in the development of deductive reasoning. *Developmental Psychology, 23,* 22–30.

Pascual-Leone, J. (1970). A mathematical model for the transition rule in Piaget's developmental stages. *Acta Psychologica, 32,* 301–345.

Pavarini, G., de Hollanda Souza, D., & Hawk, C. K. (2013). Parental practices and theory of mind development. *Journal of Child and Family Studies, 22,* 844–853.

Pelsser, L. M., Frankena, K., Toorman, J., Savelkoul, H. F., Dubois, A. E., Pereira, R. R., Haagen, T. A., Rommelse, N. N., & Buitelaar, J. K. (2011). Effects of a restricted elimination diet on the behaviour of children with attention-deficit hyperactivity disorder (INCA study): A randomised controlled trial. *The Lancet, 377* (*9764*), 494–503.

Peltonen, K., Kangaslampi, S., Qouta, S., & Punamäki, R. L. (2017). Trauma and autobiographical memory: Contents and determinants of earliest memories among war-affected Palestinian children. *Memory, 25,* 1347–1357.

Perner, J., Ruffman, T., & Leekam, S. R. (1994). Theory of mind is contagious: You catch it from your sibs. *Child Development, 65,* 1228–1238.

Perner, J., & Wimmer, H. (1985). "John thinks that Mary thinks that": Attribution of second-order beliefs by 5–10 year old children. *Journal of Experimental Child Psychology, 39,* 437–471.

Perraudin, S., & Mounoud, P. (2009). Contribution of the priming paradigm to the understanding of the conceptual developmental shift from 5 to 9 years of age. *Developmental Science, 12,* 956–977.

Perry, N. W., & Wrightsman, L. S. (1991). *The child witness: Legal issues and dilemmas.* Newbury Park, CA: Sage.

Peskin, J. (1992). Ruse and representations: On children's ability to conceal information. *Developmental Psychology, 28,* 84–89.

Peterson, C. (2012). Children's autobiographical memories across the years: Forensic implications of childhood amnesia and eyewitness memory for stressful events. *Developmental Review, 32,* 287–306.

Peterson, C., Baker-Ward, L., & Grovenstein, T. N. (2016). Childhood remembered: Reports of both unique and repeated events. *Memory, 24,* 240–256.

Peterson, C., & Warren, K. L. (2009). Injuries, emergency rooms and children's memory: Factors contributing to individual differences. In J. A. Quas & R. Fivush (Eds), *Emotion and memory in development* (pp. 60–85). Oxford: Oxford University Press.

Peterson, C., Warren, K. L., & Short, M. M. (2011). Infantile amnesia across the years: A 2-year follow-up of children's earliest memories. *Child Development, 82,* 1092–1105.

Peterson, C. C. (2002). Children's long-term memory for autobiographical events. *Developmental Review, 22,* 370–402.

Peterson, C. C. (2009). Development of social-cognitive and communication skills in children born deaf. *Scandinavian Journal of Psychology, 50,* 475–483.

Peterson, C. C. (2014). Theory of mind understanding and empathic behavior in children with autism spectrum disorders. *International Journal of Developmental Neuroscience, 39,* 16–21.

Peterson, C. C. (2016). Empathy and theory of mind in deaf and hearing children. *Journal of Deaf Studies and Deaf Education, 21,* 141–147.

Peterson, D. J., Jones, K. T., Stephens, J. A., Gözenman, F., & Berryhill, M. E. (2016). Childhood memory: An update from the cognitive neuroscience perspective. In W. T. O'Donohue & M. Fanetti (Eds), *Forensic interviews regarding child sexual abuse* (pp. 81–105). Cham, Switzerland: Springer.

Peterson, R. L., & Pennington, B. F. (2015). Developmental dyslexia. *Annual Review of Clinical Psychology, 11,* 283–307.

Piaget, J. (1950). *The psychology of the child.* London: Routledge and Kegan Paul.

Piaget, J. (1951). *Play, dreams and imitation in childhood.* London: Heineman.

Piaget, J. (1952). *The origin of intelligence in the child.* London: Routledge and Kegan Paul.

Piaget, J. (1954). *The construction of reality in the child.* New York, NY: Routledge and Kegan Paul.

Piaget, J. (1959). *The language and thought of the child, Third edition.* London: Routledge.

Piaget, J. (1968). *Six psychological studies.* London: University of London Press.

Piaget, J. (1969a). *The child's conception of time.* London: Routledge and Kegan Paul.

Piaget, J. (1969b). *Psychology and pedagogy.* Paris: Denoel.

Piaget, J. (1970). *The child's conception of movement and speed.* London: Routledge and Kegan Paul.

Piaget, J. (1972). Intellectual evolution from adolescence to adulthood. *Human Development, 15,* 1–12.

Piaget, J. (1983). Piaget's theory. In P. Mussen (Ed.), *Handbook of child psychology, Fourth edition* (pp. 103–128). New York, NY: Wiley.

Piaget, J., Henriques, G., & Ascher, E. (Eds). (1992). *Morphisms and categories: Comparing and transforming:* London: Lawrence Erlbaum.

Piaget, J., & Inhelder, B. (1956). *The child's conception of space.* London: Routledge and Kegan Paul.

Piaget, J., & Inhelder, B. (1975). *The origin of the idea of chance in children.* London: Routledge and Kegan Paul.

Pietschnig, J., & Voracek, M. (2015). One century of global IQ gains: A formal meta-analysis of the Flynn effect (1909–2013). *Perspectives on Psychological Science, 10,* 282–306.

Pijnacker, J., Vervloed, M. P., & Steenbergen, B. (2012). Pragmatic abilities in children with congenital visual impairment: An exploration of non-literal language and advanced theory of mind understanding. *Journal of Autism and Developmental Disorders, 42,* 2440–2449.

Pillemer, D. B., Picadillo, M. L., & Pruett, J. C. (1994). Very long-term memories of a salient preschool event. *Applied Cognitive Psychology*, *8*, 95–106.

Pillemer, D. B., & White, S. H. (1989). Childhood events recalled by children and adults. In H. W. Reese (Ed.), *Advances in child development and behavior*, Volume *21* (pp. 297–340). London: Academic Press.

Pingault, J. B., Côté, S. M., Vitaro, F., Falissard, B., Genolini, C., & Tremblay, R. E. (2014). The developmental course of childhood inattention symptoms uniquely predicts educational attainment: A 16-year longitudinal study. *Psychiatry Research*, *219*, 707–709.

Pingault, J. B., Tremblay, R. E., Vitaro, F., Carbonneau, R., Genolini, C., Falissard, B., & Côté, S. M. (2011). Childhood trajectories of inattention and hypera-ctivity and prediction of educational attainment in early adulthood: A 16-year longitudinal population-based study. *American Journal of Psychiatry*, *168*, 1164–1170.

Pinker, S. (1994). *The language instinct*. London: Allen Lane.

Pipe, M-E., & Salmon, K. (2009). Dolls, drawings, body diagrams, and other props: Role of props in investigative interviews. In K. Kuehnle & M. Connell (Eds), *The evaluation of child sexual abuse allegations: A comprehesive guide to assessment and testimony* (pp. 365–395). Hoboken, NJ: Wiley.

Plomin, R., & Deary, I. J. (2015). Genetics and intelligence differences: Five special findings. *Molecular Psychiatry*, *20*, 98–108.

Plomin, R., DeFries, J. C., McClearn, G. E., & Rutter, M. (1997). *Behavioral genetics, Third edition*. New York, NY: W. H. Freeman.

Poole, D. A., & White, L. T. (1991). Effects of question repetition on the eyewitness testimony of children and adults. *Developmental Psychology*, *27*, 975–986.

Porath, M. (2014). Meeting the needs of gifted learners. In J. Holliman (Ed.), *The Routledge international companion to educational psychology* (pp. 327–336). London: Routledge.

Posne, M. I., & Rothbart, M. K. (2000). Developing mechanisms of self-regulation. *Development and Psychopathology*, *12*, 427–441.

Poulin-Dubois, D., Brooker, I., & Chow, V. (2009). The developmental origins of naive psychology in infancy. *Advances in Child Development and Behavior*, *37*, 55–104.

Prado, E. L., & Dewey, K. G. (2014). Nutrition and brain development in early life. *Nutrition Reviews*, *72*, 267–284.

Prebble, S. C., Addis, D. R., & Tippett, L. J. (2013). Autobiographical memory and sense of self. *Psychological Bulletin*, *139*, 815–840.

Premack, D., & Woodruff, G. (1978). Does the chimpanzee have a theory of mind? *Behavioural and Brain Sciences*, *4*, 515–526.

Presson, A. P., Partyka, G., Jensen, K. M., Devine, O. J., Rasmussen, S. A., McCabe, L. L., & McCabe, E. R. (2013). Current estimate of Down syndrome population prevalence in the United States. *The Journal of Pediatrics*, *163*, 1163–1168.

Price-Williams, D., Gordon, W., & Ramirez, M. (1969). Skill and conservation: A study of pottery making children. *Developmental Psychology*, *1*, 769.

Provence, S., & Lipton, R. C. (1962). *Infants in institutions*. New York, NY: International Universities Press.

Qin, J., Quas, J. A., Redlich, A., & Goodman, G. S. (1997). Children's eyewitness testimony: Memory development in the legal context. In N. Cowan (Ed.), *The development of memory in childhood* (pp. 301–341). London: Psychology Press.

Quas, J. A., & Fivush, R. (Eds) (2009). *Emotion and memory in development*. Oxford: Oxford University Press.

Quas, J. A., Malloy, L. C., Melinder, A., Goodman, G. S., D'Mello, M., & Schaaf, J. (2007). Developmental differences in the effects of repeated interviews and interviewer bias on young children's event memory and false reports. *Developmental Psychology, 43*, 823–837.

Quinn, P. C. (2002). Beyond prototypes: Asymmetries in infant categorization and what they teach us about the mechanisms guiding early knowledge acquisition. *Advances in Child Development and Behavior, 29*, 161–193.

Quinn, P. C. (2008). In defense of core competencies, quantitative change, and continuity. *Child Development, 79*, 1633–1638.

Quinn, P. C., Eimas, P. D., & Rosenkrantz, S. L. (1993). Evidence for representations of perceptually similar natural categories by 3-month-old and 4-month-old infants. *Perception, 22*, 463–475.

Raaheim, K. (1969). *Opplevelse, erfaring & intelligens*. Oslo: Universitetsforlaget.

Raghubar, K. P., Barnes, M. A., & Hecht, S. A. (2010). Working memory and mathematics: A review of developmental, individual difference, and cognitive approaches. *Learning and Individual Differences, 20*, 110–122.

Rakison, D. H. (2003). Parts, categorization, and the animate-inanimate distinction in infancy. In D. H. Rakison & L. K. Oakes (Eds), *Early category and concept development: Making sense of the blooming, buzzing confusion* (pp. 159–192). Oxford: Oxford University Press.

Rakison, D. H., & Cohen, L. B. (1999). Infants' use of functional parts in basic-like categorization. *Developmental Science, 2*, 423–432.

Rakoczy, H. (2012). Do infants have a theory of mind? *British Journal of Developmental Psychology, 30*, 59–74.

Rakoczy, H. (2017). In defense of a developmental dogma: Children acquire propositional attitude folk psychology around age 4. *Synthese, 194*, 689–707.

Ramey, C. T., & Ramey. S. L. (1998a). Early intervention and early experience. *American Psychologist, 53*, 109–120.

Ramey, C. T., & Ramey, S. L. (1998b). Prevention of intellectual disabilities: Early interventions to improve cognitive development. *Preventive Medicine, 27*, 224–232.

Randell, A. C., & Peterson, C. C. (2009). Affective qualities of sibling disputes, mothers' conflict attitudes, and children's theory of mind development. *Social Development, 18*, 857–874.

Rapport, M. D., Orban, S. A., Kofler, M. J., & Friedman, L. M. (2013). Do programs designed to train working memory, other executive functions, and attention benefit children with ADHD? A meta-analytic review of cognitive, academic, and behavioral outcomes. *Clinical Psychology Review, 33*, 1237–1252.

Raven, J., Raven, J. C., & Court, J. H. (1998). *Coloured Progressive Matrices*. Oxford: Oxford Psychologist Press.

Reddy, V. (1991). Playing with others' expectations: Teasing and mucking about in the first year. In A. Whiten (Ed.), *Natural theories of mind: Evolution, development and simulation of everyday mindreading* (pp. 143–158). Oxford: Basil Blackwell.

Reeve, R. A., & Gray, S. (2015). Number difficulties in young children. Deficits in core number? In S. J. Chinn (Ed.), *The Routledge international handbook of dyscalculia and mathematical learning difficulties* (pp. 44–59). London: Routledge

Reeve, R. A., & Waldecker, C. (2017). Evidence-based assessment and intervention for dyscalculia and maths disabilities in school psychology. In M. Thielking & M. D. Terjesen (Eds), *Handbook of Australian school psychology* (pp. 197–213). Cham, Switzerland: Springer.

Reilly, D., Neumann, D. L., & Andrews, G. (2017). Gender differences in spatial ability: Implications for STEM education and approaches to reducing the gender gap for parents and educators. In M. S. Khine (Ed.), *Visual-spatial ability: Transforming research into practice* (pp. 195–224). Cham, Switzerland: Springer.

Repacholi, B. M., & Gopnik, A. (1997). Early reasoning about desires: Evidence from 14–18-months-olds. *Developmental Psychology, 33*, 12–21.

Reynolds, G. D., Courage, M. L., & Richards, J. E. (2013). The development of attention. In D. Reisberg (Ed.), *The Oxford handbook of cognitive psychology* (pp. 1000–1013). Oxford: Oxford University Press.

Reznick, J. S. (2009). Working memory in infants and toddlers. In M. L. Courage & N. Cowan (Eds), *The development of memory in infancy and childhood, Second edition* (pp. 343–365). New York, NY: Psychology Press.

Rhodes, M., & Wellman, H. (2013). Constructing a new theory from old ideas and new evidence. *Cognitive Science, 37*, 592–604.

Richland, L. E., Chan, T. K., Morrison, R. G., & Au, T. K. F. (2010). Young children's analogical reasoning across cultures: Similarities and differences. *Journal of Experimental Child Psychology, 105*, 146–153.

Richland, L. E., Morrison, R. G., & Holyoak, K. J. (2006). Children's development of analogical reasoning: Insights from scene analogy problems. *Journal of Experimental Child Psychology, 94*, 249–271.

Ricketts, J. (2011). Research review: Reading comprehension in developmental disorders of language and communication. *Journal of Child Psychology and Psychiatry, 52*, 1111–1123.

Rinaldi, L., & Karmiloff-Smith, A. (2017). Intelligence as a developing function: A neuroconstructivist approach. *Journal of Intelligence, 5*, 18.

Ristic, J., & Enns, J. T. (2015). The changing face of attentional development. *Current Directions in Psychological Science, 24*, 24–31.

Roberts, G., Quach, J., Spencer-Smith, M., Anderson, P. J., Gathercole, S., Gold, L., Sia, K.-L., Mensah, F., Rickards, F., Ainley, J., & Wake, M. (2016). Academic outcomes 2 years after working memory training for children with low working memory: A randomized clinical trial. *JAMA Pediatrics, 170*, e154568–e154568.

Roberts, K. P. (2002). Children's ability to distinguish between memories from multiple sources: Implications for the quality and accuracy of eyewitness statements. *Developmental Review, 22*, 403–435.

Roberts, K. P., & Powell, M. B. (2001). Describing individual incidents of sexual abuse: A review of research on the effects of multiple sources of information on children's reports. *Child Abuse and Neglect, 25,* 1643–1659.

Rogers, M., Boggia, J., Ogg, J., & Volpe, R. (2015). The ecology of ADHD in the schools. *Current Developmental Disorders Reports, 2,* 23–29.

Rogoff, B. (1998). Cognition as a collaborative process. In W. Damon, D. Kuhn & R. S. Siegler (Eds), *Handbook of child psychology, Fifth edition, Volume 2: Cognition, perception, and language* (pp. 679–744). New York, NY: John Wiley.

Rogoff, B. (2014). Learning by observing and pitching in to family and community endeavors: An orientation. *Human Development, 57,* 69–81.

Roid, G. H. (2003). *Stanford-Binet Intelligence Scale manual, Fifth edition.* Itasca, IL: Riverside

Roid, G. H., Miller, L. J., Pomplun, M., & Koch, C. (2013). *Leiter International Performance Scale, Third edition.* Los Angeles, CA: Western Psychological Services.

Rosch, E. H. (1973). On the internal structure of perceptual and semantic categories. In T. E. Moore (Ed.), *Cognitive development and the acquisition of language* (pp. 111–144). New York, NY: Academic Press.

Rosch, E. H. (1999). Reclaiming concepts. *Journal of Consciousness Studies, 6,* 61–77.

Rosch, E. H., Mervis, C. B., Gray, W., Johnson, D., & Boyes-Braem, P. (1976). Basic objects in natural categories. *Cognitive Psychology, 3,* 382–439.

Rose, S. A., Feldman, J. F., & Jankowski, J. J. (2004). Infant visual recognition memory. *Developmental Review, 24,* 74–100.

Rosenthal, R. (1994). Interpersonal expectancy effects: A 30-year perspective. *Current Directions in Psychological Science, 3,* 176–179.

Rosenthal, R., & Jacobsen, L. (1968). *Pygmalion in the classroom: Teacher expectation and pupils' intellectual development.* New York, NY: Holt, Rinehart and Winston.

Roth, B., Becker, N., Romeyke, S., Schäfer, S., Domnick, F., & Spinath, F. M. (2015). Intelligence and school grades: A meta-analysis. *Intelligence, 53,* 118–137.

Rothenberger, A., & Banaschewski, T. (2004). Informing the ADHD debate. *Scientific American Mind, 14* (5), 50–55.

Rovee-Collier, C., & Cuevas, K. (2009a). The development of infant memory. In M. L. Courage & N. Cowan (Eds), *The development of memory in infancy and childhood,* Second edition (pp. 11–41). New York, NY: Psychology Press.

Rovee-Collier, C., & Cuevas, K. (2009b). Multiple memory systems are unnecessary to account for infant memory development: An ecological model. *Developmental Psychology, 45,* 160–174.

Rovee-Collier, C., & Gerhardstein, P. (1997). The development of infant memory. In N. Cowan (Ed.), *The development of memory in childhood* (pp. 5–39). London: Psychology Press.

Rovee-Collier, C., Greco-Vigorito, C., & Hayne, H. (1993). The time window hypothesis: Implications for categorization and memory modification. *Infant Behavior and Development, 16,* 149–176.

Rovee-Collier, C., Hartshorn, K., & DiRubbo, M. (1999) Long-term maintenance of infant memory. *Developmental Psychobiology, 35,* 91–102.

Rubie-Davies, C. M. (2006). Teacher expectations and student self-perceptions: Exploring relationships. *Psychology in the Schools, 43*, 537–552.

Rubin, D. C. (2000). The distribution of early childhood memories. *Memory, 8*, 265–269.

Rueda, M. R., & Cómbita, L. M. (2013). The nature and nurture of executive attention development. In B. R. Kar (Ed.), *Cognition and brain development: Converging evidence from various methodologies* (pp. 33–59). Washington, DC: American Psychological Association.

Rushton, J. P., & Jensen, A. R. (2005). Thirty years of research on race differences in cognitive ability. *Psychology, Public Policy, and Law, 11*, 235–294.

Rushton, J. P., & Jensen, A. R. (2010). Race and IQ: A theory-based review of the research in Richard Nisbett's intelligence and how to get it. *The Open Psychology Journal, 3*, 9–35.

Russell, J. (1999). Cognitive development as an executive process—in part: A homeopathic dose of Piaget. *Developmental Science, 2*, 247–270.

Rutter, M., Graham, P., Chadwick, O., & Yule, W. (1976). Adolescent turmoil: Fact or fiction? *Journal of Child Psychology and Psychiatry, 17*, 35–56.

Saine, N. L., Lerkkanen, M. K., Ahonen, T., Tolvanen, A., & Lyytinen, H. (2011). Computer-assisted remedial reading intervention for school beginners at risk for reading disability. *Child Development, 82*, 1013–1028.

Salminen, J., Koponen, T., Räsänen, P., & Aro, M. (2015). Preventive support for kindergarteners most at-risk for mathematics difficulties: Computer-assisted intervention. *Mathematical Thinking and Learning, 17*, 273–295.

Salmon, M. H., & Zeitz, C. M. (1995). Analysing conversational reasoning. *Informal Logic, 17*, 1–23.

Sameroff, A. J. (2010). A unified theory of development: A dialectic integration of nature and nurture. *Child Development, 81*, 6–22.

Sameroff, A. J., Seifer, R., Baldwin, A., & Baldwin, C. (1993). Stability of intelligence from preschool to adolescence: The influence of social and family risk factors. *Child Development, 64*, 80–97.

Sasser, T. R., Kalvin, C. B., & Bierman, K. L. (2016). Developmental trajectories of clinically significant attention deficit/hyperactivity disorder (ADHD) symptoms from grade 3 through 12 in a high-risk sample: Predictors and outcomes. *Journal of Abnormal Psychology, 125*, 207–219.

Saxe, R., & Carey, S. (2006). The perception of causality in infancy. *Acta Psychologica, 123*, 144–165.

Saywitz, K. J., & Nathanson, R. (1993). Children's testimony and their perceptions of stress in and out of the courtroom. *Child Abuse and Neglect, 17*, 613–622.

Scammacca, N. K., Roberts, G., Vaughn, S., & Stuebing, K. K. (2015). A meta-analysis of interventions for struggling readers in Grades 4–12: 1980–2011. *Journal of Learning Disabilities, 48*, 369–390.

Schaafsma, S. M., Pfaff, D. W., Spunt, R. P., & Adolphs, R. (2015). Deconstructing and reconstructing theory of mind. *Trends in Cognitive Sciences, 19*, 65–72.

Schank, R. C., & Abelson, R. P. (1977). *Scripts, plans, goals and understanding*. Hillsdale, NJ: Lawrence Erlbaum.

Schiff, R., Bauminger, N., & Toledo, I. (2009). Analogical problem solving in children with verbal and nonverbal learning disabilities. *Journal of Learning Disabilities*, *42*, 3–13.

Schiff, R., & Joshi, R. M. (Eds) (2016). *Interventions in learning disabilities: A handbook on systematic training programs for individuals with learning disabilities.* Cham, Switzerland: Springer.

Schneider, W. (2015). *Memory development from early childhood through emerging adulthood.* Cham, Switzerland: Springer.

Schneider, W., & Bjorklund, D. E. (1992). Expertise, aptitude, and strategic remembering. *Child Development*, *63*, 461–473.

Schneider, W., Niklas, F., & Schmiedeler, S. (2014). Intellectual development from early childhood to early adulthood: The impact of early IQ differences on stability and change over time. *Learning and Individual Differences*, *32*, 156–162.

Schulte-Körne, G. (2010). The prevention, diagnosis, and treatment of dyslexia. *Deutsches Ärzteblatt International*, *107*, 718–727.

Schultz, T. R. (2003). *Computational developmental psychology.* Cambridge, MA: MIT Press.

Schulz, L. E., & Gopnik, A. (2004). Causal learning across domains. *Developmental Psychology*, *40*, 162–176.

Schunk, D. H. (2012). *Learning theories—An educational perspective, Sixth edition.* Boston, MA: Pearson.

Seehagen, S., Schneider, S., Miebach, K., Frigge, K., & Zmyj, N. (2017). "Should I or shouldn't I?" Imitation of undesired versus allowed actions from peer and adult models by 18- and 24-month-old toddlers. *Infant Behavior and Development*, *49*, 1–8.

Service, V., Lock, A., & Chandler, P. (1989). Individual differences in early communicative development: A social constructivist perspective. In S. von Tetzchner, L. S. Siegel & L. Smith (Eds), *The social and cognitive aspects of normal and atypical language development* (pp. 23–49). New York, NY: Springer.

Shaul, S., & Schwartz, M. (2014). The role of the executive functions in school readiness among preschool-age children. *Reading and Writing*, *27*, 749–768.

Shayer, M., & Wylam, H. (1978). The distribution of Piagetian stages of thinking in British middle and secondary school children: II. *British Journal of Educational Psychology*, *48*, 62–70.

Shaywitz, S. E., Morris, R., & Shaywitz, B. A. (2008). The education of dyslexic children from childhood to young adulthood. *Annual Review of Psychology*, *59*, 451–475.

Shaywitz, S. E., & Shaywitz, B. A. (2013). Making a hidden disability visible: What has been learned from the neurobiological studies of dyslexia. In H. L. Swanson, K. R. Harris & S. Graham (Eds), *Handbook of learning disabilities, Second edition* (pp. 643–657). New York, NY: Guilford Press.

Shaywitz, S. E., Shaywitz, B. A., Pugh, K. R., Fulbright, R. K., Constable, R. T., Mencl, W. E., Shankweiler, D. P., Liberman, A. M., Skudlarski, P., Fletcher, J. M., et al. (1998). Functional disruption in the organization of the brain for reading in dyslexia. *Proceedings of the National Academy of Sciences*, *95*, 2636–2641.

Shechner, T., Britton, J. C., Pérez-Edgar, K., Bar-Haim, Y., Ernst, M., Fox, N. A., Leibenluft, E., & Pine, D. S. (2012). Attention biases, anxiety, and development: Toward or away from threats or rewards? *Depression and Anxiety, 29,* 282–294.

Sheingold, K., & Tenney, Y. J. (1982). Memory for a salient childhood event. In U. Neisser (Ed.), *Memory observed: Remembering in natural contexts* (pp. 201–212). San Francisco, CA: Freeman.

Shuttleworth-Edwards, A. B., Kemp, R. D., Rust, A. L., Muirhead, J. G., Hartman, N. P., & Radloff, S. E. (2004). Cross-cultural effects on IQ test performance: A review and preliminary normative indications on WAIS-III test performance. *Journal of Clinical and Experimental Neuropsychology, 26,* 903–920.

Sibley, M. H., Kuriyan, A. B., Evans, S. W., Waxmonsky, J. G., & Smith, B. H. (2014). Pharmacological and psychosocial treatments for adolescents with ADHD: An updated systematic review of the literature. *Clinical Psychology Review, 34,* 218–232.

Siegal, M. (1991). *Knowing children: Experiments in conversation and cognition.* Hillsdale, NJ: Lawrence Erlbaum.

Siegal, M., & Beattie, K. (1991). Where to look first for children's knowledge of false beliefs. *Cognition, 38,* 1–12.

Siegler, R. S. (1994). Cognitive variability: A key to understanding cognitive development. *Current Directions in Psychological Science, 3,* 1–5.

Siegler, R. S. (2000). The rebirth of children's learning. *Child Development, 71,* 26–35.

Siegler, R. S., & Jenkins, E. (1989). *How children discover new strategies.* Hillsdale, NJ: Lawrence Erlbaum.

Sigman, M., & Whaley, S. E. (1998). The role of nutrition in the development of intelligence. In U. Neisser (Ed.), *The rising curve* (pp. 155–182). Washington, DC: American Psychological Association.

Simcock, G., & Hayne, H. (2002). Breaking the barrier? Children fail to translate their preverbal memories into language. *Psychological Science, 13,* 225–231.

Simkin, Z., & Conti-Ramsden, G. (2006). Evidence of reading difficulty in subgroups of children with specific language impairment. *Child Language Teaching and Therapy, 22,* 315–331.

Singer-Freeman, K. E., & Bauer, P. J. (2008). The ABCs of analogical abilities: Evidence for formal analogical reasoning abilities in 24-month-olds. *British Journal of Developmental Psychology, 26,* 317–335.

Skeels, H., & Dye, H. B. (1939). A study of the effects of differential stimulation on mentally retarded children. *Proceedings of the American Association of Mental Deficiency, 44,* 114–136.

Skinner, B. F. (1969). *Contingencies of reinforcement: A theoretical analysis.* Englewood Cliffs, NJ: Prentice-Hall.

Slater, A. (1995). Individual differences in infancy and later IQ. *Journal of Child Psychology and Psychiatry, 36,* 69–112.

Slater, A., Cooper, R., Rose, D., & Morison, V. (1989). Prediction of cognitive performance from infancy to early childhood. *Human Development, 32,* 137–147.

Sloutsky, V. M. (2003). The role of similarity in the development of categorization. *Trends in Cognitive Sciences, 7,* 246–251.

Sloutsky, V. M. (2015). Conceptual development. In R. M. Lerner, L. S. Liben & U. Müller (Eds), *Handbook of child psychology and developmental science, Seventh edition, Volume 2: Cognitive processes* (pp. 469–518). Hoboken, NJ: Wiley.

Smith, L., Fagan, J. F., & Ulvund, S. E. (2002). The relation of recognition memory in infancy and parental socioeconomic status to later intellectual competence. *Intelligence, 30,* 247–259.

Smith, L., & von Tetzchner, S. (1986). Communicative, sensorimotor, and language skills of young children with Down syndrome. *American Journal of Mental Deficiency, 91,* 57–66.

Smith, M. M. (2005). *Literacy and augmentative and alternative communication.* London: Academic Press.

Snowling, M. J. (2013). Early identification and interventions for dyslexia: A contemporary view. *Journal of Research in Special Educational Needs, 13,* 7–14.

Sodian, B. (1994). Early deception and the conceptual continuity claim. In C. Lewis & P. Mitchell (Eds), *Children's early understanding of mind* (pp. 385–401). Hove, UK: Erlbaum.

Sokol, B. W., & Martin, J. (2006). Good fences make good neighbors: A response to Overton and Ennis. *Human Development, 49,* 173–179.

Sommer, D. (2012). *A childhood psychology: Young children in changing times.* New York, NY: Palgrave Macmillan.

Southgate, V., Senju, A., & Csibra, G. (2007a). Action anticipation through attribution of false belief by 2-year-olds. *Psychological Science, 18,* 587–592.

Southgate, V., & Vernetti, A. (2014). Belief-based action prediction in preverbal infants. *Cognition, 130,* 1–10.

Spanoudis, G. (2016). Theory of mind and specific language impairment in school-age children. *Journal of Communication Disorders, 61,* 83–96.

Spearman, C. (1927). *The abilities of man.* New York, NY: Macmillan.

Spelke, E. S., & Kinzler, K. D. (2007). Core knowledge. *Developmental Science, 10,* 89–96.

Sperber, D. (2001). In defense of massive modularity. In E. Dupoux (Ed.), *Language, brain and cognitive development: Essays in honor of Jacques Mehler* (pp. 47–57). Cambridge, MA: MIT Press.

Spitz, R. A. (1946). Hospitalism: A follow-up report on an investigation described in Volume 1, 1945. *Psycho-Analytic Study of the Child, 2,* 313–342.

Steinberg, L., & Chein, J. M. (2015). Multiple accounts of adolescent impulsivity. *Proceedings of the National Academy of Sciences, 112,* 8807–8808.

Stern, D. N. (2007). Applying developmental and neuroscience finding on other-centred participation to the process of change in psychotherapy. In S. Bråten (Ed.), *On being moved: From mirror neurons to empathy* (pp. 35–47). Amsterdam, NL: John Benjamins.

Sternberg, R. J. (1997). The triarchic theory of intelligence. In D. P. Flanagan, J. L. Genshaft & P. L. Harrison (Eds), *Contemporary intellectual assessment* (pp. 92–104). London: Guilford Press.

Sternberg, R. J. (2015). Multiple intelligences in the new age of thinking. In S. Goldstein, D. Princiotta & J. A. Naglieri (Eds), *Handbook of intelligence:*

Evolutionary theory, historical perspective, and current concepts (pp. 229–241). New York, NY: Springer.

Sternberg, R. J., Grigorenko, E. L., & Bundy, D. A. (2001). The predictive value of IQ. *Merrill-Palmer Quarterly, 47*, 1–41.

Sternberg, R. J., Grigorenko, E. L., & Kidd, K. K. (2005). Intelligence, race, and genetics. *American Psychologist, 60*, 46–59.

Stoltz, T., Piske, F. H. R., de Fátima Quintal de Freitas, M., D'Aroz, M. S., & Machado, J. M. (2015). Creativity in gifted education: Contributions from Vygotsky and Piaget. *Creative Education, 6*, 64–70.

Stotz, K. (2008). The ingredients for a postgenomic synthesis of nature and nurture. *Philosophical Psychology, 21*, 359–381.

Suddendorf, T., Oostenbroek, J., Nielsen, M., & Slaughter, V. (2013). Is newborn imitation developmentally homologous to later social-cognitive skills? *Developmental Psychobiology, 55*, 52–58.

Sullivan, K., Zaitchick, D., & Tager-Flusberg, H. (1994). Preschoolers can attribute second-order beliefs. *Developmental Psychology, 30*, 395–402.

Sundet, J. M., Barlaug, D., & Torjussen, T. M. (2004). The end of the Flynn effect? A study of secular trends in mean intelligence test scores of Norwegian conscripts during half a century. *Intelligence, 32*, 349–362.

Sutton, J. E. (2006). The development of landmark and beacon use in young children: Evidence from a touchscreen search task. *Developmental Science, 9*, 108–123.

Swingler, M. M., Perry, N. B., & Calkins, S. D. (2015). Neural plasticity and the development of attention: Intrinsic and extrinsic influences. *Development and Psychopathology, 27*, 443–457.

Symons, D. K. (2004). Mental state discourse, theory of mind, and an internalization of self-other understanding. *Developmental Review, 24*, 159–188.

Tadić, V., Pring, L., & Dale, N. (2009). Attentional processes in young children with congenital visual impairment. *British Journal of Developmental Psychology, 27*, 311–330.

Talwar, V., Arruda, C., & Yachison, S. (2015). The effects of punishment and appeals for honesty on children's truth-telling behavior. *Journal of Experimental Child Psychology, 130*, 209–217.

Talwar, V., & Lee, K. (2002). Emergence of white-lie telling in children between 3 and 7 years of age. *Merrill-Palmer Quarterly, 48*, 160–181.

Talwar, V., Murphy, S. M., & Lee, K. (2007). White lie telling in children for politeness purposes. *International Journal of Behavioral Development, 31*, 1–11.

Tamm, L., Nakonezny, P. A., & Hughes, C. W. (2014). An open trial of a metacognitive executive function training for young children with ADHD. *Journal of Attention Disorders, 18*, 551–559.

Tannock, R. (2007). *The educational implications of attention deficit hyperactivity disorder.* Toronto, Ontario: Literacy and Numeracy Secretariat.

Tannock, R., Frijters, J. C., Martinussen, R., White, E. J., Ickowicz, A., Benson, N. J., & Lovett, M. W. (2018). Combined modality intervention for ADHD with comorbid reading disorders: A proof of concept study. *Journal of Learning Disabilities, 51*, 55–72.

Tessler, M., & Nelson, K. (1994). Making memories: The influence of joint encoding on later recall by young children. *Consciousness and Cognition: An International Journal, 3*, 307–326.

Thomas, R. M. (2005). *Comparing theories of child development, Sixth edition.* Belmont, CA: Wadsworth.

Thommen, E., Avelar, S., Sapin, V. Z., Perrenoud, S., & Malatesta, D. (2010). Mapping the journey from home to school: A study on children's representation of space. *International Research in Geographical and Environmental Education, 19*, 191–205.

Thoresen, C., Lønnum, K., Melinder, A., & Magnussen, S. (2009). Forensic interviews with children in CSA cases: A large-sample study of Norwegian police interviews. *Applied Cognitive Psychology, 23*, 999–1011.

Thoresen, C., Lønnum, K., Melinder, A., Stridbeck, U., & Magnussen, S. (2006). Theory and practice in interviewing young children: A study of Norwegian police interviews 1985–2002. *Psychology, Crime and Law, 12*, 629–640.

Thrasher, C., & LoBue, V. (2016). Do infants find snakes aversive? Infants' physiological responses to "fear-relevant" stimuli. *Journal of Experimental Child Psychology, 142*, 382–390.

Tillman, C. M., Bohlin, G., Sørensen, L., & Lundervold, A. J. (2009). Intellectual deficits in children with ADHD beyond central executive and non-executive functions. *Archives of Clinical Neuropsychology, 24*, 769–782.

Tomasello, M. (2005). "Cultural constraints on grammar and cognition in Piraha: Another look at the design features of human language": Comment. *Current Anthropology, 46*, 640–641.

Tomasello, M. (2016). The ontogeny of cultural learning. *Current Opinion in Psychology, 8*, 1–4.

Tucker-Drob, E. M., Briley, D. A., & Harden, K. P. (2013). Genetic and environmental influences on cognition across development and context. *Current Directions in Psychological Science, 22*, 349–355.

Tucker-Drob, E. M., Rhemtulla, M., Harden, K. P., Turkheimer, E., & Fask, D. (2011). Emergence of a gene × socioeconomic status interaction on infant mental ability between 10 months and 2 years. *Psychological Science, 22*, 125–133.

Turkheimer, E., Haley, A., Waldron, M., D'Onofrio, B., & Gottesman, I. I. (2003). Socioeconomic status modifies heritability of IQ in young children. *Psychological Science, 14*, 623–628.

Turnbull, W., Carpendale, J. I. M., & Racine, T. (2009). Talk and children's understanding of the mind. *Journal of Consciousness Studies, 16*, 140–166.

Udwin, O., & Kuczynski, A. (2007). Behavioural phenotypes in genetic syndromes associated with intellectual disability. In A. Carr, G. O'Reilly, P. N. Walsh & J. McEvoy (Eds). *The handbook of intellectual disability and clinical psychology practice* (pp. 488–528). London: Routledge.

Ullstadius, E. (1998). Neonatal imitation in a mother–infant setting. *Early Development and Parenting, 7*, 1–8.

Uzgiris, I. C. (1999). Imitation as activity: Developmental aspects. In J. Nadel & G. Butterworth (Eds), *Imitation in infancy* (pp. 186–206). Cambridge: Cambridge University Press.

van den Bos, W., Rodriguez, C. A., Schweitzer, J. B., & McClure, S. M. (2015). Adolescent impatience decreases with increased frontostriatal connectivity. *Proceedings of the National Academy of Sciences, 112,* E3765–E3774.

van der Donk, M., Hiemstra-Beernink, A. C., Tjeenk-Kalff, A., Van Der Leij, A., & Lindauer, R. (2015). Cognitive training for children with ADHD: A randomized controlled trial of cogmed working memory training and "paying attention in class". *Frontiers in Psychology, 6,* 1081.

van der Maas, H. L., Kan, K. J., & Borsboom, D. (2014). Intelligence is what the intelligence test measures. Seriously. *Journal of Intelligence, 2,* 12–15.

van IJzendoorn, M. H., Luijk, M. P., & Juffer, F. (2008). IQ of children growing up in children's homes: A meta-analysis on IQ delays in orphanages. *Merrill-Palmer Quarterly, 54,* 341–366.

van IJzendoorn, M. H., Palacios, J., Sonuga-Barke, E. J., Gunnar, M. R., Vorria, P., McCall, R. B., Le Mare, L., Bakermans-Kranenburg, M. J., Dobrova-Kroll, N. A., & Juffer, F. (2011). Children in institutional care: Delayed development and resilience. *Monographs of the Society for Research in Child Development, 76,* 8–30

VanTassel-Baska, J., & Stambaugh, T. (2008). *What works: 20 years of curriculum development and research.* Williamsburg, VA: Center for Gifted Education.

Vasilyeva, M., & Lourenco, S. F. (2012). Development of spatial cognition. *Wiley Interdisciplinary Reviews: Cognitive Science, 3,* 349–362.

Vaughn, S., Roberts, G., Wexler, J., Vaughn, M. G., Fall, A. M., & Schnakenberg, J. B. (2014). High school students with reading comprehension difficulties: Results of a randomized control trial of a two-year reading intervention. *Journal of Learning Disabilities, 48,* 546–559.

Vendetti, M. S., Matlen, B. J., Richland, L. E., & Bunge, S. A. (2015). Analogical reasoning in the classroom: Insights from cognitive science. *Mind, Brain, and Education, 9,* 100–106.

Vicario, C. M., Yates, M., & Nicholls, M. (2013). Shared deficits in space, time, and quantity processing in childhood genetic disorders. *Frontiers in Psychology, 4,* 43.

Vig, S. (2007). Young children's object play: A window on development. *Journal of Developmental and Physical Disabilities, 19,* 201–215.

Vinden, P. (2002). Understanding minds and evidence for belief: A study of Mofu children in Cameroon. *International Journal of Behavioral Development, 26,* 445–452.

Vissers, L. E., Gilissen, C., & Veltman, J. A. (2016). Genetic studies in intellectual disability and related disorders. *Nature Reviews Genetics, 17,* 9–18.

von Bastian, C. C., & Oberauer, K. (2014). Effects and mechanisms of working memory training: A review. *Psychological Research, 78,* 803–820.

von Tetzchner, S. (2009). Suporte ao desenvolvimento da comunicação suplementar e alternative. In D. Deliberato, M. deJ. Gonçalves & E. C. de Macedo (Eds), *Comunicação alternative: Teoria, prática, tecnologias e pesquisa* (pp. 14–27). São Paulo: Memnon Edições Científicas.

von Tetzchner, S., Rogne, S. O., & Lilleeng, M. K. (1997). Literacy intervention for a deaf child with severe reading disorder. *Journal of Literacy Research, 29,* 25–46.

Vulchanova, M., Foyn, C. H., Nilsen, R. A., & Sigmundsson, H. (2014). Links between phonological memory, first language competence and second language competence in 10-year-old children. *Learning and Individual Differences*, *35*, 87–95.

Vygotsky, L. S. (1962). *Thought and language*. Cambridge, MA: MIT Press.

Vygotsky, L. S. (1978). *Mind in society: The development of higher mental processes*. Cambridge, MA: Harvard University Press.

Vygotsky, L. S. (1935a/1982). Undervisning & udvikling i førskolealderen. In *Om barnets psykiske udvikling* (pp. 89–104). København: Nyt Nordisk Forlag Arnold Busck.

Vygotsky, L. S. (1935b/1982). Spørsmålet om undervisning & den intellektuelle udvikling i skolealderen. In *Om barnets psykiske udvikling* (pp. 105–124). København: Nyt Nordisk Forlag Arnold Busck.

Wai, J., Cacchio, M., Putallaz, M., & Makel, M. C. (2010). Sex differences in the right tail of cognitive abilities: A 30 year examination. *Intelligence*, *38*, 412–423.

Wai, J., Putallaz, M., & Makel, M. C. (2012). Studying intellectual outliers: Are there sex differences, and are the smart getting smarter? *Current Directions in Psychological Science*, *21*, 382–390.

Wainryb, C., Shaw, L. A., Langley, M., Cottam, K., & Lewis, R. (2004). Children's thinking about diversity of belief in the early school years: Judgments of relativism, tolerance, and disagreeing persons. *Child Development*, *75*, 687–703.

Walker-Andrews, A. S. (2008). Intermodal emotional processes in infancy. In M. Lewis, J. M. Haviland & L. Feldman-Barrett (Eds), *Handbook of emotions* (pp. 364–375). New York, NY: Guilford Press.

Wallin, A. R., Quas, J. A., & Yim, H. S. (2009). Thysiological stress responses and children's event memory. In J. A. Quas & R. Fivush (Eds), *Emotion and memory in development* (pp. 313–339). Oxford: Oxford University Press.

Wang, Q. (2001). "Did you have fun? ": American and Chinese mother – child conversations about shared emotional experiences. *Cognitive Development*, *16*, 693–715.

Wang, Q. (2004). The emergence of cultural self-constructs: Autobiographical memory and self-description in European American and Chinese children. *Developmental Psychology*, *40*, 3–15.

Wang, S., Kaufman, L., & Baillargeon, R. (2003). Should all stationary objects move when hit? Developments in infants' causal and statistical expectations about collision events. *Infant Behavior and Development*, *26*, 529–568.

Wang, Z., Devine, R. T., Wong, K. K., & Hughes, C. (2016). Theory of mind and executive function during middle childhood across cultures. *Journal of Experimental Child Psychology*, *149*, 6–22.

Wang, Z., Wong, R. K. S., Wong, P. Y. H., Ho, F. C., & Cheng, D. P. W. (2017). Play and theory of mind in early childhood: A Hong Kong perspective. *Early Child Development and Care*, *187*, 1389–1402.

Warren, A. R., Hulse-Trotter, K., & Tubbs, E. C. (1991). Inducing resistance to suggestibility in children. *Law and Human Behavior*, *15*, 273–285.

Warren, A. R., & Tate, C. S. (1992). Egocentrism in children's telephone conversations. In R. M. Diaz & L. E. Berk (Eds), *Private speech: From social interaction to self regulation* (pp. 245–264). Hillsdale, NJ: Erlbaum.

Wason, P. C. (1977). The theory of formal operations: A critique. In B. Geber (Ed.), *Piaget and knowing: Studies in genetic epistemology* (pp. 119–135). London: Routledge and Kegan Paul.

Wass, S. V., Scerif, G., & Johnson, M. H. (2012). Training attentional control and working memory – Is younger, better? *Developmental Review, 32*, 360–387.

Watanabe, H., & Taga, G. (2006). General to specific development of movement patterns and memory for contingency between actions and events in young infants. *Infant Behavior and Development, 29*, 402–422.

Waterhouse, L. (2006a). Multiple intelligences, the Mozart effect, and emotional intelligence: A critical review. *Educational Psychologist, 41*, 207–225.

Waterhouse, L. (2006b). Inadequate evidence for multiple intelligences, Mozart effect, and emotional intelligence theories. *Educational Psychologist, 41*, 247–255.

Waters, A. M., Lipp, O., & Spence, S. H. (2008). Visual search for animal fear-relevant stimuli in children. *Australian Journal of Psychology, 60*, 112–125.

Waxman, S. R., & Gelman, S. A. (2009). Early word-learning entails reference, not merely associations. *Trends in Cognitive Sciences, 13*, 258–263.

Wechsler, D. (2014). *Wechsler Intelligence Scale for Children*, Fifth edition. San Antonio, TX: NCS Pearson.

Wellman, H. M. (1990). *The child's theory of mind*. Cambridge, MA: MIT Press.

Wellman, H. M., Cross, D., & Watson, J. (2001). Meta-analysis of theory of mind development: The truth about false belief. *Child Development, 72*, 655–684.

Wellman, H. M., & Lagattuta, K. H. (2004). Theory of mind for learning and teaching: The nature and role of explanation. *Cognitive Development, 19*, 479–497

Wells, G. (2008). Dialogue, inquiry and the construction of learning communities. In B. Lingard, J. Nixon & S. Ranson (Eds), *Transforming learning in schools and communities: The remaking of education for a cosmo politan society* (pp. 236–256). London: Continuum.

Welsh, M. C., Friedman, S. L., & Spieker, S. J. (2006). Executive functions in developing children: Current conceptualizations and questions for the future. In K. McCartney & D. Phillips (Eds), *Blackwell handbook of early childhood development* (pp. 167–187). Oxford: Blackwell.

Wertsch, J. V. (1991). *Voices of the mind: A sociocultural approach to mediated action*. London: Harvester Wheatsheaf.

Whitaker, S. (2017). Assessing the intellectual ability of asylum seekers. *International Journal of Developmental Disabilities*, DOI:10.1080/20473869.2017.1322343.

Whitman, T. L., O'Callaghan, M., & Sommer, K. (1997). Emotion and mental retardation. In W. E. MacLean (Ed.), *Ellis' handbook of mental deficiency, psychological theory and research, Third edition* (pp. 77–98) Mahwah, NJ: Lawrence Erlbaum.

Wilkening, F., Levin, I., & Druyan, S. (1987). Children's counting strategies for time quantification and integration. *Developmental Psychology, 23*, 823–831.

Willatts, P. (1989). Development of problem-solving in infancy. In A. Slater & G. Bremner (Eds), *Infant development* (pp. 143–182). Hove, UK: Lawrence Erlbaum.

Willingham, D. T. (2004). Reframing the mind. *Education Next, 4*, 19–24.

Wilson, R. S. (1983). The Louisville twin study: Developmental synchronies in behavior. *Child Development, 54*, 298–316.

Wimmer, H., & Hartl, H. (1991). Against the Cartesian view on mind: Young children's difficulty with own false beliefs. *British Journal of Developmental Psychology, 9*, 125–138.

Wimmer, H., & Perner, J. (1983). Beliefs about beliefs: Representation and constraining function of wrong beliefs in young children's understanding of deception. *Cognition, 13*, 103–128.

Winsler, A. (2009). Still talking to ourselves after all these years: A review of current research on private speech. In A. Winsler, C. Fernyhough & I. Montero (Eds) *Private speech, executive functioning, and the development of verbal self-regulation* (pp. 3–41). New York, NY: Cambridge University Press.

Winsler, A., & Naglieri, J. A. (2003). Overt and covert verbal problem-solving strategies: Developmental trends in use, awareness, and relations with task performance in children age 5 to 17. *Child Development, 74*, 659–678.

Woolley, A. W., Aggarwal, I., & Malone, T. W. (2015). Collective intelligence and group performance. *Current Directions in Psychological Science, 24*, 420–424.

Woolley, G. (2010). A multiple strategy framework supporting vocabulary development for students with reading comprehension deficits. *Australasian Journal of Special Education, 34*, 119–132.

Yang, D., Sidman, J., & Bushnell, E. W. (2010). Beyond the information given: Infants' transfer of actions learned through imitation. *Journal of Experimental Child Psychology, 106*, 62–81.

Zelazo, P. D. (2015). Executive function: Reflection, iterative reprocessing, complexity, and the developing brain. *Developmental Review, 38*, 55–68.

Zigler, E., & Valentine, J. (Eds) (1979). *Project Head Start: A legacy of the war on poverty*. New York, NY: Free Press.

Index

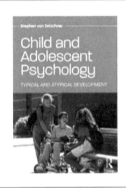

The **Topics from Child and Adolescent Psychology Series** is drawn from Stephen von Tetzchner's comprehensive textbook for all students of developmental psychology, *Child and Adolescent Psychology: Typical and Atypical Development*

Table of Contents

Praise for *Child and Adolescent Psychology: Typical and Atypical Development*

'An extensive overview of the field of developmental psychology. It illustrates how knowledge about typical and atypical development can be integrated and used to highlight fundamental processes of human growth and maturation.'

Dr. John Coleman, *PhD, OBE, UK*

'A broad panoply of understandings of development from a wide diversity of perspectives and disciplines, spanning all the key areas, and forming a comprehensive, detailed and extremely useful text for students and practitioners alike.'

Dr. Graham Music, *Consultant Psychotherapist, Tavistock Clinic London, UK*

'An extraordinary blend of depth of scholarship with a lucid, and engaging, writing style. Its coverage is impressive . . . Both new and advanced students will love the coverage of this text.'

Professor Joseph Campos, *University of California, USA*

'Encyclopedic breadth combined with an unerring eye for the central research across developmental psychology, particularly for the period of its explosive growth since the 1960s. Both a text and a reference work, this will be the go-to resource for any teacher, researcher or student of the discipline for the foreseeable future.'

Professor Andy Lock, *University of Lisbon, Portugal*

It is accompanied by a companion website featuring chapter summaries, glossary, quizzes and instructor resources.

CPSIA information can be obtained
at www.ICGtesting.com
Printed in the USA
LVHW081421190922
728744LV00017B/177